6/10

DORR TOWNSHIP LIBRARY (DOR)

3 1341 00072 3339

c/5/11

D0879582

BE The Change

Morning Dove

authorHOUSE®

DORR TOWNSHIP LIBRARY
1804 SUNSET DR.
DORR, MI 49323

AuthorHouse™
1663 Liberty Drive
Bloomington, IN 47403
www.authorhouse.com
Phone: 1-800-839-8640

© 2009 Morning Dove. All rights reserved.

No part of this book may be reproduced, stored in a retrieval system, or
transmitted by any means without the written permission of the author.

First published by AuthorHouse   12/1/2009

ISBN: 978-1-4490-3035-3 (e)
ISBN: 978-1-4490-3033-9 (sc)
ISBN: 978-1-4490-3034-6 (hc)

Printed in the United States of America
Bloomington, Indiana

This book is printed on acid-free paper.

To the only one who can love me this way and has loved me with the purest love I have ever known.

CONTENTS

ABOUT THE AUTHOR

Their came a time in my life, when I found a destiny altering moment and I could no longer simply exist. *I had a vision of life far above what we currently experience and that vision became my dream to reveal it to the world.* I felt the Ascended Beings along with my spiritual teachers, asking for help to tell the Greater Story of mankind. My name is in *honor of my Cherokee ancestry.* In God's eyes we are not different because of ancestry but we are all His children. My genealogy consists of Ralph Waldo Emerson, Betsy Ross, and King James I, and my family has served in every war ever fought in America, with honors. My family has come from Germany, France, and England coming to this continent in the 1500's. But the truth is *we are all* from God and so in God's eyes *we are ONE people.* I have longed to write all my life and so as I speak to you I want you to know that what is written has come from my soul. God has always given me the words to write.

Every season has a place, and when the harvest is ready, the fruits come forth. I have taken what is Within me, and God has multiplied and now I share with you. Life is more than we have understood in days gone by. Life on earth is about becoming one with Our Creator.

INTRODUCTION

~ Within you right now is the power to do things you never dreamed possible. This power becomes available to you when you align yourself with God. ~

Today I challenge you to love yourself more than anything in this world. Your life has incredible potential to awaken you and change your course. Everything about your life experience, good or bad, easy or difficult, holds the key to why you came to earth and what you came to do. If you doubt what I have come to tell you, that's ok, but take a walk with me for a time and when the book is over, you make the choice of where you go from here. Like a ship that is safe in a harbor, you, too are safe by living the way you live right now. You can convince yourself that you are safer not doing anything different and just living to get by.

~But ships were not built for the harbor and your life was not designed to just stay in one place~

You were created in the image of God and God is always changing, always becoming more but it's **NOT** because He stays in a safe harbor. God is everywhere, from the cave to the open seas. God is always changing like the clouds in the sky. ***God is willing for the storm***

1

because He knows the beauty after the storm and knows that the storm will help us grow. Our growth is very important to God. He loves us very much and wants us to be more by becoming one with Him. When we become one with Him we help others become one. Our growth is important to God because He created us so we could be co-creators with Him and everything we do can help God in multiplying His love.

~God's love is eternal and always they're for you, and He will never leave us~

God loves based on **NO conditions** and so **no one or nothing** has to live up to a certain set of standards or rules, to receive God's love. God's pattern shows us how to live our lives. When I say pattern I ask you to open your understanding and look at the pattern in nature, alone.

~Nature is always changing, always revealing miracles, always opening new doors and always transcending~

The pattern of our lives is about becoming MORE than what we currently are right now. Because God created man far above his creating purpose behind nature, and if nature is always transcending, doesn't it make sense that *we have a greater potential in our lives*. But religion and many human beliefs try to keep us from going beyond our "mental box" of what we think our life is about.

~God's love is unconditional and that means there is nothing you can possibly do to loose God's love~

Do you understand what that means? Have you lived all your life on eggshells because although you have heard of unconditional love, you have been taught that God's love is given when you meet certain conditions? Has this been reinforced by earthly relationships of love or of teachings in church?

This is where **the truth must be re-established** in the hearts of all people. This is where the greatest misconception on planet earth is found, in how our hearts hold God's truth but our "minds", or our "mental boxes" have been given different teachings. **The greatest loss is that the heart and the mind have separated** and lost connection. The heart knows your true identify meaning who you are and why you are here but has been overcome by the mind, that which is programmed by the experiences of life and how you **interpret** them. The true way to heal and really see who you are and the beauty of your life is to reconnect the heart with the mind. And the only way to do that is to see how the mind needs to rewrite what it believes as truth about "Y-O-U". You see our minds hold certain beliefs and those beliefs have attached to other beliefs. The beliefs have become our reality as we see them through the mortal mind, the carnal or the ego. We have allowed them to be our "reality" only because of ignorance. I speak with a heart of love for you. Your life has incredible power and **you will find it when** you begin to look at what you have allowed yourself to believe and then rewrite the lies you have told yourself to be true. **We were created in His image to do the same things as He does.** We have the potential to become a vessel in which we are co-creators with God.

So as I begin, how can I tell you in this introduction how important the journey of your life is? The truth is that each of our lives are as important as the life that Jesus lived and many other incredibly gifted spiritual men and women that walked this earth. **This book is not about "religion" but about "spirituality" and who you are as a spiritual Being.**

God has asked you to sit a spell and re-think about your life and it's meaning. I wonder if you are one who has experienced enormous pain and struggle in recent years and you are even wondering why you are here on this earth in the first place. Or maybe you have been given many blessings but you just want to find greater purpose in understanding how you can reach out and help the world. This book has the "potential" to help you become a force in this world for change **but the only way it can be affective is that you take hold of your own learning.** When you are willing to re-look at yourself and your beliefs, only then can you be the change. I cannot do anything for you and none of the words I write can potentially do anything for you. ***My words have power only if you are the doer of change.*** I encourage you to use this book as a tool to help you see that there is more to life than what you currently understand. I encourage you to believe that you are the only one that can create the change you need in your life and only when you see that, will you be the change. This is about ***courage to find the real you and to love who you are*** and to see that you are more than what you believe.

Many of us walk long and lonely roads with struggles that often overwhelm our daily living and to you I want to give you the courage to pick up the pieces of your life and re-look at them **"differently"**. The way your life has been lived and experienced by you ***is to help you to learn***, to grow, and to become what you need to become in order to manifest the spiritual plan laid out before you came to earth. ***Sometimes the journey we have been on has greater meaning when we take off the colored lenses that we have been judging our path with, and put on new lenses.*** It is my deepest desire to help you take hold of your life today and begin to walk ***toward "your own destiny"*** and ***believe*** that all you have experienced in life is for your learning and for your growth. It is not to destroy you or make you miserable. Sometimes many of us go thru much more difficult paths than others and we wonder why are we so unlucky. Are we the unlucky ones? Maybe we go thru far more, because we have more to overcome in order to fulfill our spiritual plan. Don't get discouraged when I say this. If you have far more to overcome than many then you can know you have a very important mission on earth. If your life has had enormous obstacles, then when you understand how to rise above them, you will accomplish great things and the blessings will be enormous. We have the greatest ability to really bring change and our complicated journey is trying to keep us from ever being who we are and doing what we came to do. Obstacles are thrown on our path to discourage us. But you can rise over them quickly ***when you really see the truth of your life.***

This is my hope in that you will have the courage to move mountains. What does God need, you may ask? He needs people ***who are willing***

to walk the journey they have volunteered to walk, and then to formulate within themselves how they can take all the pieces of their lives, in this lifetime, and bring forth richness and meaning. When we pick up the pieces of our lives, we have the potential to help ourselves and in turn a vast number of people who can take courage for their lives.

Maybe the path that has brought enormous pain and struggle and loneliness is a path that has been trying to teach us things we were not willing to learn and grow from. You can become a force in which you can help the world change themselves by the example of your "own courage." You may ask yourself right now what do I need to learn and why am I not willing. Like anything in life, learning is part of growing. Maybe it ***appears*** you are not willing because ***you don't understand the value*** of the troubles and so you hang on to fear. Growing often comes as a result of change. Change is what the world has done from the beginning and change will always precede greatness.

Why is change so hard on this planet? Is it because many are just set in their ways? Do they know that "their" ways will one day be changed to new ways of doing things? ***How about us changing before we leave this lifetime so that a foundation of future change can be quicker?*** One of the core problems of humanity is that we divide and conquer over everything that will never matter one bit in the Spiritual realm. We divide and conquer over everything because ***humans have such a need to be right***. Instead of arguing with our brothers and sisters ***lets try to understand them and see it from a different viewpoint***. Is it really going to hurt if you realize your way isn't the only way of seeing things? I have known some who argue all the time and condemn anyone who doesn't see it their way. They are often very insecure and so they get their good feelings when they feel right about everything. Whether it is political, religious, or any disagreement we need to get rid of the ***mindset*** that takes us down from uniting as one people under God. The "mindset" is simply how we have chosen to believe our way is the only way. Our way may be very valid and beneficial but ***everyone sees things from their viewpoint and it doesn't hurt to see something thru the eyes of another***. Our mindset is affected by factors that have affected us in our lives. When two leaders argue for centuries, I think all of us can agree that the original issues are long gone and what is left is simply a ***mindset. A mind set in stone, where nothing is changeable which keeps everyone fighting for their own way.*** The issues aren't the problem, for the problem is the EGO, the dualistic way of doing everything. God wants us to put away childish things and if we differ from one another then understand the reasons and find a common ground. Many leaders who fight battles for centuries have forgotten the original issue that brought the arguments in the first place because the people involved have been gone for a long time.

~Change comes when courageous people are willing to take off the colored lenses they have viewed our world through and pull the beam out of their own eyes~

In God's eyes color of skin, nationality, religious beliefs, geographical location, and political preference ***does not stop Him from empowering anyone that is willing to become one with Him.*** Men divide because of pride and selfishness but ***God loves unconditionally. To serve the God within you and The God Almighty you must put away childish things and become wise.***

~God calls forth a people with a pure heart that want all people to have the same abundance~

What you might need to learn could be very simple and might just be the way you "view" something. The way we "view" things can bring us to a change in our lives that is able to take us down a road in which we always dreamed. It might be a simple belief, it might be something that would take courage, it might be many things but change comes as a result of learning something and in turn becoming MORE of who we are. Maybe you are one who has lost a child recently and you cannot find the reason why this awful thing has happened. That child is now your guardian angel and has the ability to help you become MORE of who you are. ***Don't spend too much time being angry or feeling crippled because when you are ready the teacher will come.*** The teacher might very well be your child who has "only" moved into another realm. What you need to learn will be given to you as you ***begin to walk*** the road of empowering who you are spiritually. As far as why you have not been willing for this in the past, I can only say that for me ***my unwillingness was based on my lack of understanding*** that my life was important. My unwillingness was a result of me feeling a fear of change, and I felt I was unworthy, and that my life was insignificant, and that my place was to remain doing what "seemed" to be safe.

Like the ship was not built to dwell in the harbor, you and I are not created to simply exist and just fulfill the human desires we accumulate on earth as we live here. We are created out of God as individuals, which have God dwelling in us. We have been given power to use our free will to co-create MORE of God. God wants us to embrace the "importance" of our lives and the "importance" of what we can do to change our world so that God's abundance can be so great today and forever. But like all things, ***we must first begin with ourselves.*** We must first pull the beam out of our own eyes in order to really see the truth. I believe that when we see the truth, and when we work towards eliminating the false beliefs we have about ourselves, and our world, this is when we will have the power to not only change ourselves, but also change will become a force in our world. If we could see that there is more power in unconditional love than all the hate and pride that ever existed from the beginning of this earth, ***then we would not waste time or energy on the things that bring nothing into our lives.***

As you read this book remember that I don't have all the answers and many things that I express are not new to mankind. Even today in our world there are many gifted, and spiritual men and women that speak the same things. ***See this book as a tool that is able to open up your own toolbox of solutions to your life.*** See this book as stepping-stones for you to find more of what your life is about. See this book as a way to encourage you to look beyond what is currently known to mankind and find an even greater purpose to life on earth. The greatest tool you have is what is within you. Your intuitive, inner voice, is your spiritual being that you brought with you into this world, and that being, **which is you**, can guide you. This is critical for you to know because when I say that my words or my thoughts cannot change you, what I mean is that as you read, the inner voice **within you will alert you** to what you need to pay attention to. **Don't put that voice aside but hear that voice, and respond with love in your heart to think on what it might mean for you.**

This is a personal journey of transformation. One of the dangers of any book, including the Bible, is that you believe that the words written are "everything there is to know" and nothing can be added or changed. Another danger is that the words written are the only thought on the matter and the only answer to the path you need to take. Jesus emphasized the "living word", not the written word. The written word can be dead if you use it to understand your life. The written word speaks to the people it was written for, at that time in history, but can be a challenge to those who walk thousands of years later. Times change, God is always changing. But what remains the same yesterday, today, and forever is the **Living Word. The Living Word is what your heart hears within thru intuitive connections, thru God within you, thru your I AM PRESENCE, your spiritual being.** The Living Word has the ability to breath life into your soul and help you become one with God. **The Living Word has the ability to help you understand how these teachings apply to you and your life, personally.** The Living Word is breathing in and out and has the ability to sense your needs and what will help you to draw closer in oneness with Our Father. The Living Word flows with the river of life that is always seeking for more abundance.

As you read my words, **use them to re-connect to what is within "You" and then hear the voice of God speaking to your own heart.** You are an individualization of God and God created you with the same ability to co-create and bring more to this earth. You may wonder how God trusts humans to do something so profound. It is because He believes in you being able to take the pieces of your life and turn them into the blessings and learn and become full of knowledge and wisdom.

God has faith that you will find everything you need from within. God gives you full reign because He knows you have His heart of love built in. God knows who you are and loves you unconditionally. God's love for you is so complete and so fulfilling that when you embrace His love and open your heart to Him, ***nothing in this world will ever satisfy you again.*** What humans long for on earth is love and to find God and when they find these two parts of which ***"they think they are missing"***, they will then find complete wholeness and this is when they can be all and more of what God created them to be. ***What joy there will be when all of God's children believe they are worthy, feel the love of their creator and create enormous abundance on planet earth.*** God hopes you will take a chance and find that your life is more important than you imagined and begin to live as you wrote your spiritual plan.

I challenge you to look beyond all the teachings that you currently know and believe ***there is far more to learn***. Become attuned to the inner person you are and follow your own intuition so that you can begin to see the things that you need to overcome in order to rise above a ***"limited"*** belief system. God gave all of us the same ability to see the plan of our lives that was given from the beginning. Jesus, Buddha and many other spiritual teachers who have walked on this earth and have left messages had the same struggles of finding out who they really were and reconnecting with the spiritual being they were. They had victory and they want more than anything else for us to also have victory. They are the Keepers of the Eternal Flame of God's Love. Again, I also ask you to ***not attach to the outer teachings*** of what is written here as "all-inclusive". What I mean is that the words written are to ***help "you"*** take courage of your own destiny and are not everything you need to learn and understand. As you tap into your own inner being, you will find new and ***just as important*** teachings on your own. God will begin to teach you things that are uniquely for you. This is where your own ability to go inside and learn from the inner teacher that dwells within you, is so critical.

Everyone is different and everyone sees things according to their own understanding. For example a child will see the same situation that an adult sees and yet have a whole different interpretation. The reason for this difference is an illustration given to you in which you can understand how the mind interprets things according to their level of consciousness. Consciousness is the awareness or perception of something by a person or the state of being awake and aware of one's surroundings. So when I speak of Consciousness I want you to understand that how you perceive something can be determined by your understanding, your culture, and even the times in which you live. A good example is that the Bible was written to people who understood things a certain way but if they understood as we do today, **the Bible would have to be written to a higher understanding**. As in school you cannot expect a kindergartner to see things the same as a senior in High School. Religion has drilled us to believe that each one's interpretation isn't always correct and a particular religion will often cling to theirs as being the "only way" to see something. But God gave us individuality and free will so that we can explore what is here on earth and **formulate our own understanding**. For any group to say they have the only understanding of something is their way of trying to create a fear in differences and ultimately their greatest fear is that they are wrong in believing they know everything. But our differences are the essence of free will and in giving all of us FREE WILL God is saying our differences can help us to become more and to improve on what is, right now. God trusts that we can come full circle and really see for ourselves why it is better to do something a certain way.

~When an action is born out of fear, it can only take us down a road where fear must keep us doing the same action, because more fear is required to keep control over our beliefs. But when an action is born out of love, it will take us down a road where love keeps us doing the same action~

This is the key to abundant life. When you see why doing something **for the right reason is really in your own benefit** and will ultimately give "you" life eternal, **then no one has to convince you to do the same again and again**. Some might say that this is dangerous and can only lead to error. But the truth is that when we understand something, we have the potential to make things better. ***When we understand something we can build on it because knowledge helps us to let go of fear.***

God needs all of us to take hold of our lives and to learn the value of things that are from the heart. God needs us to correct the things that are wrong because we want life to be better. When we understand things, we see the value in change and we no longer see it as something we "have" to do but we now ***see it as something we "want" to do*** because we want life more abundantly. ***This is the difference between doing something out of fear and doing something out of love.***

I believe that if we truly connected to the Father, as Jesus and many other Ascended Beings did, we wouldn't wander off because what we would find would be so beautiful that we would desire nothing more than the perfect love for God and mankind. ***It will be a feeling like we have never experienced in this life*** and our hearts will desire to do everything we can to help others and to receive more of God's love.

~When we love like God that same love is returned unto us and we are then made whole~

When we experience this we take a bold stand for ourselves and no longer desire childish or foolish things. We feed on the truth of God's love and we want more of it. It sets us on a track of oneness with the Father and no one or nothing can change how we feel. That is when the power of God heals us from within.

Sometimes we do have to go down roads that are very harmful but there is always a way out if we honestly take hold and take courage to make the necessary changes. Sometimes that means we must ask for help, but if asking for help gets us started on a road that will forever change our lives for the good, ***then wouldn't you want it?*** If we need counseling and we need the strength from another to re-look at our own reasoning's, then doesn't this seem to be a good place to start? ***There is nothing wrong with getting help.*** God allows us the freedom to journey ***as we choose,*** so that when we resolve the things in our lives that need resolving, we also gain courage and strength within. When we take hold of decisions that need to be made in order for us to ***begin*** a journey of change, then we are saying ***we are taking back control of our lives***. We are making a statement that this is our life and no one has permission to live it for us. We begin to see we truly do have control over our lives. ***We find that we are not victims of circumstances but we are victors waiting to embrace our lives.***

As you begin to read, think of yourself as a Treasure Hunter. You are on a quest to find out more of why you do what you do, and who you really are in the eyes of God. You may find interesting artifacts that intrigue you but also cause you to see the foolishness of the illusions you have kept on the filmstrip of your mind. As you begin to put the pieces of the puzzle together in your life, and you find incredible beauty on the roads of your past, remember that ***you are very special in God's eyes*** and your story can inspire others to do the same. Even though at one time you saw those roads as failures or as traps that kept you in a survival mode, you now can see them as ***tools*** and as you uncover the real reason why those roads had to be walked by you, you begin to unlock the potential of the spiritual being you really are and the mission of your life. Keep in mind as you uncover your path that every step of the way, even if it is painful, has beauty when uncovered. As a Treasure Hunter, why is there such joy in finding ancient treasures buried so long ago? For some, the treasures are family heirlooms or keys to the past that have been so long ago forgotten. For others they are long forgotten stories of people who lived, who loved, and who died in their life struggles. And many times the treasures unearthed of the past lead to lost civilizations, to medical marvels, to ancient secrets and to treasures waiting for someone to find them. Why are these treasures so important to those alive now and in this time period? For the stories that we find of the past, when we die they will die with us and because they are only stories, how will they change our own future?

~They change our future by how they change our hearts and how we view things~

Our hearts then have the ability to change the desires within us convincing us it is time to take hold of our own destiny. As we take hold of our own destiny we have the ability to change future generations and become the change in our lives and in those who look on or who will live in the future. The treasures of the past, good or bad, *are keys to unlock a treasure chest full of incredible wisdom* waiting to be embraced and waiting to assist us in changing our world. But if you remain unwilling to uncover the treasures of your past, then they will haunt you and those that walk after you. Take courage and know that knowledge is freedom.

As I think on the treasures of wisdom of the past, I am reminded that each of us hold within our being, incredible truths that were given to us before we set foot on this earth. We are spiritual beings having an earthly experience so that we can be a reflection of God's light and love and can bring change to a world waiting for answers. And even more important we are Spiritual Beings that have lived many lifetimes and in this life we bring with us the wisdom and the strength but remain human. Have we lost this understanding as we find our lives go in a downward spiral? I believe with all my heart that *we have forgotten but we haven't lost anything*.

Everything about us is waiting to be re-awakened. Before we came to this earth we had help from a spiritual teacher in formulating our purpose and mission. The plan was made into a blueprint and that blueprint is still intact. *It has not been marred; it has not been changed, but is as plain as the day we made it.* The reason we loose sight that it exists is because we get so caught up in the journey of life on earth, that we have simply covered it over with layers upon layers of ways to see things *that are far from beneficial to us as spiritual beings* but we believe they are beneficial for us on earth. These layers are created slowly, year after year, by our interpretations of why things are happening. We see things differently as we walk in life because we are trying to survive in a world that is often focused on *immediate gratification*. We can't change the world and we have definitely lost sight of our blueprint but the hope with this book is that maybe some of us can get past the things that ***cloud our vision and pull the beam out of our own eyes.*** Maybe some of us will see the blueprint, and take the courage to leave behind the things that hinder our walk, and believe the power waiting for you to embrace.

The power to change your world and how you see your life is within you right this very moment. ***No one needs to tell you that it's there and nothing can change its mission, accept you. No one can take away what is within you and you will be able to reconnect as soon as you let go of the things that cloud your vision.*** Many things cloud our vision but most importantly it's our belief of deserving love and of loving ourselves. Fears, frustrations and needs to control others, keep us in a struggle and take us down roads that only lead to more trouble. Going within and taking hold of our own lives is the number one task you must accomplish. You can't change the beliefs of anyone outside of you. You can't stop their opinions no matter how powerful they are in trying to hurt you. ***You are only in control of Y-O-U. Therefore focus on going inside of yourself.***

Use your inner wisdom and be honest with yourself. You ***don't have to share anything about you with anyone***, but be honest and ask yourself the questions that come to the surface as you begin an honest evaluation of the reasons why you feel the way you do. If you feel anger with your parents, your children, or your spouse then allow yourself to feel that anger but then ask yourself if they changed would it really change your world. Many times we, as humans, tend to blame our struggles on how others have hurt us or done things to us. But the truth is that there will always be others that will hurt or betray us. And if those that hurt us change, could you change from living it over and over? Do they have a hold on your future by taking away the power of your free will to live as you choose, even if they changed? We blame outside people, circumstances, and scenarios for our troubles but really the truth is it's not the troubles that determine how we feel ***but our interpretation of the troubles*** and how we can't move past them and learn the lesson. If someone runs his or her car into the back of your car, how do you react? Yes you have a right to be angry but anger won't change what happened. Do you hang on to something for the rest of your life because it gives you permission to be angry or can you see the value of letting something be the way it is and finding a reason to see the blessings of the rest of your life. Thankful people that understand life isn't perfect and always will contain loopholes, find a joy in the good things that life has brought. We can't dwell on the negative and ***expect joy*** in our lives. If we always have a gloomy outlook of why this or that is happening and we always blame someone for making us unhappy then we are only doing ourselves wrong. We are the only ones that are unhappy. We create our own sense of struggle and our own unhappy attitude.

~Our sense of struggle is the struggle itself~

When we see that we are in control of our own destiny then we realize that it is only in our own hands to change our future. Look at the bright side instead of the gloomy side. There is a saying that says:

~I can complain because rose bushes have thorns or I can rejoice because thorn bushes have roses~

Take control by starting with every day little things that happen and use these as opportunities to see more of who you are and what you need to do in your life to make it more abundant. It is all about how we see things and that comes back to our mindset or our consciousness. Our mindset is simply how we view our lives, our world, and our future. Our mindset is directly related to our level of understanding. It is my hope that you will understand more thru what I write and in turn your mindset will change. ***If we always see the negative and always find why something can't work then we will never embrace the potential awaiting for us in our individual lives and in our world as a whole to see life as a beautiful opportunity of transcendence.*** Believe that God created you for a purpose and your life mission is waiting to be embraced. Whatever struggles, of your past, has hindered you; see them as lessons to learn by. See anything that has been hard on you, which has created enormous heartache, as something you must move past and gain wisdom from within, in order to reach the next level of your understanding. ***The troubles we go thru are only there to teach us and NOT to stop us.*** Sometimes they do stop us for a while and sometimes ***they send us on a different road*** in which we must walk for a while. But all troubles can cease when we see them differently.

Think of a child who is dying of cancer, being strength to an adult who has lived a privileged life and for many years. Why does this child, who never can grow up, who never can enjoy the simple things of life, and who has no future, have the ability to bring joy and compassion to people who have lost sight of the many things they have to be thankful for. Because this child has stopped looking at his own struggles and has been able to look into your heart and see what you need to change so that you can be happy, you also can see beyond your current circumstances. This child is giving you a new perspective on what you are currently going thru by showing you that there is more to your own life. Everything we need to become the people God intended us to become is within our own being. Nothing and no one outside of our being can or should have any control over our destiny. If you feel someone or something is responsible for your attitude or outlook in life, or is hindering your ability to walk in this life, then you need to look at yourself. It is you and ***how you see it*** that is hindering you, and not them. No one has any control over you, unless you give him or her control.

Let us begin to open up our hearts and re-look at our lives so that we can become the people we are destined to become. You have the power to re-look at your life and see it differently. No one is stopping you unless you count your own inner voice. If your own inner voice is the one stopping you from finding the joy of life, then lets change the way you talk to yourself. Take the courage you have within and begin today to take a new step towards finding the joy God so much wants you to have. ***Begin by taking the responsibility that you are the only one who can take charge of your life.*** Take charge and stop looking for help somewhere outside yourself. Be the Change by starting with yourself

GOD

In explaining God to you I need you to understand that how you see things will determine how you understand the reality of God. Your level of consciousness or understanding is determined by how open your heart is to different ways of seeing things.

~God is Spirit and those that worship Him, worship Him in Spirit and in truth~

You might see God as an old man that sits on a throne or you might see him as one who is ready to judge and bring judgment upon your every wrong move. I don't know what your understanding is and so it is my desire to help you see Him in a new, and universal way. For years I had seen Him as most people and yet I feel that God has led me to this point where there is a need for Unity in this world and it is my desire that you will embrace a Universal Way in which all people on this earth can unite as ONE.

To understand God you need to understand that God created from a basic substance, which is described in the Bible as *Light*. But we can now understand through science that light is another word for energy and this is where my thoughts are going. Keep in mind that understanding some of what was written many years ago in the Bible could take on a new view in today's world. The message has more to understand than what was revealed so long ago. ***God is about always becoming more and so the Bible, as written so long ago, has hidden messages that can now come forth because God knows people are ready for a higher understanding.*** What I am saying is that the same concept of the different levels of energy, is similar in the different levels of understanding. So if you lived in the days of the Bible, lets say the Old Testament, you would have read certain truths that were written for your understanding but the same truths written today can be written for you to have a ***higher understanding****.* In the world God created a pattern and yet in the pattern He created form. Form comes in many different ways. From living to non-living, forms have patterns but beneath it all, everything is made from energy or God's light.

When I speak of energy I want you to begin to envision energy on different levels. Let's envision the steps in a ladder to make it simple. Each step represents energy of different vibrations. Our material world is made up of spiritual energies that have been lowered in vibration in order to take on the form God needed to create. So what I am saying is that there is a layered structure of energy in this world. Each layer is a different vibration. So if we keep going towards higher vibration we will ultimately rise to the very substance that created this earth, which is Light. But you may ask where did this light come from? I can only say that God created the light because in the beginning there was nothing but God. The Bible says,

> ***"All things were made by Him; and without Him was not any thing that was made." (John 1:3)***

God was all that existed in the beginning. I believe that God created the light out of his own being and therefore it is not different from or apart from God. The word "apart" will be used over and over again in this book because it is critical that you know you are not apart from God and never have been.

~Light is simply God wearing a mask in the form of many different created substances~

To see God and to know God, you need to open your eyes, for He is all around you and is *in* everything. Only the carnal mind or the ego tries to prevent you from seeing God in everything. To see God in his fullness you need to have the Christ mind. The Christ mind is a level of understanding that you can attain by growing closer to oneness with God.

God in His highest form is a state of pure Being, a state of pure consciousness. Since a lot of this book will refer to consciousness let me define it for you.

~Consciousness refers to your perception of something or the awareness you hold in your mind of yourself, the world and God~

Take for instance how there is a difference in the understanding between a child and an adult. A child sees things according to their level of understanding and an adult sees things according to their level of understanding. Understanding and perception is based on what they know about something and is influenced by experience, emotions, family, country, and nationality. So there are not only differences in understanding or consciousness between age groups but also in nationalities. Take for instance someone arriving from China and coming to the United States for school. Many times even language and choices of words for the same actions have different meanings as a whole, in different countries. This is why many things can be lost in translation. It's not always intentional but is how we explain the same thing in a different language or culture. Take a look at music. If you put the same words and the same notes with different key signatures, you have a different composition and the mood that it creates will be different. The same is with language.

~Language barriers exist because of our different understandings of the same expression~

Which is often according to the levels of understanding where we live and when we live on this earth. We could go on and on and write a book about "our differences" but my goal is to help you see *why* we see things at *different levels of understanding* and *know that these different perceptions aren't necessarily all there is to know about something*, nor are they the final analogy.

So if you take the picture of God and you ask 10 people who God is and what does He look like, and then you chose those 10 people from different religions and countries, you are going to get many different interpretations. The truth is that there is a Universal picture of God and this is where we as humans need to *join hands and come together* to understand God. Let's find a greater understanding of God and allow our Consciousness to be raised so that we not only see God better, but *we draw close to Him in a Universal way*. Let's understand that we might each have a different way of seeing God because of the different levels of understanding we are at. That's ok, because our differences in how we see things actually adds a broader view of the Greatness of God.

~We are all from the Creator and we are all capable of becoming one with Him~

We are all as important as another. So walk with me through some thoughts and let's see if we can open up more understanding.

As I said God is a state of pure Being, and this side of God has no form. *God is also a self-conscious being that has individuality and does have a sense of form*, as we see form. Just in understanding these two aspects of God or two levels of seeing Him, we know God created form out of His own being. This is critical to understand in understanding the different aspects of God.

Let's look at something that we do understand in order to have a clearer picture of what I am saying about God. H2o is what we commonly call water, in a liquid form, but H2o can be seen in different forms and each form serves a purpose. If you freeze H2o it becomes a solid and is called ice. If you boil H2o it becomes a vapor such as steam. Each form is still H2o but ***each is created from its original being, namely H2o.*** It is not created ***apart*** from the main basic state of Being. So to understand this further, think about which form of H2o can be turned into ice. ***Only the liquid form or the self-conscious being of water can be actually made into another form.*** But the vapor or the steam cannot be made into ice, and this can represent, as an example, the same as God, with no form. ***God can only use the self-conscious being that has individuality and a sense of form, to created a form from His own being.*** God cannot create something that is apart from itself. God takes a part of Himself and creates the form He desires. So this also is very important to understand in knowing God. God is creative and with imagination and when He created all forms of life, He created them with His own vision of what He desired. ***That is why the Bible states that without Him was not anything made that was made.*** In other words, to create the world of form ***He put a part of himself into this world and all that is in this world. He is in everything*** in this world and cannot be separate from anything that is created and that includes non-living forms such as rocks.

This is very important to understand. Many people feel like God is somewhere else, some place unreachable and this creates a sense of separation, a sense of unworthiness, etc. The truth is ***God is inside of you.*** He lives in your being and is not separate from you at all. ***God is a permanent part of "you" and so cannot be separate from you.***

~God took a part of him and made you and so you are a part of God~

Do you understand how important this is? Everything that was ever created is really God wearing a disguise. Everything was created by God and from God and therefore has God's consciousness within it. We are **not separate from God** and **never have been**. If you could grasp this alone, it would help you to know that everything you need, to change your life, to build upon your understanding, and to go beyond your current struggles, is right inside waiting for you to tap into. **God is within**. Jesus said,

"The Kingdom of God is within".

You can feel a sense of comfort to know God is in you and you are a part of Him. So many times when we struggle in this life, we feel like there is no one that cares and we feel so alone. *This "alone" feeling is one of the most devastating emotions.* When a person feels alone they also feel unloved and this connects our hearts to the one who created us. When we feel alone and unloved we loose belief in God and in the purpose of our lives. This will cause us to become so desperate. So, today as you read on, *keep the warm feeling inside that God is in you* and *you are a part of Him right now*. You always have had him and so as you begin to grasp this reality, know that He knows everything you are going thru and He loves you no matter what. He will **never leave you** and he **never has** in the past. *The reason we feel so alone is because we have been taught that God is somewhere outside and we have to find him.* We have believed that we are separated from God and so we have to find him and invite him to come into our hearts. *But the truth is He has always been in our hearts and all we have to do is open our hearts to see Him.* We have been taught that God won't accept us unless we are repentant and willing to turn our lives around into a "perfect scenario", "that we envision we must have". You see, the "alone" feelings are *created by our own lack of understanding.* We have a picture of God in our mind that has been created by the world. We have believed it to be true and *we have shut off our connectedness to God by our beliefs.* What I'm saying is that we have shut off our communication so that God can help us see the truth. *When you believe that you don't have God in you and never will, this creates a vacuum that can never be filled until you change your belief.*

To know that everything in the material universe is made from God consciousness, you will then know why Jesus said *that if men should hold their peace, even the stones would cry out.* However, not everything in the material universe has the *same level* of consciousness. God created a world of inanimate forms and then created a number of self-conscious to inhabit the inanimate world. Human beings were created to descend into the material universe and to gradually work their way up through the different levels of the world of form, until they expand their self-awareness, their sense of identity, to the ultimate level. What's very important for self-aware beings to understand and what gives them *meaning to their existence* is that they recognize *they are a part of God* or an extension, an individualization of God.

Look at a rock. A rock is an inanimate form but is still from God. A rock has God's consciousness embedded within it, but because it *isn't self-aware*, it doesn't realize that God created it. Therefore it will never be any more than a rock. *But we as humans are self-aware beings and we have the ability to go beyond what we are right now and draw more of God's light into our being.* If we are willing to learn and grow and expand our awareness then we can become very helpful to the spiritual world.

~The spiritual world cannot force help on the human world but if asked to help they are more than willing and that is when the two vibrations connect~

That is when a higher vibration brings light into the material world.

~It will take human beings that are willing to have the mind of Christ and be examples to bring more light to this world~

You see we have often heard of the Second Coming of Christ and I believe *that*

~The second coming of Christ is when the spirit world is invited by willing human beings to give assistance to manifest a higher vibrational light on this planet~

The Christ mind is what we can have while here on earth and is what the spiritual beings have already. This mind comes when you are willing to give up the human sense and take on the mind of Christ or spiritual understandings that draw you closer to becoming one with God. The mind of Christ raises your light, or your level of vibration and when this happens and it happens to enough people, the Second Coming of Christ will be made manifest.

~You see the difference between heaven and earth is a difference in vibration or energy~

In helping you to understand God, it is important to understand why religion has been so much a part of our world. God wanted religion to help human beings fulfill their potential and recognize themselves as sons and daughters of His.

~When people recognize the truth about things, it brings peace in many ways~

However, sometimes when the truth is made known it brings fear because it disproves your beliefs as you have seen them in the past. Take for instance, that you were raised in a religion and now you find that the teachings are not **all** true. This truth made known can actually cause a fear of so many things. And furthermore it can create a fear within you because you are questioning the doctrine.

So knowledge or truth can be liberating only if you are **open** to receiving it. But if you are stuck in a belief then truth can be fearful. Letting go is hard in this world.

~Many times our sense of security is based on things of this world and when those things no longer exist, we actually feel lost and very alone~

The fear we feel is a fear of whether we are doing the right thing or on the right path.

~Anytime a rug gets pulled out from under you, you will loose your sense of balance~

When this happens keep in mind that God is always changing and he never stays the same. So if you were in a certain belief for many years, and now everything seems to be wrong and you are jumping ship, so to speak, you have the right to feel that your world has fallen apart. Don't fear changing your understanding of a teaching. Because there are many levels of understanding or consciousness, **give yourself the "ok" to learn more than what you have currently learned in the past.** Don't fear God because you are now questioning a belief of the church you have gone to.

~A church doesn't save you but our relationship with God saves you~

So if you currently don't have all the right understanding of a teaching, **don't you think God would want you to have it.** Looking for it and changing what you once believed is what God wants because God wants all to come to Him and sometimes we have to leave behind the things that hindered our vision in the past. What I want to assure you with, is that even though these feelings **are valid at this time in your life**, you need to be able to move past them and look to the future and then all that you are experiencing at this moment, will pass. A new view of things will emerge on the horizon as you begin a new journey, a new path, **where truth is the most important thing you desire.** This is where faith and trust, that **God will help you and not leave you** *destitute* is important. ***The unknown or the unexplainable brings unrest and fear and this creates a void in each of us.*** But if you have faith that these times are teachers for you to learn something from, then you can see a deeper understanding of why difficulties happen in life.

So when people do recognize themselves as sons and daughters of God, God can experience this world through them. God can experience what it is like ***to be inside his creation*** and not only ***be the creator*** of it, who is looking at it from the outside. God has more than one purpose for the creation of human beings. If you really think about this, you will realize how much ***God wants to be a part of you and how much he wants you to be a part of him***. You are one with God but the only thing that keeps you from feeling this oneness is ***your mind*** and how it sees things. It puts up walls in which you cannot see the truth. It is our ego or carnal mind that we experience as a challenge when coming on this earthly visit. When we see through this carnal mind, we see the world as the only home we have and the reason for what we do is justified by a "limited" view.

~But we are more than this life and we have more to do than just work, eat and sleep~

We live for the things of this world because this ***is*** our life but we don't need to be living ***only*** for the things of this life.

This is what happens when we come to earth. Just so you know, all of us when coming to earth, forget we are spiritual beings and we forget that we are here to experience something in this life that will help us in our spiritual being to become more of God. We also forget the plan we laid out with our spiritual teacher to help us give optimal growth in this life. Yes, this life is about taking responsibility for what we are given and working at growing in many aspects but we cannot forget ***we are spiritual beings FIRST*** and this life is a classroom in which we can advance, through our experiences in this life, to a higher understanding and achieve a greater closeness with God.

Take life serious but don't forget to be the spiritual being and don't forget that your first love is for your creator and how you can help him and become a co-creator with Him. ***When troubles come, try to learn the lesson, grow in understanding, show compassion and move beyond it.*** Some troubles are very difficult but each one is important and when the lesson is learned, you can move on and gain greater understanding. Don't give up and don't let things get out of hand. Just regroup and find friends that can help you in moving past things. The greatest gift is that you are on earth and you now have an ability to expand your spiritual awareness through the experiences you encounter at this time in this lifetime.

God wants to walk with you and He wants to experience them with you. Maybe it would be a wonderful privilege if you could see, ***God in you,*** going thru the same heartache and then talk with Him, and ask Him how you should deal with it. Go inside and become one with God, ***who is in you.*** You are not alone and your struggles are not to take you down.

~Allow God to love you and as you both experience the same heartache, you both can help each other, by being each other's best friend~

Jesus said, my father and I are one. This is the greatest privilege and this is being one with The Father.

~God wants to experience His creation through those He created~

As you are always striving for more understanding of things in this world naturally that you might already know about, God also wants to live thru us and ***understand the feelings and struggles we have thru the experiences, thru His creation.*** Some might say, this seems like an odd way of explaining God. I mean shouldn't God be telling us how to get out of our struggles. But the truth is that God created us from himself and God wanted us to experience life in different aspects and

~He wanted to experience life thru us so that He too, would become more~

So when you go thru an experience you go thru many things including what you become from the experience. God wants you to not just go thru things that are difficult but He wants to see how the experience helps you to become more of who you are at this time in your life. *God put a part of His reasoning in our minds and so doesn't it seem possible that the answers to our problems might already be inside of us but waiting to emerge.* Maybe all we have to do is look inside. This is why knowing these things can give you courage and courage can help you look at the God within you for the answers.

Another important part of God's reason for creating is that he wanted change to be always present not only in our lives but also on planet earth. He wanted *movement* so that all of His creation *could* be MORE. Just think of one atmospheric presence that you see every day. The clouds. God created the clouds to constantly change and never stay in one place. If God is a God of "never" changing and always remaining the same, as religion often teaches, *then why is everything in creation always changing.* It's just not logical!

So when God created the world of form, He also set in motion certain natural laws that would guide the constant change or evolution of the world. *These laws make it possible that the universe could evolve without any input from God.* The universe could grow in the mechanical fashion that is currently envisioned by modern scientists. But one might wonder what good does the mechanical universe serve? Wouldn't God in all His creative powers become bored by watching the universe unfold according to mechanical laws that would make everything so predictable?

I remember when I was a young girl and my parents gave me a train set for Christmas. I had so much fun with it but then I became bored of watching it go around the track, the same track over and over. I think the best part of getting the train set was in building the track and putting the track and the decor on a huge piece of wood. So the fun was in building the train tracks and not in watching it run around the same predetermined track that never changed. Now think of God and how He wanted to create a universe that is alive and vibrant and can change continually in ways that can be surprising even to him.

"His joy is in watching His creation and the adventures we go on, so to speak."

What I mean is He didn't make us like robots that did the same things over and over, *He made us to be ever changing and ever growing and at the same time God was experiencing through us*. So when God finished creation He wanted us to co-create, and to do this without any input from Him. In other words He wanted to step back to see what He could see and what *we could do*. God created us in his image and likeness and He is an incredible creator and so doesn't it only seem logical that He would want to watch us do the same. Doesn't this sound familiar? Yes, it sure does. Just look at the natural ways we live our lives.

In life, teachers teach students and then they let the student go on their own for a time and create. They watch the student use the skills that they taught them, to be co-creators. God is our teacher, our creator but He wants us to be more than robots. He wants us to use our imagination and our creative abilities and He is excited to see *what we can create, what we can do with this world*. This is why beliefs that trap you into thinking *inside a little box* and never let you experiment or exercise your skills, is *not of God* but of man's ego, man's way of thinking.

The reason God created human beings in His own image and likeness was to give them the ability to always be able to create more, just like Him. And because God has proven thru the vast intricacies of His creation that He does have the imagination, He wants to see what we might create. We simply are human beings with the ability to co-create with God. God is the external creator who creates the universe from the outside. But we, as humans are meant to be *internal creators who help co-create the universe from the inside.* Think of it this way. God created planet Earth as a starting point, a foundation in which *it can become so much more.* Then God sent human beings with the command to multiply and take dominion. I explain all of this to help you understand that *God is your friend and He longs for a relationship with you.* He knows a relationship out of fear would never work if you were going to be partners with Him. If you can grasp just a few things about the reasons why God created us and for what purpose, *you will see that any kind of fear or judgment can never serve a purpose in what God meant when He took a part of Him and created us.* Use your logic, use your reasoning and then open your heart and see for yourself that God longs for you to see Him as the loving God He is and then to take the opportunity He has given you *to be everything He wants you to be.*

Keep in mind that in Genesis it says God created the earth in six days and then on the seventh day He rested. When I was young I learned in church that this was the reason we were to go to Church on Sundays. I carried that belief all thru the years but the truth is it isn't really stated that way but religion has used that to get people to believe that on the day of rest we are to rest with God at church. Does that make sense? So, God wanted you to rest as *He was resting.* Later in life I challenged this by thinking out of the box, so to speak. I wondered if maybe God rested because He wanted to see what His creation could do on the seventh day. As I mentioned earlier God enjoys watching His creation and experiencing life thru them and so this theory I believe is very possible. *We are co-creators and so* could it be possible that God "resting" meant that God temporarily stopped His creative work on planet Earth *so that humans would take the opportunity to continue the work themselves.* I believe we are to take *an active role* in bringing God's kingdom into full manifestation on this planet. Creation is long past but the *pattern* of God is still the same. To bring God's kingdom to earth is to have the same desires as God, to have the light in which all creation came into being from and multiply our talents.

~Send into the cosmic universe the God within us and in return we will receive more of God~

Today He wants us to be co-creators and to believe that we are still given an opportunity to create.

~I think God really is hoping that in this New Age, a few that are willing to listen will hear His voice and understand that He still wants us to take upon ourselves the ability to be in His image and likeness~

What does this mean? It means look at what God has done and now take what He has given to us and multiply our talents. Send unto the universe the same and use the talents that are given to us as a reminder we are in His likeness and become partners, co-creators, and of the same mind of God.

I know this isn't what you have been taught. In my search for the rest of God's truth, I felt over and over that many religious teachings had ***partial*** truths in them, but often led humans down a road ***where all the pieces didn't fit together***. And the roads they were lead down, took away the power of taking hold of their lives. If you can see that we, as humans, are co-creators and Jesus is an example and we are to take responsibility of our lives, growing spiritually and becoming as Jesus said, one mind with God, then the seventh day, might make sense to you.

Another thought about creation is that sometimes we wonder that if God created the animals with abundant life naturally, why don't we also have abundant life? Again, this is about free will. We are human beings with free will to do as we wish. So if we want abundant life then we need to create that life thru the love of living the life God gave us freely.

~God wants humans to build upon the foundation He laid in creation and watch as we create more abundance for us. It truly is the Father's good pleasure to give you the abundant life~

This is the natural state of affairs on planet earth, namely that all human beings have abundance of every good and perfect gift. Jesus said, **" That ye may be the children of your Father which is in heaven: for he maketh his sun to rise on the evil and on the good, and sendeth rain on the just and on the unjust."**

But even more, Human beings are not *just* created to experience the universe and to help co-create it but God also wants us to grow in consciousness and self awareness, constantly becoming more than we were before. God wants us to reach the highest possible spiritual level we can attain but this only comes with understanding.

~Sometimes to reach a higher understanding we must go through tough experiences~

Earth is like a classroom in which we come here with how far our spiritual beings have grown to this point, we learn from the experiences we go thru in this lifetime and we rise above and beyond them. This is where we must look at our troubles as tools to grow from and to become more, by understanding the lessons from them.

~No experience is to destroy us or to stop our growth~

Growth in anything is in levels. Just look at a tree and how there are rings in the wood, which represent levels of growth.

So even in the most imperfect conditions on planet earth we can learn the lessons and move on. We can become MORE of who we were before. This is about keeping love in our hearts and growing with oneness in God.

~Becoming more in God's eyes requires giving up selfish desires and gain~

Becoming More is about growing as a spiritual being. I am not saying that certain conditions on earth are easy to deal with but what I am saying is that we can open our hearts and make the best of every situation. For the truth is ***when we change the way we see things, the world changes around us.***

~When we get a vision of a better future, it catches on like wildfire and before you know it there are many who have the same vision~

~There will always be opposition in this world but when enough people become the CHANGE, opposition looses its power~

The way to a better world is to know that God wants' us to believe we can make it happen by opening our hearts and becoming the co-creators He wanted us to be. Be The Change and Take hold of your destiny and your world.

~Always do everything for the betterment of the whole of mankind~

If you do things for selfish reasons, or for your gain, then it will affect the "whole" of mankind and create an imbalance. I am not saying you can't have a better life but the ***motive*** behind what you do is sent into the cosmic universe and ***what you send out will return unto you.*** So if you do something with a selfish motive and send it out into the cosmic universe, then imbalance will be returned unto you. But if you do something with unconditional love for the "whole" of mankind, then you will have a positive affect on this planet and others around you.

~The key to changing our world comes when you first focus on changing yourself~

When you change yourself to match the mind of Christ, you begin to bring more and more light into the world of form, and this will raise the vibration of the planet to a higher vibration. If enough people do this, then the planet will overcome many things and light will consume the darkness. Keep in mind that if you enter a dark closet and strike a match to see, that little light will lighten the whole closet. You can't get rid of evil or darkness like you can get rid of many things on this earth.

~The only way to get rid of darkness or evil is to bring in more light~

~Be the Change and Bring the light to planet earth and then you will know God as who He is~

Let's take a journey back to when we first arrive on earth through the birth process. We know deep inside that we are connected to something outside of our human bodies. In other words I believe although we have forgotten our "I AM" presence and our Spiritual Being from which we came from, we really didn't forget everything.

~The key is to be aware there is more to your life than you currently know and this alone will begin the journey of discovery you need to go on~

We also know there is a God. Deep inside we know this because God is in us and we are a part of His pure Being. When we think of humanity, we cannot forget a Son of God that came to be **an example.** Jesus' entire earthly ministry was meant to **demonstrate the path** where a human being, a son or daughter of man, could potentially grow in self awareness until it **manifests the full identity as a Christed being and accepts his or her identity as a son or daughter of God.** When you manifest this sense of identity, you can permanently ascend to the spiritual realm. This is the journey I am speaking about.

But for many it might take more than one lifetime. This is why the reference of reincarnation is in the bible, to explain in greater depth your opportunity in life. Briefly you can know that reincarnation was taken out of the bible by religious church officials years ago and this was done so that they could have control over the people and in turn benefit the church. There is a reference that was left in the Bible about reincarnation. It says that John the Baptist was indeed Elijah come again. If John was Elijah, then he would have had to been reincarnated. John did not suddenly appear but he was born of a woman just like all the rest of us. The fact is that Elijah returned as John the Baptist to help Jesus in his Galilean mission. *The reason I want to emphasis this is because, to manifest the highest level of self-awareness sometimes you must live many times.* It is God's desire that all of us raise our level of consciousness to the point of entering the spiritual realm. This is Salvation. And because we have "free will" *we can choose if we want to return to earth* and become more. Nothing is forced on us and that is why it is important to see that *we are in control of our destiny*.

God created us in his likeness and image, with free will and creative abilities just like He is. We are truly created in His image and likeness. The purpose is so that we can do many wonderful works.

~What you believe you can achieve~

We have the potential to put aside any and all things that hinder our *greater purpose* in life. Whatever stands in our way of not being who we are then we need to face it, and look beyond it. It is our choice.

Emotional struggles can be the most trying and block the greatest effort made for change in your life. It is easy to feel sorry for ourselves when going thru trying times. I don't think anyone that ever walked this earth can say they never felt sorry for themselves. But the key is found in understanding *the value of the emotion or the reason we are going through what we are going through.* Yes, some emotions must run their course but after this happens *wouldn't it be to our advantage to move past them* and begin to walk on, *to stronger purposes ahead?* If we keep on going on the emotional roller coaster of life, then nothing can be accomplished. *This is where it is your choice.* You can chose to continue on the same endless cycle of going no where with the same traumas of life and how unfair things have been and *I can guarantee nothing much will change* and *all you will do is feel more hopeless and angry and fearful*. *Or* you can go thru the problem, and then say, ENOUGH! You can get the emotion out of your system and *then plan the rest of your life*.

I bring this up because many people blame God for their trials in life. Who is really stopping your growth if *you won't move on*? It's you and you alone. It's your choice to believe the false things about God or to see Him as the greatest help and the greatest friend you will ever have. Life is happening while you are weeping. Weep and then move on. I say this out of love. *I want you to find the greater joy that is waiting for you to embrace*. But if you continue on a dead end path, you will loose out on seeing what is ahead.

~You will never know what you could have achieved if you remain at an emotional impasse~

You might say, but you don't understand. I *do* understand. Life has given me some very important lessons. I have learned what it is to suffer and to weep. To lose the love you long for and to never find you were loved. I have learned that life isn't fair or so it seems and that people judge you harshly when all you did was love them.

~But if I had remained in the "suffering mode", I wouldn't be writing to you right now~

I loved myself enough to say, *"this isn't the end of my story"* when bad things happen. I loved myself and said, *"Get up and show others they, too, can get up and make a difference in this life."* Together, we move on to victory. I speak to you out of love and tell you that I believe you can make a *major difference for good on this planet*. Work thru what hinders you and love yourself enough to believe that anything can be done out of pure unconditional love, and this begins with yourself.

So in knowing that when we come to earth, we are connected to something outside of ourselves, which I call the spiritual self, we also become aware *we have lost a sense of self and what we came to do*.

A wise soul will overcome this lack and take every experience as an opportunity to grow in self-awareness and build a stronger sense of identity. In this day and age much opportunity is given if a person is willing to become aware of his higher spiritual self, but *remain in a physical body*. This is how the kingdom of God can manifest itself on earth. When someone was willing to take on his or her spiritual self and yet remain unascended, they brought incredible change and great light to this planet. We can help raise the consciousness of the entire planet if we realize that we are chosen of God, all of us. Do you understand that God wants to fill you with His light while you are still in the human form? Do you understand what this means and how important this mission is? *If God can find human beings that are willing to be the Change by bringing light to earth while still in embodiment, this will create the greatest coming of the Christ*. This is the Second Coming. It is through the co-creators when they bring so much light, the kingdom of God will be brought to the earth.

So let's go back to creation and understand that God created physical matter in which we are all a part of. Physical matter has the *memory in the form of a seed* of God's self-aware being. You are physical matter. This is a "pattern" in God's creation.

~All living things that God created have a memory built within them so that life will continue and never end. The memory is God's way of saying to multiply and that there is always More~

The same memory is built into us in our Spiritual Being and this is God's way of saying there is much to do, multiply and take dominion. Just look at the memory of a single seed and you will see what I mean.

~A seed we plant in the ground will lie dormant, waiting for something to add energy and cause it to grow~

A natural seed needs water to begin the transformation. Once water is given, the seeds present form must die so that new life can begin. For you, the energy that will cause the seed you carry in your being to grow is the universal Christ mind or the Christ consciousness. *You also must leave behind the mortal, human way of understanding and come to a higher understanding.* Just like the seed planted deep into the earth, the pattern for new life within you that is waiting to emerge can only come when you allow your old self to die and you are reborn. So what I am saying is that another purpose for the creation of human beings is that they can serve as the intermediaries for helping the entire material universe become self-aware, *by beginning with themselves and their own transformation.* When a soul manifests full Christ Consciousness, it can permanently ascend to the spiritual realm and become an Ascended Master. However, even after a soul permanently ascends, the growth doesn't stop. That is why Jesus said. **"My Father's house has many mansions."** There are levels in the spiritual realm just as there are levels in the material realm.

This would explain why God always wants to become more and why God wants us to also become more. Nothing stays the same and everything is constantly becoming more. The Bible states, *"Ye are Gods"* and what this means is that we are God's "in the making" and because any part of God has the potential to expand its self-awareness, we also have the same potential. This is how we become one with our creator,

~by merging our beings with God, we begin an active role in God's creative force~

I have tried to spend some time explaining God's creation but now I want to try and give you another view of God. In the Old Testament times people had a primitive relationship with God and then Jesus came to give us a more mature view of God. In the Old Testament times, God was seen as a remote being, watching and ready to punish people if they sinned and also as someone we could ask, that would fulfill the wishes of those who pleased him. In pleasing Him we are conditioned to believe we have to earn God's love and acceptance. They were taught that if you worshipped God, prayed, performed sacrifices and did whatever your religion dictated, then God would make sure that everything you wanted was granted. ***But this lead to more disappointment and doubts*** in the eyes of believers and ***it created a greater division between them and God.*** When not everything worked well, they blamed God. ***It was an approach that became mythical, like some fairytale because it wasn't realistic and it only set people up for heartache.*** They believed God would punish or reward, but no one knew when God would do that. Often people would be so upset that they would wonder why bad things happened to good people. People would experience much disappointment and would grow angry with God. Oftentimes even if you did all the outer things right, God wouldn't always reward you and so people either rejected the love of God or they feared God was punishing them. Either way ***it created a division from God.***

~Keep in mind the division was not created by God but by how they saw God~

To see God in the right way, we will loose the chains that bind us and we will find a relationship with a pure Being that loves His creation as much as He loves himself. This is not to present God as egotistical but to remind you that in order to love God you must first love the God in you.

~You have a part of God in you and if you don't love yourself, then you can never love God~

Jesus said, ***"Love thy neighbor as thyself,"*** because Jesus knew the key was to love God more than anything else. To love thyself, who is a part of God, connects you to a oneness with God because you love the God within.

Jesus came to bring a higher understanding of the Father. He came to reveal the truth in that

~God wanted us to take hold of our own destiny and become an active force that would give us the abundant life~

Jesus wanted to do this by showing us the ***inner path*** to God. In Matthew 6:1, it says, **"Take heed that ye do not your alms before men, to be seen of them: otherwise ye have no reward of your Father which is in heaven."**

Jesus wanted to explain to us that the ***inner path would lead to a transformation in consciousness.*** To have a good relationship with God and to totally understand Him and His love for you ***means you must transform your state of consciousness or in simpler terms change your understanding of God.*** God is not an external being in the sky, but ***one that lives in the hearts***. Jesus explained by saying the Kingdom of God is within. God is ***not*** an angry being who is ready to crack the whip and punish the moment you do something wrong. God is ***not*** a genie in the bottle where you can ask what your heart desires and he will give it to you if you are obedient in every way. God is ***not*** one who decides whether good or bad things will happen to us. Jesus came to explain and to give an example that we need to take responsibility for our own lives and our own salvation. We create our own circumstances in our lives by the choices we have made.

~So in a nutshell God wants us to become one with Him and Jesus came to show us how~

But let's look at many of the world's statements about God that have no truth in them. One is that he is a remote being in the sky that is beyond our reach and beyond our comprehension yet is watching every move we make. Another is that God is an angry being in the sky that is ready to judge us harshly at any moment and punish us for an eternity. Another is that God is an unjust being who condemns some people to a life of incredible suffering while giving others a life of incredible luxury. Another is that God supposedly wants us to follow his laws, yet some who live a God-fearing life, experience great suffering. While others break the laws of God and man and get away with it and also attain great riches and power. Some believe that God is like a "genie" in a bottle that will supposedly give everyone that prays to Him what they pray for but never seems to be around when they need Him the most.

Why are our beliefs of God so far from reality, even in our present world? Why do we tend to see God, as some fairytale that we know isn't realistic? I thought about this and wondered if it is because we simply don't have a personal relationship with Him and we don't "see" Him as a real being. I feel it is understandable why we keep these beliefs instead of searching for the truth. Don't get me wrong about not having a personal relationship because I believe many *feel* they do have one. But if they believe Him to be any of the views I have already discussed then their relationship is superficial. It's superficial because those foundational truths don't manifest closeness and in fact manifest fear or separation. Love and fear cannot coexist. All of this is a result of never seeing Him as *we think* He looks like. Because humans *see the world form* and *that is their confirmation that something is real*, it is hard for them to believe and have a relationship with someone they have never seen. Think about someone you know and the personal relationship you have with him or her. You easily see them in a real way and with no effort. I think this is why we tend to believe unrealistic stories about God because *we really don't believe Him to be real or we don't really understand Him so we can't get to know Him.* However, we won't let go of the possibility He is real. I would like to help you have a different understanding of God and when you understand how you can see Him by understanding Him as a spirit, you will begin to develop a personal working relationship with Him. When you understand that God is in everything, you then realize that His presence is everywhere and *His visibility is through His creation.* To know this will help you have a greater love for all He has created and along with that you will have a respect.

Many believe that God loves them but they are taught by religion they are to fear God and his punishment for their sins. *Again, there is no fear in love*. So if God's foundational message is of His unconditional love, then surely He doesn't want us to fear Him. We are also taught that God is perfect but then why did he create imperfect beings that are sinners by birth. And for one final thought. God supposedly creates our souls when we are born or conceived; yet he is still punishing all of us for what Adam and Eve did thousands of years ago.

So because of all these very definite definitions of God *by religion, we are more confused than ever.* God is Spirit and we worship Him in Spirit and in truth. So what is the truth about God? If most Christians have been brought up with a distinct and deep seated fear of God and we as humans tend to run away from what we fear, *then how are we going to get close to God in a very real way.* Due to all these beliefs many Christians do not really want to come closer to God, let alone achieve oneness with this frightening being and they actually feel safer leaving Him as a distant being in the sky. In order to follow the path of oneness that Jesus came to demonstrate *we must make peace with God.* We must begin to *wash the lies from our heads and find out how to know him in truth and in spirit.*

Paul often spoke of the carnal mind and I will refer to it as the ego. A brief explanation of the ego is a person's sense of self-esteem or self-importance that mediates between the conscious and the unconscious and is responsible for reality testing and a sense of personal identity. The ego is the part of your thinking that can often be in alignment with your experience on earth *but not with your spiritual self* and actually can *keep you from connecting to your true spiritual identity.* The ego is born out of a belief that we are separate from God and it is in this separate feeling that our fears arise. The ego doesn't want us to come into a sense of oneness with God and it wants to keep us clinging to the *image of a remote God in which we need to fear or hide from.* The reason Adam and Eve hid from God is because they allowed the ego to make assumptions about God and so they feared him. They weren't willing to take hold of the responsibility of changing their own lives so they ran from God and called him judgmental in their minds.

The truth is that Christianity has distorted the facts *to fit their goals.*

~ *If they can create fear among the people then they can control the minds of the people*~

Christianity has gone against what Jesus came to do and that was to have a oneness with God. Instead we have become separated. In Christianity, we don't always see things as clearly and a lot of that is because *we fear to look beyond the teachings of religion.*

I would like to briefly share an experience I had with religion. I belonged to a strict, non-denominational church with no name that preached strictly from the bible and had rules to live by. No TV and no movies, no social events and no dancing whatsoever. Women wore dresses, never cut their hair, and always wore it up with no jewelry whatsoever. No make-up and no bows in the hair. Children were encouraged to not have friends outside the fellowship and to not play sports as it took too much time. The dress was at or below the knee and woman could NOT wear pants. Many rules were not spoken of but if you crossed the line someone would bring up how you needed to correct your ways. They preached that there were no rules and didn't force anything on anyone, but they lied. I walked for 26 years and I can tell you that the people had little choice over many things. The ministers, if asked would deny this, but the truth is if you didn't follow strict rules you would not be allowed privileges.

My point here is very simple. *Fear is often created in religion without you even knowing it.* In my situation the ministers might deny certain things but underhandedly they have you boxed into their ways of doing things and of their teachings. It's a control thing and when a minister does something wrong, they just say they are human. I argued once with a worker/minister about a rule. They denied their was any rule and then when I said, so it's ok I do this or that, and they answered me by saying, Do you think God would want you to do that? Because of the intimidation, I questioned my own need to exercise free will and so they had me trapped because they also accused me of not wanting to be an example as Jesus was. *It's cunning and it's not of God.*

God wants us to be free to choose and to grow and so many religions are the *greatest hindrance to growth*. The truth is when you have a better understanding of what Jesus came to represent, and that he is not the only son of God, then you stop worshiping an idol and you start walking on the path that Jesus came to show us to walk. **When your eyes are open, you realize that the path churches teach is not the path that Jesus taught.** Of course, some religions are not as strict but nevertheless most believe that Jesus is the Only Son of God and we cannot do anything for ourselves because He did everything for us. They teach we need to bow before Jesus and submit everything to him. **The sad part of this teaching is that it takes away your ability to live your life and grow into Christhood.** Jesus came to show us how we can become the Christ. He showed us how to live and he said we could do greater things than he ever did. How clear does it have to be?

When we awaken to the real truth about God and all of His sons and daughters, that is when we can have a beautiful relationship with God and that is when we take the rightful role as co-creators. This is God's plan for us. This is why we are here and God wants us to take hold of our purpose in life.

In the Old Testament humanity had a lower level of understanding and as a result, people couldn't receive a very sophisticated concept of God and so they constructed the angry being in the sky. But Jesus came to bring a loving image of Our Creator.

~Jesus wanted us to see God as a loving father figure who took pleasure in giving us his kingdom~

Jesus said the kingdom is within us, which means that we don't need an outer church or religion to enter the kingdom.

~Religion is not an avenue in which it creates an end to our own abilities to understand on a deeper level~

The core of the message of Jesus is to help us stop looking on the outer appearances or the external God and **to look within and see God as an internal presence.** God is a personal and internal friend to become one with. The sad truth is that the message that Jesus came with was lost somewhere in translation. But how in the world could a religion that claims to represent Jesus ignore and twist Jesus' own concept of God?

I think the easiest answer is that people at the mythic level of consciousness dominated Christianity. The ***intuitive ability in our minds was hindered*** because they taught that Jesus was the only one that could communicate with the Father. They convinced us that Jesus ***was an exception*** and we could only communicate with God by praying thru Jesus' name.

~The truth is that the only way to rise above the teachings laid out by the churches is to understand more fully how the pieces fit together~

When you compare the laws of nature, and you look at the traits of humans, you will see that all of these interpretations of God make no sense.

~Humans have the incredible ability to create and to advance their learning above and beyond what they currently know~

We are in the image and likeness of God and so all the teachings that put God in a fear-based setting where we have no power over our own lives and our own destiny, have to be wrong.

~To know God we must not be angry with Him~

We must heal our anger by finding out the real truth about God. But one very important part of healing is in ***confronting fear***. Anger in religion is suppressed because most don't want to acknowledge it. As "good" Christians we were brought up in the institutions of church to have fear of God and through fear we attained anger against God.

~I am a firm believer that you cannot change anything without confronting it first~

We have been brought up to not question church doctrine and so **our fears become internalized.** We want the answers to our questions but yet we have been also brought up to believe that if we question doctrine we are not faithful to the Christian religion, and we will not be saved but will burn forever in hell. And so we are caught in a catch 22 in which we cannot run away from the fearsome God. We cannot run and at the same time we feel enormous guilt if **we question** things because we are taught that would be blasphemy and we then would for sure go to hell.

~This trap within our being, keeps us going in circles. We can't grow and we can't even understand. If we can't understand we will never become the co-creators God created us to become~

We "feel" we are caught between an "angry" God and the fiery hell below. The truth is that when you cannot run away from a threat and cannot destroy it, you feel trapped and you become so frustrated. This is why you will find some very courageous souls leaving all the churches in search of God. It takes courage if you feel you might go to hell, for questioning but you make a stand anyway. You hope that maybe by seeing things the way they are, you are leaving a door open where one day a better understanding will enter in.

Frustration builds up pressure where you can ultimately change the outcome. This is a great example of how trying times can ultimately bring you abundant life. However,

~...if you do nothing, then all you do is build walls around yourself~

and the frustration continues along with anger. Christianity keeps you in a box by dictating that to be a good Christian you are not supposed to have any negative feelings and so frustration leads to fear and fear leads to anger against God, which ultimately is ***anger against yourself.***

We must allow ourselves the freedom to get to know God and ***our willingness to reach for a higher understanding is a result of true loyalty towards God.*** What do you love the most?

~When it comes right down to knowing God, are you willing to really know Him as He is?

I came to this point in my own life. Do I want to know the truth that Jesus came to bring about His Father and about our lives? I found thru the years that the teachings of churches and of Jesus were not always parallel. I saw many loopholes and I wondered if maybe I was misunderstanding what Jesus came to reveal.

~I always believed that the message of Jesus was far greater and had a deeper meaning~

I had to ask myself if I was willing to jump ship and plunge myself into the river of life in order to find the whole message that Jesus came to bring us.

~If I was to attain a higher understanding I had to let go of the beliefs I had been comfortable with all my life~

To tell you the truth this was rather frightening to me. I felt I was loosing a part of myself and I worried at first if I would be lost forever. But I knew that in order to see the deeper message of Jesus I would have to pull away from all that I had allowed myself to believe and have faith to walk a path unknown to me at the time. It was my love for Jesus that would lead me to the truth and in turn I would find God and his great love for us.

~For the truth is that perfect love is the only thing that will cast out fear and anger~

When you are absorbed in fear and anger it is hard to find perfect love and so the only way to find it is in the intuitive level of consciousness. But even more profound is that most people don't realize they have fear and anger towards God because they are so accustomed to not question doctrine and so everything they feel is hidden in the subconscious. For me I will say again, it was my love for Jesus that convinced me that no matter what I found when stepping away from lies, I would follow Jesus.

So what is the intuitive level, which we can raise above limited beliefs and which can ultimately help us get in touch with the truth and God Himself? When we are at an intuitive level of consciousness we can find answers but we can't prove them, as we just know they are true.

~It's a deeper understanding of something in which you cannot find physical proof but you know for a fact it is truth~

When you reach the intuitive level of consciousness, you experience that your identity is far more than both the physical body and the outer personality.

~You know that you are a spiritual being who is only residing in this physical body for a time~

This is where it becomes logical that you have lived before and some people at the intuitive level actually experience memories of past lives. The intuitive level is the only way to rise above the intellectual impasse that so often results from rational thinking.

This not only resolves the question of reincarnation but also of whether God exists. You can only find a final answer to whether God exists at the intuitive level. Jesus came to this earth to teach us how to go within and experience the truth through an inner knowing and this confirms why he sent us the Comforter and talked about the key of knowledge.

~Jesus knew God was real because he experienced God as a Living Presence inside himself~

And as any true teacher, he wanted all of us to experience the same. My point here is that we need to rely on our intuition in order to rise above the teachings put out by Christianity. The only way to take Christianity to a **new level** and know that God exists is to go directly to the intuitive level giving people an internal certainty.

So let me go over some of this again only a little differently. I know that for all of us we have our own struggles with knowing God and relating to Him in a personal way. It's not because we don't love Him or appreciate Him but it's because He is Spirit and we cannot see spirit and so knowing God takes an intuitive feeling of a deep understanding.

~We live in a world where outer doctrine becomes almost godlike because it is taught through churches. Our world also bases confirmation of an existence on a "form"~

We learn to not question church authority or even God Himself. You cannot resolve your relationship with God through outer doctrines, by using the relativity of the human intellect or the reasoning of the ego. So the only way you can really know the truth is if you are willing to look beyond outer doctrines and apply the inner way of seeing things, which is your higher self- emerging to help you come to the truth.

How does one prove that God does "not" exist? Many have tried to develop theories to explain that there is no intelligent creator and yet they can't explain how an incredibly complex universe could have evolved through a process that is completely random and without intelligence.

~We can prove something does exist but you cannot prove that something does not exist~

All we can really say is that we haven't yet found or proven God's existence. And this is our dilemma. In religion this is a frustration. People find it hard to understand why God has not settled the question of His existence. Why doesn't He just come right out and make it clear so there is no doubt? Maybe it has to do with "free will" and if He were to prove His existence, then God would actually violate people's free will, in which they go within, intuitively and see the truth. Whatever the reason, at this time, God chooses to leave it that and on a broad scale there would be no positive proof. ***However, on an individual scale people could know through intuitive knowing.***

Maybe it has to do with the fact that God wants us to gain the understanding of ***going within***, as Jesus came to emphasize.

~God knows that if we develop the skill of intuition and going within our own being for answers, we will grow in many areas~

Our life on earth has the potential to create many wonderful experiences in which all humans can enjoy and live in peace but much of the knowledge waiting to emerge comes from using our intuitive skills in which we can tap into the God within us. God might never provide a worldwide, unquestionable proof of His existence.

~For the real proof will be given to those who are willing to go within and apply the inner approach to knowledge~

Just so you know many have solid proof of God's existence by this approach. Some call it a mystical or spiritual experience. But whatever they call it, the fact remains that *any human has the capacity to receive this same experience.* You open your heart and mind to God, resolving all conflicts in your own view of God and the door or key of knowledge will open up so that what is within you will tell you everything you need to know. It is a skill that *needs* to be learned.

There is one thing that is very important in this book and that is the importance in knowing that God created *a pattern for life on earth*. The reason I address religion, Jesus, God, The Bible and Salvation is because I want to pull together the picture of life. The pattern I want to make is that in knowledge it is more than just words on paper, *it is about how you can take your own life and apply the "same pattern" found from God's creative forces and find the purpose and the plan of "your" life.*

God's existence is without question but what happens is that we as humans take our abilities here on earth and try to find proof. Proof sometimes is not reachable when we use *the tools of human reasoning* and this is why Jesus came. He came to show us to *go within* and *use an intuitive process to reach conclusions.* God's existence isn't dependent on whether you can prove it but to know of His existence we are given an opportunity in learning a new skill that can be applied in everything in life.

This chapter was hard for me because I felt that I knew God but how can I help you know God. So I ask you right now to go within your own being and put aside the logic and reasoning of the human mind. Go within and find the God within you, because God is in you. As I have already said, we live in a world in which everything is defined by having some kind of form.

~God created the entire world of form but God is beyond the world of form~

The important part of knowing this is in understanding that you cannot describe or picture God by using any ideas, words, concepts, or images from the world of form. Keep in mind that you can illustrate some of the characteristics or qualities of God *but the only true way of knowing God in the ultimate sense is to go beyond the world of form.*

Remember the commandment in the Old Testament, **"Thou shalt have no other Gods before me."** And what about another commandment, **"Thou shalt not take unto thee any graven image."** I believe with all my heart that God was trying to help you understand that *He understood where your lack of understanding might hinder your ability to see Him in the totality.* God asked those that wrote down the words to convey a message that *might prevent* people from setting up an idol created in the world of form and an attempt *to help people find the true God by always seeking to look beyond any images from the world of form.*

Through the years there have been many teachings about the I AM Presence and this is because of the importance of the spiritual self. The spiritual self is your I AM Presence, and an individualization of the presence of God, the I AM THAT I AM, that enables you to know the true presence of God. Even the many spiritual experiences from all cultures and traditions of experiencing God, is very hard to describe by using words or images. You just cannot describe what it is like to experience the living God. I think the most important part of trying to describe it, is that it *encourages others to seek their own inner experience.* We are all individual co-creators and we all have the potential to be what God needs us to be. The individuality of our lives and the experiences we need to go through is critical in our own growth. So if you are to hear of someone else's mystical experience, keep in mind to *never* turn it into an unquestionable doctrine. In other words don't see it, *as all there is to see.* It is important to know that what that person saw is according to his or her own level of consciousness and that if we were to see the same experience, we might see a different picture.

This unique way of seeing *thru our own understanding is to confirm that God is always becoming more and there is never one picture of something* but there are many pictures and each picture enhances the whole of the experience.

~So every experience seen thru different eyes and with different understandings is meant to enhance the beauty and the complexity of the experience and to help you see that turning anything into a doctrine takes away from the experience~

Enjoy what you see, and find out how it helps you *as an individual*. Grow from it and draw closer to God but *don't make it a belief that it is all there is to know.* I want you to accept with full assurance that it is good to see something but know that what you see, isn't all there is about it. Believe that everything in life has more about it than what is seen through your eyes.

Remember that the level of consciousness causes you to see things according to how *you are able to understand it.* For instance, the lower mind has caused people to create and *accept many concepts about God that have nothing to do with the reality of the divine being.* People have described God with human characteristics, which can be seen as flaws by the way they interpret things in their mind and this has caused many conflicting ways to see God. Remember the saying that God is not mocked. This means that *God is not affected by human beliefs or opinions.* God is who God is or I AM WHAT I AM. When Moses asked God for his name, he was told that it is "I AM THAT I AM" in Exodus 3:14. What does this really say, you may ask. *It says that God himself is a conscious being who is very aware of his own existence.*

Evil in our world is something that we experience every day and so I feel it's very important to give you a better understanding of how evil is in relationship with God. Many ask why there is evil in the world and they even wonder if its God's will that there is evil in the world. Intuitively I sense it isn't God's will at all. Many think that if God created everything then it only proves that He created evil. Many religions say that evil is the opposite of God. The truth is that *evil was not created by God*, but in fact was created by conscious beings, including but not limited to human beings. *These beings use their free will to choose*

to go against God's laws and this in turn creates the illusion of evil forces. God could not give people free will without giving them the ability **to go against the laws** used to create the world.

~The existence of evil is not in alignment with the divine plan of God for this world and God did not create evil~

But the freedom to use free will allows people to go against and misuse it and the result is evil. So in other words God's laws are given **to give freedom to choose** but God had no intention that we would create evil.

~If people could not go against God's laws, they don't truly have free will and yet if they do go against God's laws they will eventually self-destruct~

God's laws are designed so that the world of form continues to evolve in a sustainable manner and yet if anything violates these laws, the violation is not sustainable. Let me clarify this.

~God never intended that human beings would use their free will to destroy themselves or parts of His creation~

Even though free will is God's will, the results of **misuse** is not what God intended. What I am trying to say is that these things are not God's fault but in fact our fault because of our own choices. So if we want a better world, then we need to make better choices.

Think a moment about our children and how we raise them or at least we try to raise them. We allow them the freedom to choose and when they get older they are on their own and their choices will either help them or hurt them. The same is with God. He is our Father and He loves us very much. But He knows that we were created **to be independent** so that if we choose to do what's right we will experience greater abundance in our lives. God allows human beings to create imperfect manifestations even while continuing to hope that they will someday realize that they are not acting in their own best interest.

~*God hopes that people will see the wrong choices that don't help them, and decide on their own, by their own free will to make better choices*~

This is the beauty of the power of free will and how if used for the good of all mankind, it will help bring incredible growth to planet earth.

~*Choices are important to God because He believes if we knew better we would do better and He believes in us*~

When you understand the power of choices in free will, you must also understand that when bad things happen because of poor choices, ***it is not God's fault***. Anything that is created against the basic laws of God is predestined to self-destruct. ***Evil is only a temporary manifestation that is a result of a poor choice,*** like a house built on sand. It will only last for a season before it destroys itself. God is not mocked, because all of the energy used by the forces of evil will eventually be raised to its original purity. To us as humans we do feel that evil goes on for so long but as a cosmic perspective it will be gone in the blink of an eye. Keep in mind that everything is energy and

~*....evil can be erased by simply purifying the energy*~

We purify the energy by bringing light to this planet. The best way to look at it is to remember how the sand castles so intricately built on the shores can be erased in one wave rolling in from the ocean. This is very important when you wonder if your good works can make a difference.

~*Yes just one person can make a difference like no one else*~

Look at the life of Jesus. Even though many of his teachings are lost and many were not understood like they should have been, He has made a difference in this world like no one else.

Nothing in this world is permanent and so the experimentation of the choices of mankind cannot destroy it. Human beings might take great pride in the sand castles they build on the beach, just as certain evil forces might think they have messed up God's plan. ***But God knows that these forces have built their castles and when the tide rolls in, even the most powerful castles will be erased by one wave of spiritual energy.***

When talking about God's laws we need to address the judgment that people put on God himself. They claim he is an angry and judgmental God who seeks to punish. Many carry fears that God doesn't love them unless they do everything perfect. They believe they are unworthy and miserable sinners by nature. I can only see someone pounding his or her head on a cement floor and then blaming someone else for a headache. Whoever put the floor in had no intention of someone pounding his or her head on it. That is their choice if they do so ***but it's no ones fault but their own.***

~God created a set of laws to guide us but those laws are a freedom in which we can choose how we want to experience life~

If ***we*** choose to use the laws to harm others, or ourselves it doesn't make any sense to blame God. The truth is that we each have a spiritual teacher that we consulted with before we came to planet earth. But if we use God's laws to make choices that go against the spiritual plan we designed before we came, then we must remember it is by our choice, our plan is not being fulfilled. When a soul is ***not*** open to inner instruction from his spiritual teacher, that soul has become his own teacher and the material world is a classroom in which the soul can learn from. ***Thru all thy getting we will get understanding, is God's hope and we ultimately can reconnect to our true spiritual identity.***

So let's continue to look at God and why He felt it important to tell us to not create a graven image of Him whether by statue or a mental image in our mind. When we create an image of God, *we start to worship a god that never changes--a dead god is what it becomes.* Think about it. If you have a picture in your mind of something, then that picture is complete and permanent and so it becomes a graven image. Many times we read of a living God and this is where something is changing.

~Something living is always growing and becoming more~

Life is defined as something that is changing and this is how *we need* to see God. Why is this so important, you may ask? Because this understanding that God is living and ever changing,

~will keep you from falling into the trap that what you know is all there is to know~

Once you begin to see some of the very important things of spiritual teachings from an intuitive level you will be more willing to receive new insights and revelations. You will begin to experience new growth for yourself and *the God within you will teach it to you.* This is a major step in taking control of your own life and destiny and in helping others to do the same. You will then realize that as long as you are in a human body, you will never know everything there is to know about God and so this alone will give you the courage and the excitement to be open to a higher understanding.

~You will then always be looking for the LIVING PRESENCE of God that is hiding behind outer descriptions~

All my life I found it rather exciting to look at some of the teachings from churches and then see if I could see beyond what was said. It was almost like finding a needle in a haystack but it was a wonderful challenge. I love puzzles and so when I would hear particularly the teachings of our brother, Jesus, I knew they were **not** the whole story **but rather fragments that told so little.** What I hope you can see for yourself is that this is your opportunity to not be afraid to take what you have heard and learned and then ponder them, turn them over and see the back side, step away from the picture and then look at it afresh. Use your intuition and see what you can see without anyone telling you. It's ok to not put something into a form but **allow your mind to see beyond all form.**

Do you realize that all thru the ages the teachings you have heard and have read were given from this very process, the intuitive process? In our world we often feel like we can't obtain something unless it is concrete or has already been revealed. We don't believe we could receive a teaching that may have never been given before. But we can! **How do you think all the teachings that have been given since the dawn of man, came? They came from what is within, from intuitive voices that inspired the truth to be written.** You have the same knowing of what is true and what is necessary to be revealed to the world. This is where my own words and my understanding have come from. I have listened to my inner voice, and I have put together the pieces as I have seen them thru the eyes of God. God is within and He inspires all of us. We are co-creators and have the same ability to create as God has done. That is what it means to be in the image and likeness of God.

~Take back the power of which you are and enjoy the gifts God has given you~

Keep a right heart and a right intention and know that what you receive is not for selfish gain. Keeping a pure motive will help the teaching to be of the right kind. And remember that God has more to reveal to all of mankind. Don't believe for one minute that God has told you everything there is to know.

~Do you think that God, who has revealed in nature everything always changing, has really told you all there is to know about life and the future?~

As we have already spoken about in how people understand and their level of comprehension at different times in earth's history, so it is a fact that God has so much to reveal to us, when we are ready. **When the student is ready the teacher will come.**

~ Be ready because God needs humans that are willing to be vessels of change~

God needs humans that love Him and His plan for all creation enough to take an active role in advancing their ability to comprehend more and in turn more will be given. Life on earth is far more than what we see today.

~Life has no limits and God wants you to know that He has so much more to give you when you are ready. BE READY!!!!!!!~

Through the ages we have often wondered ***where God lives?*** Our children have asked us and we have often been scrambling for an explanation. In the Old Testament the people of the time wanted to have a picture of where God lived and so ***they constructed a view of the world*** that placed the Earth as the center of the universe. ***Their view was formulated by their understanding to the best of their ability.*** To them the earth was flat with a dome above it and the stars were attached to the inside of the dome. But it was ***on the outside of the dome that they placed God's domain***. Even then they separated God from themselves ***by placing Him on the "outside"***. But God has never been separate from us but is within and God has never been on the outside, for the truth is ***God is within His creation***. It was basically a belief that God was high up in the sky and when Jesus rose again, He

59

rose physically to that height. As we think of this thought we get many different opinions. Sometimes we find people would rather just get rid of the fact that there is a God. But in today's world we understand things much different and so the words of the Old Testament, even though many cling to this in religion, are just not real. *It was real to those that lived in those days, or rather as real as they could comprehend.* Just think about it. If you were to travel back to that time in history and present technology as it is today, *you would loose their attention in the first sentence,* for they would be so utterly confused. They simply didn't have the ability to understand. Don't think for one minute they didn't have the intellect because they were very smart. Like anything in the process of life, we grow thru hands on experience. Inventors have the ability to produce something that is seen in their mind but not ever been made into form. This is proof that they have God within them. They can take an unbelievable image they hold in their mind, but the world cannot see it no matter how hard they try, and bring it to life. The people in the Old Testament were just average people *but their world was different than our world today.* They had all the abilities that we have but they didn't have the *progressive technology* that we have. *Their world had not possessed the stepping-stones to where we are at this moment in time and so they weren't able to comprehend.* God gave them the information that could help them at that time in their lives but often their primitive view caused them to wander away from the things God tried to reveal to them. Their understanding was based on the ego and they often wandered farther away from God and created a greater separation. *God wanted them to understand to the best of their ability and He knew the message wouldn't quite be complete but it would lead them down the correct path and eventually He could give them MORE of what He wanted them to know.* It seems that we are now at a time in man's history where we can really grasp the bigger picture and so today God has much to reveal to us. We are in a different time in history and the knowledge we have is far more advanced than what they had but we still don't have all there is to know. I explain this to you in detail so that *you can embrace the future.*

~GOD NEEDS YOU AND YOU ARE THE FUTURE~

There is so much ahead if only we are willing to love God for who He is, and to see Him with open eyes and open heart. There is so much more to life and God's vision of what His creation can be is greater than you can even imagine in your wildest dreams.

To understand how we can see more than what we currently see and how God can reveal more, we need to look again at light and why God created everything from one basic substance.

~The truth is that this very substance, light, would hold the key to opening up our understanding~

As I have already said everything is energy and we have many teachings that reflect how important this is. Think about Einstein and his theory. It **simply stated** that everything was energy. Our eyes see only certain types of energy or light waves **but there are many light waves and they all vibrate at different frequencies than what our eyes can detect**. You may ask why do our eyes see only certain frequencies and I will tell you that this is linked directly to how you understand things or your level of consciousness. So in other words in order to see more of God's truths that are waiting to be revealed when the student ready, you must broaden your ability to see higher frequencies of light and in order to do that you must raise your level of understanding. To raise your level of understanding you need to be willing to walk the path of knowledge and learn more. As you learn more you can take in more. **I think if you really ponder just this fact you will know intuitively that what you don't see, isn't all there is. We live in a universe that has different dimensions that are set apart by their different vibrational properties**. So to make it simple I think it is fair to say that these different dimensions or vibrational properties can also be referred to as different frequencies and it is these frequencies, higher or lower, **that determine the levels of energy that come into your mind and into our world**.

*~If you don't think your life is important THINK AGAIN.
You see when YOU BECOME THE CHANGE; you raise
your own light by the path you are willing to take~*

When you raise your own light, you are given more light from God. Then You begin to give back to God all that He has given and when others help you and you give back to them, **you start a circle that begins to spin so fast that incredible light is given off from it**. It's like a top that is spinning so fast that it begins to give off images of things you have never seen and yet they are so beautiful. *Those images are a small picture of the MORE that God has waiting to reveal to all of us.*

*~We will never know what CAN BE unless some of us
are willing to take a chance and know the future is more
beautiful than imaginable in the greatest imaginations that
ever walked this earth~*

So as your light becomes brighter it will fill the world with more light and *from just your light,* that you are willing to give, the whole world can **begin to experience the higher frequencies of God's light.** As you walk and they watch your life change and feel greater abundance, many will do the same and when enough people become the CHANGE, that is when the world will change.

*~You see YOU are the hope of change. Your life is as
important as the life of Jesus~*

Jesus did this very thing with His life. He is our EXAMPLE. This was what Jesus came to help us understand. His whole life's message was for us to see who we are and how we can be the CHANGE. When He realized that if He took what He knew and built upon it, He could begin to raise the light of the world. *He was the Light of The World* but you are also able to become the Light Of The World.

We have talked about levels of energy in this world but I want you to understand that there are levels of energy in the spiritual realm, which also progress to higher frequencies until they reached the highest possible frequency. This frequency is light or energy in its *purest* form, namely what the creator created as the first act of the creative process. Genesis 1:3 ***"And God said, Let there be light: and there was light."*** We already know that everything in our world has a "form" and that before the creator could create anything with form, it had to create a medium that could be molded into the form desired. Our modern science calls that medium, "energy" and the Bible calls it "light". ***"All things were made by him; and without him was not any thing made that was made."*** (John 1:3) The creator began with energy at the ***highest possible vibration*** and then created a number of levels made of lower vibrations. Kind of like a ladder. Each level progressively was lowered in vibration. ***Each level was interdependent of the other.*** Picture a beam of light from God with the purest and highest light at the top and then watch as levels like the steps of a ladder stream downward from the highest realm to the next lowest realm until it reaches the material universe, being lowered in vibration along the process. ***This is how spiritual energy is lowered in vibration and becomes available for creating form in the material world.*** And this is the best way to envision why our world has a ***need to bring back into its realm, light of a higher vibration.*** The world was created so that it could be a place in which humans could grow and become the spiritual beings they had the potential to become.

~Now it is time to bring God's light back to the world. It's time to bring the Kingdom of God to earth~

This is what Jesus spoke about when He spoke of the Second Coming of Christ. The Second Coming of Christ is when the people in embodiment become the Christ and bring the light of God back in the highest vibration. The Second Coming is not with outward show but is within. When we embrace what is within us and become the light of God, the Christ will return to earth in a different form. When Jesus was the Christ, He was THE light of the world as one man, this time the Christ will be embodied in many people in the world and the light that will come to earth will be greater than any light man has ever seen. Jesus will come on a White Horse to welcome His brothers and sisters home because *they will have understood* that what was within them *was the Light of The world*, and HOME is to know you are already home. Change comes from within and the message has not changed. BE THE CHANGE.

So when understanding this you might see the complexity of God and how we all come from the same source of light. The existence of planet earth is dependent upon the existence of the higher spiritual realms because *that is where the energy that created this world comes from* and continues to come from. Don't you see? We are still receiving God's light in order to sustain life on this planet.

~He has not left us; He feeds us His light and his love EVERYDAY~

With these thoughts to be true you now can see that there is *no barrier between God and Man*, except what man thinks by the understanding he has in his MIND. The difference between Heaven and Earth is only a matter of vibration. This is why we all can have an inner and very personal connection to all who are in the spiritual realm and we can actually live on this earth and yet ascend to this realm *by our level of consciousness*. Again this is where the kingdom of God is within us. When you understand this you can see what hell is. Hell is the lowest vibration where your level of understanding is so far from God's mind *that you literally feel alone and you are in hell.* The reason this is so hard and you feel so alone is because *you are a part of God* and when you remove yourself this far from God, *you loose a part of your wholeness* and there is no other way to feel than simply ALONE. So the answer of where God lives is clear. He lives all around us and inside of us. *There simply isn't a place where He doesn't live.*

Before I leave this chapter on God I want to give you a way in which *you can bring peace in your heart of God and His great love and care for your individual life.* It is more than just knowing God in words but God is a relationship that you will always treasure and in order to have that you need to make peace with God. Jesus came to show us the path of oneness with God, and oneness with all life.

I have already covered these points but I want to repeat them so that you understand *you need to let go of what you have currently believed God to be.* God is not a remote being in the sky that is beyond our reach and beyond our comprehension. God is watching every move we make but this is because *He loves his creation.* Yes God created our souls but *He is not ready to punish us for what happened in the illustration in the Garden so many years ago.* God wants us to become more aware of our own capabilities and *so any trials are really not punishment but tools to learn by.* When we pray, how can we even believe that our prayers are likened unto the Genie in the Bottle mentality? Where did this analogy come from? And when we don't get our every request why do we automatically believe He doesn't care, and is simply not around? We believe these things because we have been programmed that this "is God".

⁓Let go of these restricting thoughts and see the God that loves you more than life itself⁓

Another sad belief we take on is that God supposedly loves us but we must fear Him and expect He will punish us if we don't live perfect lives. This is so restricting.

⁓How can anyone get to know someone if fear is always on the platter?⁓

Think of your own parents. If a father or mother was feared in your home, were you really able to get to know them? Weren't you afraid to even ask questions? This is simply the greatest obstacle in religion.

~The teachings are to keep you in a controlled relationship with God and you cannot possibly get close to Him. What an INJUSTICE to God!!~

How can any loving spiritual teacher teach that God is to be feared when really God wants a close and loving relationship with you so that you can become all He longed for. Again God is not an angry being in the sky that is ready to crack the whip when we get out of line. God is not waiting to judge our every move and then find justification to send us to a lost eternity. If you just think about this along the lines of a loving parent in this world, how can you even believe that God is worse than any parent that has the same compassion given from God? *It just doesn't add up.* We have blindly continued to believe lies about God *that do not even add up in our own reasoning.* And what about justice? We watch those that live in God-fearing life experiences, following every law and yet still have great suffering. Then we watch others break every law of both God and man, but they seem to get away with it and attain great riches and power. I think for myself this was one of the greatest revelations because when I saw this happening over and over again, I knew that the teachings of God were far from true.

One last thought I would like to share. We are indoctrinated that God is perfect in every way and yet we wonder why did *he create us as imperfect beings* that are sinners by birth? Does that really make sense?

~Why would God create humans as sinners and what purpose does He have in watching us begin as sinners and walk an impossible path in which there is no hope~

Is this *some kind of cruel joke* in which God wants to watch his creation stumble around in the dark? If one is born without legs, do you think it's easy to watch them struggle? God loves you so much and He doesn't want you to struggle but He wants you to have the greatest abundance. God did not create you as a sinner and He doesn't want for one minute us to suffer. Our suffering and our wrongdoing are a result of our free-will choices, and not God's plan. God loves you and you are born as an extension of your spiritual being in which God longs for you to become even more. You chose to come to this earth to co-create because being a Co-creator is your identity. You are a part of God and you are a co-creator.

These beliefs have led you to a faulty perception of God *and in turn you have withdrawn from the reality*. It's as if you have been given a delusion of who God really is and it's created a *sense of mental fragmentation*. The contradictory and inconsistent elements with which you define God in your mind has *led you to a breakdown in the relation between your thoughts, your emotions, and your behavior to the reality of God*. Because you have been brought up with a deep fear of God, your natural tendency, if you face the reality of what you have been taught, *is to run*. *God never wanted you to fear Him*. Anyone that faces fear will run or hide and that is how you have reacted to the presence of God. Many preachers further their teachings by saying *you cannot run from God* and **so there is no way out**. If you believe you are born "no-good", and you experience life as we all do, you don't do everything perfect. Then you are told God is angry and judgmental and so whether you are portraying some kind of saint or not, *you are always in a fear zone with God because you're never really taught anything else about Him*. This alone explains why many don't really want to get too close to God or achieve oneness with Him because they are fearful of Him and so they would *rather believe* He is a remote Being in the Sky. Or they just don't understand Him and they feel they never will.

To become One with God, as Jesus taught throughout his life, it is essential that we make peace with Him. But to do that, it is first necessary to really know Him and understand Him. I haven't really covered a lot about the ego, as of yet but I want you to understand that the ego is *born out of a sense of separation from God and so it will naturally fear God*. An example of how the ego came into being is in the illustration of the Garden. When Adam and Eve separated themselves from God, they also lost their spiritual teachers that knew the plan of this embodiment and they felt alone. It says they hid themselves from God. In feeling alone they created the ego, the part of them that took the place of their spiritual teachers and this part was their way of survival. The ego became their reasoning in life and it was seen thru their understanding. Remember we loose our level of understanding the farther we get from God. So the ego is the part of us that Jesus spoke about in referring to the Carnal mind. *The ego is what keeps us from self-destructing and feeling totally lost*, but also keeps us from really knowing God or remembering why we came in the first place. It's kind of like something that keeps us between here and there.

> *~The ego takes on a mind of it's own and that mind isn't in alignment with God or the Spiritual Being you are and so your Ego becomes a voice that sees as the world sees~*

However, they also became separated from God and the Light that God wanted them to possess. This is why I have said that the greatest scenario God sees in which we can bring the most change on this earth is *when we are still in the human form, still able to mingle on earth but have let go of the ego and have taken on the Spiritual Self we truly are.* The ego is a lower vibration or a lower level of consciousness.

> *"The ego doesn't want us to keep a sense of oneness with God because deep down the ego is the part of us that came into being because we were angry and fearful of God."*

This is why the ego really wants us to hang onto the image of a remote God and to see God as someone to fear so that we will continue to hide from him, because the ego's greatest fear is death to itself. That explains why Paul spoke about dying daily. It was necessary for the ego to die in order for us to become one with the Christ Self within us. But the fear in the ego is so great that it becomes evident that *the very key to your transformation* is found in letting the ego die.

The flat out truth is that when we define God as we have, and all that we understand comes from religion or Christianity, I think we really have to wonder *why Christianity promotes beliefs that are in direct opposition to Jesus and His life purpose.* Jesus' main goal in His life was to show us a "oneness" with the Father and to take back our own free will to achieve that oneness, and yet Christianity has portrayed the loving, gentle Father that wants to be one with us, *as someone who is far away and judgmental and to be feared, which keeps us from using our God given free will.*

In the Old Testament this was easier to understand because the level of consciousness was at a lower level. However, Jesus came to show us a different picture. He came to show us that His Father is a loving father figure who takes good pleasure in giving us the kingdom. Then Jesus explained the kingdom was within and by this teaching he was trying to relate to God *in a personal way and NOT as a being far removed in the sky somewhere out there.* Jesus came to tell us that His Father is an internal presence that lives within us and has always lived within us. We often believe in religion that we have the correct translations of the "truth" but because we see that the concept of God in today's churches is far removed from the "truth", we then know something is either lost in translation or is misinterpreted so badly that the churches that preach Jesus have lost the loving relationship between God and one of his sons, Jesus.

So to sum up Christianity in today's world we can draw the conclusion, by the teachings that are basically dominate in this century and what Jesus tried to make obsolete, *mainly the mythic picture of God, is not logical nor consistent and creates nothing but fear in the minds of human beings.* The truth is, these teachings have created fear against our loving Father.

Any psychologist or doctor that is trying to help you sort through things that stop your healing, will acknowledge that *the first step to healing is to see the problem that needs healing.* This is why I feel that *knowing God as He really is, is the first step to your own healing.* You must let go of any anger or fear of God in order to get to know Him. As I speak these words about you having anger with God, I believe that *many of you will not feel you have this problem*. Keep in mind that Christians are brought up with teachings that they are *conditioned to not question* for fear that they will not be called faithful servants. They are taught *they cannot fight God and so questioning the teachings is like blasphemy* which this is also taught will take you to hell.

~So when you cannot run away from a threat or a doubt and you cannot destroy it, you feel trapped and this leads to frustration~

Frustration can be helpful because it creates *enough pressure that you choose to face the fear and overcome it* but if no action is possible because you fear you are questioning God himself, *then frustration continues to build which will eventually create anger within you*. This creates a subconscious anger against God and because you are a part of God and God is within you, *it also creates anger against yourself.*

Many people deny they have anger with God but often those are the ones who will lash out at other religions or organizations that don't believe the way they do. *They do this to others because they are using them as scapegoats.* And even though *they preach to love your enemies they are quick to condemn anyone who doesn't totally believe as they do.* This is proof of a deep subconscious anger against God. It is a frustration they feel because deep inside they know the beliefs they have been taught *don't add up.* This way of taking your anger against God out on other people might help you relieve some of the pressure, but it will never do anything to resolve the real cause of your anger. And furthermore it will never help you to draw close to God and feel a oneness with Him.

There are people in today's world that have taken courage to re-look at what their churches have taught and begin to really get to know God. *They are spiritual beings that are willing to stand against the multitude and claim the message of Jesus again.* They are willing to accept the false teachings as false and take on a stand in which I know Jesus is so very thankful for. When I belonged to a very strict religion that had many of these beliefs, often the thought crossed my mind, "what if all they teach is far from the truth?" *Somewhere deep in my spiritual being I knew the truth*. I say to you this day stand up for the truth and no matter what you have let yourself believe in the past, let go of it and re-look at what Jesus taught. Jesus wrote years ago, *"With men this is impossible; but with God all things are possible."* (Matthew 19:26)

He wrote this to help us understand that to solve a problem through the carnal mind or the ego, it is nearly impossible to have success.

~The ego just doesn't see things in the light~

The ego sees things through a dualistic filter and this is what truly makes the task impossible. Jesus wanted us to see that the ego is born out of separation from God and so it can't really help us develop a loving relationship with Our Father.

~Jesus came to show us how to have a Christ mind, a Christ consciousness because he wanted us to reach beyond the ego for the one vision of the Christ mind~

This is the only way to salvation, see the truth of Our Father and develop a oneness with Him.

We must ask ourselves a question when we have decided we want to have peace and growth for our future with God. Do we love the teachings of Christian churches more than we love the teachings of Jesus? *Do we desire the outer churches that we often attend, more than the inner path to God?* Even if we are comfortable in the church we follow, are we willing to take one step higher towards a better relationship with Our Father, if that meant leaving behind all that we currently believe is true about God?

When the church chose to lie about reincarnation, there motive was to get people to rely on the church for salvation and so the truth about reincarnation had to be kept out of the scriptures. For if it weren't kept out, then the people would know that their salvation was independent of the church. In other words people would see that everything they needed to be saved was already within them. If people were taught reincarnation and of course believed it, this would mean they would have more than one lifetime to win their salvation and they would be less likely to give unconditional obedience to the outer church or give their money to the church. But on the other hand if the church left out this teaching, then the people would believe salvation is only in this lifetime, which would cause them to have reverence to the leaders of the church and in turn give the money to the church, or they would be sent to hell.

~Leaving out this teaching created a separation from the real truth about life on earth~

and then fed the ego or the world the treasures they desired. Each teaching that was left out caused a greater gulf between us and God and when other questions came up we saw the answers thru the filter of whether we knew our Father or not. ***Things became very distorted and that is why we often depend on outer doctrine because we really can't fit all the pieces together.*** There are too many pieces kept out of the picture or at least out of the picture we think is true. There are too many critical pieces missing in our vision or our mind. Yes, I will say it again.

~The pieces missing are really there but how we see things keeps the critical pieces invisible to our eyes~

Most Christians have a very hard time accepting the teaching of reincarnation. Without accepting this teaching we find **alternate reasons** to explain the struggles of this life. We sometimes have the reaction, that God is punishing us and Why? We not only ***don't understand*** that we might have created this reaction from something we have done in this life, but also it might be a result of something we have to heal from a past life that affects us now.

72

~Christianity took away the power we had of how we are able to be responsible for our destiny~

by making Jesus the savior of the world who died and took all our sins upon himself. This doctrine takes away the true message of Jesus that we are able to become one with the Father, because we are able to be co-creators and it takes away our *personal accountability* by saying Jesus did everything for us and so we can't do anything more. *This doctrine takes away our power to be who we are but the underlying problem of this doctrine is that it has tried to remove God's universal law, FREE WILL.* When anyone disturbs God's laws, and their power, they will have to reap what they sow. This is where religion can be very crippling. It takes away our spiritual identity and it was never and I repeat NEVER Jesus' intention. If we understand reincarnation correctly then we understand that all responsibility of our lives is placed *on ourselves.*

~The conditions we face in this life are a direct result of our choices in this life or in past lives~

You might be feeling a little queasy when you first hear this because now there is only *one* to blame, *namely yourself.* But don't beat yourself up too badly. There is a way to learn and move beyond anything in life. God *doesn't* want you to feel like you are a sinner by nature and you have no control over your destiny, and you will never be able to take back control over your life.

~You must face your fears and only then you will rise above them~

Reincarnation is actually where the buck stops and in knowing this *it will liberate you in ways you never dreamed.* Reincarnation answers your own questions of God being unjust or one to fear. Because the universe returns to us what we send out, we realize **we are in control** of what our future can be like.

~We will understand that if we want more abundance then we need to send out more abundance~

This is where we can neutralize the negative causes of our actions. Doing the right thing, we can accumulate positive consequences and when something from a past life comes back to us, we will be able to cancel it out by drawing upon what we have accumulated in positive actions in this lifetime. Jesus explained this very concept in the following verse: **"But lay up for yourselves treasures in heaven, where neither moth nor rust doth corrupt, and where thieves do not break through nor steal."** (Matthew 6:20) God does not punish anyone but the truth is we punish ourselves by violating God's universal and impersonal laws. **When we violate them, we actually set in motion a cause that in time will come back to us as an effect.** So if a child is born with cancer, it is possibly the effect of a cause set in motion in a past life, because no one is born a sinner and this child couldn't have done something to cause this in this lifetime. Another possibility is that the child came to show people the greater part of life with the love he or she possesses in spite of the suffering or his or her life is to help bring a cure. There are endless possibilities. Another thought is that if a person leads a good life but terrible things seem to follow them, it is because the effect from a past life has come back to them. Keep in mind these are opportunities to clear them up and move on. Also, if this person had not lived a good life in this lifetime, the results might have been much worse. Now on the other hand if a person lives selfishly and against the will of God in this life and achieves great success with riches and power, this person might have earned this in a past life. However, you can be sure that this person will not escape the selfish consequences of this lifetime and will either have to deal with them in this lifetime or in another lifetime these consequences will return unto him or her. I explain all these possibilities to show you that when you see that reincarnation is a master key in the totality of our lives, you will see that you then can go within and understand your own life better and in turn become empowered taking a hold of the future of your destiny. *It will all make sense when you have the greater picture of life on earth and the Father that created you out of a pure stream of the highest light and love possible.*

In knowing and understanding the concepts of the truth behind reincarnation, we can then remove the desire for vengeance.

~Vengeance will only reap our own punishment because what we send out into the universe will return unto us again~

So if we seek revenge, we only set in motion a cause that will haunt us in a future life. *When Jesus said to turn the other cheek he wanted us to avoid creating negative consequences that could create more trouble for us in the future.* The truth is reincarnation makes it very obvious that God is *not unjust*, which in turn helps us to overcome any anger we might have against God. To help you understand that Jesus did in fact teach reincarnation and put to rest any doubt you might have. Think on the verses in John 9. *"And as Jesus passed by, he saw a man which was blind from his birth. And his disciples asked him, saying, Master, who did sin, this man, or his parents, that he was born blind?"* The disciples presented this question to Jesus because they *did know the concept of reincarnation*. They asked Jesus whether the man sinned or his parent's *because they saw it was a possibility the man was reaping from a past life.* Jesus often taught or expounded on things with the disciples, away from the multitude and so they had an understanding of reincarnation. *Jesus knew that unto those that are willing to have a higher understanding, the mysteries of the kingdom of God would be revealed but to those that were stuck at a lower level of consciousness, they would be given parables, that seeing they might not see and hearing they might not understand.*

I understand this concept of reincarnation may not be acceptable to many who read this book but I want to explain to you so that you can think on it and eventually find a rational explanation that has the potential to help you move past your limited understanding of God.

As you think about the loving God that created you and you find yourself willing to lay aside some or all of the beliefs you once had, *I believe with all my heart that you will find a deep love for your Father that will grow with every passing day.* God isn't looking for perfection but for a willingness to really look at the truth. God loves you more than you can even imagine. God is with you always. *Become one with God and love Him with all your heart and soul and you will find the kingdom of God that is within you and in turn you will bring God's Kingdom to earth.*

AN EXAMPLE: JESUS, "THE CHRIST"

For all of us, the more we understand the better we can make our own conclusions. We are truly God's creation and His handiwork reveals we are gods in the making. If you can re-look at the life of Jesus and really understand how his life was to help you become all you are, this alone will empower you to live as rightful heirs of the Kingdom of God.

You will notice that I titled this chapter, as Jesus, the Christ because Jesus is a Christed being and "Christ" ***wasn't his last name or part of his name***. How interesting we have assumed that Jesus Christ was his full name but "the Christ" is what he came to bring to your attention so that you will know what will save you and who you potentially can be. Let's get to know the real Jesus.

You know Jesus as you have been taught and that is where we will start. ***Nothing is lost*** by what you know and believe, but all things will be revealed as you begin to take hold of a new perspective of his life on earth.

~The life of Jesus is the most well known life in the world and yet it is truly the most misunderstood~

Many religions grasp onto Jesus and have there way to put "him" into their teachings. Jesus came at a time in human history where people *were waiting for him* because the scriptures wrote about how he will save his people but when he came, the message he had, that would help them become the spiritual beings they potentially could become, *was hard for them to grasp*. It was *their current level of consciousness that kept them from really seeing his life purpose*. What happened was that the people took what they saw and *interpreted it according to their level of understanding?* On top of that the church had their own agenda and chose to write the life of Jesus down so that it would *benefit their earthly desires*. I cannot speak for everyone that lived because in my heart most people want to know and want to be empowered. The problem with the life of Jesus today, is that much of what he taught has either been distorted *to fit another picture or has been lost*, either in translation or by a motive from outside forces.

One major false teaching of Jesus is that *he was an exception in the human race*. By this I mean we are taught that Jesus was the "only" Son of God and not just a son of God. Jesus came to teach us by example that we *can escape* how the human mind sees things and that death is *not the end of our soul* but why does religion teach differently. *Jesus came to teach by example that we can all have the Christ Consciousness and that is the only way we can be saved*. Jesus was an example of the "the Christ", the Christ mind that is the only way to be one with the Father. It is taught in religion that Jesus was the "only" Son of God, the only one who could escape death. Then how can he be an example? Isn't an example one that shows you how you can successfully *achieve the same in your life?*

> *~Would God really send a Son in which we could never match up to and never be able to do the same?~*

If religion is telling the truth *then did God mock our very existence?* When Jesus called himself the Son of God, the Jews cried blasphemy but when the Christians looked down on the Jews for this statement, they turned around and called Jesus the Only Son of God. Doing this they created a greater blasphemy!

~Why would Jesus say that we could do greater things than him if he is an exception to God's creation? ~

Why would Jesus say we are god's? If Jesus is the **only one** that can manifest the life **God accepts** then why would God send him to us? Wouldn't that be an insult?

~If we are made in God's image then why did God only create one Son?~

These questions are obvious and they are the very reason so many are tired of all the arguing. **Let's get down to the truth and start living our lives.** If religious people would rather teach something that doesn't make sense, then let them. They have Free Will, but let us go on to a higher understanding. We give them permission to remain in the trapped beliefs that don't take them any further and we will walk on to the greater understanding that Jesus wants us to know. Jesus didn't come to insult us because he was "supposedly" better than us or better than we could ever possibly be.

~Jesus came to be the inner savior but the world sees what is outside and will swear up and down that what they see is all there is~

But the truth is that Jesus saw in his life that whatever man saw on the outside ***was always in danger of being turned into an idol.*** Jesus is representative of the only begotten Son of God in the form of the "Christ Consciousness", what is within, the inner Christ. ***To see Jesus as an exception, and not the example he came to be, only creates walls around "your" thinking, a prison within that "traps you" into never understanding any more.***

I don't even recall Jesus saying in his own words, that he was the Only son of God because if I remember right he always referred to us as his brothers and sisters or friends. And when we remember the words written, "that without Him was not anything made that was made", and if we believe Jesus to be God's only Son, ***then where do we fit in?*** I think we have allowed ourselves to believe a "***circle of lies***" that the religious world has written in their books. ***Some of us have questioned the interpretations of man and have been accused of blaspheme.*** And others have just accepted that all of this is the truth, because they choose not to stand up and fight for the truth.

> *~The power of the life of Jesus only comes to you when you understand the whole picture and get rid of the lies~*

If you loosely believe in teachings ***that don't create a vehicle in which you can travel*** to far away places and learn and grow and become all that God desires of you, then you will never be empowered to do anything.

> *~The true mission of Jesus was to empower everyone, in every walk of life, in every religion; to become the co-creators God created them to be~*

> *~Many religions have distorted the real mission of Jesus and have taken basic writings and twisted them to fit their story~*

The truth is that we really have to step back and ask ourselves if maybe we have misinterpreted the messages Jesus came to bring. If we have, ***then are we willing to honor his life by getting down to the truth.*** For me, I am not willing to watch the life of Jesus ***be misinterpreted anymore.*** If we have misinterpreted, is it because of how his life was interpreted by the people of the time when he lived and because it was written by church in a book we call the Bible? We must take a stand and not allow the messages to carry on without questioning them. Jesus often spoke of God's word as "Living" and so if we just think about a ***living word***, then we can see that the Bible is a word that is set in stone ***but not a word that is living***. The living word is always able to become more. The Bible can contain teachings you can put in your heart, and those teachings ***are not the end of what is to be revealed because they are meant to be living***. Putting the teachings of the bible into our hearts, that are warm and ready, the teaching becomes a living presence that will grow and grow. I believe that Jesus wants to tell us more about his life. Not because he wants attention ***but because his life was an effort to help us become one with the Father and to take control over our own destiny.***

~I believe Jesus is tired of the false teachings in which the power of his example is gone~

Jesus wants us to see the Father as ***a Father that loves our ability to create.*** Jesus came to really show us how to live and yet his life and death seems to have mysteries that haunt us. If truly the words written so long ago, were an interpretation of the level of Consciousness of those times, and the words have remained as a false idol, something written in stone that is not changeable, then are we willing to hear Jesus in this day and age? We must take courage. We can live this way for as long as we want, and know deep inside that what we know, doesn't add up to giving the life of Jesus ***the power it was intended to be,*** or we can take a stand for his life and give Jesus an opportunity to speak again to us.

In religion we are taught that the Bible is the final word and that creates a fear within us to not question anything. The words in the Bible are not complete. I have spoken about how ***a message is an open door to an understanding*** but if you hear ***just*** the words and then close the door by believing that is all there is to be said, then you will only hear part of the message. A living word is when you hear the words, and then you hear God speaking within your heart. God is in you and He will build upon the teachings.

~The living word of God is the only word that will help us grow closer to God and become the Christ within~

The Bible was written many years ago and it related to things that were common in that day and age. We often try to apply it to our lives and it is one of the ways preachers teach sermons. This is understandable and ok to some degree but the life of Jesus is very important and *we also need to see the deeper meanings behind the messages*. It's not just about applying simple things as to how to deal with people in this world. *The life of Jesus is about a greater picture that affects our eternal destiny and our growth in the spiritual world, which connects us to our Father in Heaven.* It is a very important message then and today. In those days it was written in the Bible to be interpreted according to their lives then. However, in our day, we have the ability to have a higher understanding and the same teachings have the ability to connect us to the deeper message with which Jesus lived and died for. Jesus did warn us in the scriptures of these very thoughts I am sharing. When he said that **"except our righteousness exceed the righteousness of the scribes and Pharisees, we would not enter into the kingdom,"** *he was warning us that the words would one day not have the same meaning.* He knew that to intellectualize our way into heaven, *would not give us the ability to know the truth* and that is the very reason he used the example of the scribes and Pharisees. When Jesus said that God is spirit and we must worship Him *in spirit and in truth*, he didn't want us to become comfortable with the rituals or even interpretations of the church. Jesus wanted us to understand the nature of Spirit and that is it is *always transcending and becoming more* and so we must always want to learn more of God.

Before Jesus left this world he left a very important message to his disciples. You can read John 14:15-18 and find the message is about the Comforter. To understand these verses better *you need to remember that there is an outer way and an inner way to God.* The outer way is how the Pharisees and Sadducees, the lawyers and priests taught and lived. Many Christian churches think *they are not like these that followed in Jesus' day*. I wonder if they feel they aren't like them because their religion name isn't theirs. I remember the church I went to, that thought they were the only way to heaven and they often spoke against these that followed an outer way. ***But the truth is they also were following an outer way.*** The outer way is based on the belief that you can enter Heaven by observing certain rules given by religious teachings on Earth. You believe that as long as you follow certain doctrines that are defined by your church leaders you will be saved. It is also about being obedient to the leaders and the doctrine, and going to church, and living a certain way, and dressing a certain way. It entails a list of rules that guide you and ***if you deviate from them, you will be judged.*** The truth is that it really is reinforcing the belief that you will be saved only by ***changing your outer actions*** without changing yourself or your state of consciousness. Keep in mind that many of these churches also teach about changing what is within and they say that if you are right on the outside then it will be proof you are right on the inside. ***I think the ego can go in circles about this and argue till the end of time.*** Jesus came to talk about how you can be saved and his message was that the ***"only begotten Son of God was the Christ Mind"*** or consciousness and only when you have this mind in you, will you be saved.

~The outer appearance had nothing to do with it then and has nothing to do with it now~

How we dress and look, what we drive, where we live and anything else has nothing to do with going to heaven.

~It is what is within, having the mind of Christ, the Christ consciousness is what will save our souls from being lost.~

The Christ Consciousness holds a high vibration of light, which is how we draw close to God. So feeling lost, simply means we are separated from the ability to be close to God because we have shut off the mind of Christ and therefore have a lower vibration of light, which keeps us from drawing close to God. That is the "lost" feeling and it feels like a lost eternity. We are made in the image of God and God is within us but to draw close to His ongoing being, we have to open our hearts within to receive the light within from our inner being. God is within but *if we turn off the ability to receive His light from within, then we will feel empty and separated*. Think of being in a dark room. The light is within the room but you must turn it on to benefit from it.

> *~The light is available but unless you really want light then it will only remain a fixture and never benefit you.~*

We are in control of our destiny, because that is how God made us and

> *~Jesus came to tell us we do have control.~*

Jesus saw how so many had lost their understanding of who they were and how powerful their lives are. Jesus wanted us to know we also can be the Christed Beings and we can do the same things as God.

> *~We are created as co-creators and yet mankind simply turned off what was within them, because they didn't understand what it was that could empower them~*

I have noticed for many years the nature of humans. I noticed they naturally wanted to learn, grow, take charge, and make a better world. I noticed the ambition, the intellect, the creativity and the imagination. I noticed how many people that have lived had made such a difference in our world even in their single lives. Inventors, philosophers, explorers, scientists and the list goes on and on of those that contributed to make a better world. This is the nature of mankind and this is exactly the nature of God. He truly did make us to be like Him. But then I noticed how religion tried to control the natural abilities by keeping them under lock and key. Religion has taken away the power of free will and the ability to create any way we want. *Religion has taken away the power of the life of Jesus.* Religion uses doctrine to put controls on people. *But Jesus was not of religion and he was not here to put controls on us. He wanted us to experience life and to exercise our God given free will.*

To add more injury to the true message of Jesus, they take his dying for your sins as his way of paying a price for your salvation and the only thing you need to do is be obedient to him and you will be saved. This takes away the power of your life and detaches your need to become the Christ or to do anything that can help you grow and become what God needs you to be. *This essentially says that Jesus did everything for you and you will never be able to do anything for yourself.* So if you take the rules of the individual church, then add the death on the cross, and the obligation to Jesus, you get a formula of outer doctrines saving you. *What I mean is that you have no power over your life because essentially Jesus did everything for you and now your life is that of a puppet.* Do you really think this was Jesus' motive for coming here? Many Christians judge other religions but fail to see theirs *is as faulty as those they condemn.* Could this be the common denominator where we still have the mote or the beam in our own eyes and yet we preach that *they* are blind?

~I have felt a message for many years that Jesus needs people to really understand why he came to earth and how it can really help them~

What if your religion has taken you down a similar road to those you have judged to be wrong, would you *be willing to re-look at everything* and make a fresh start?

The inner approach is what Jesus referred to when he said the Kingdom of God is within you. What this means is that the door to the kingdom of God, the door to understanding, the door to the master key that opens all the locks, is waiting within you. *It also means that you cannot obtain entry through any other way, including outer rules and doctrines.*

~It means that the kingdoms entrance lies waiting within you and only by changing your state of consciousness will you gain access to open the door, because this is the only way you can see the real Jesus~

Paul spoke about dying daily and putting off the old man and putting on the new man. But was that in correlation to the same messages of Jesus where he spoke of the Kingdom within.

~I believe it was a direct attempt to teach the people how to change their state of consciousness~

Paul also spoke much of the carnal man and we will call this the ego. Paul was willing to go thru many difficult situations to examine himself and put off the part of him *that hindered his walk with the Christ.* He was willing to let his carnal self, or ego die *because he understood within that he could not take this old man with him to a higher level of consciousness, which is called heaven.* He knew that he had to put on the wedding garment which is the Christ consciousness or as it was referred to in those days, the mind of Christ. *This is the true explanation of being born again.* In those days as well as in our days it is preached that to be born again we must accept Jesus as Lord and Savior, with just our lips.

~To be born again means to allow the mind of Christ to be born within you~

Are you aware that the ego or the carnal mind cannot see the Living Christ when it stands in the flesh? This is why they didn't recognize Jesus 2000 years ago. *The truth is that the carnal state of consciousness will not allow you to see the door to the kingdom of God that is within you.* Do you also know that this is why you are more likely to accept the teaching that the Savior will do all the work for you? *When you don't understand and when the abilities to understand are not there, you settle for what you do understand. It's as simple as that.*

The inner way, the inner Savior, the Christ Mind is the king who is sitting on the throne in the kingdom of heaven *that is within you*. So how do we get the mind of Christ? *Jesus wanted more than anything for us to have the same joy of entering the Kingdom and so he sent his own Spirit, his Christ mind, to every person on the face of the earth, through the Comforter.* Jesus knew that the only way to put on the wedding garment that would allow you to enter the kingdom, would be to absorb a portion of the Christ mind, which would have the ability to raise your level of consciousness, until you have put off the old man, the carnal mind and put on the new, the Christ mind. Jesus wanted you to put off the human self that you were born with and re-connect with the spiritual being that God created in His image and likeness. Before Jesus left this earth He promised to send you a comforter, the Holy Spirit. *The only way the Holy Spirit can be given to us is through a Being in Heaven who is willing to let his own Spirit, the part of his spiritual self, come down to this earth.* I will speak to you later but this same concept is true about the Ascended Host, that is made of Beings that have reached their spiritual higher self and are waiting in the spiritual realm to help all who still are on earth. The Comforter is a part of the Spiritual Being of Jesus who is willing to send to us a part of Himself that can guide us and counsel us on how to attain our salvation. The "Christ Self" is not in the Bible and I believe that it is because the people of those times wouldn't have been able to fully grasp the connection to Jesus. *The wording would have confused them.* The Christ Self is a part of Jesus, a portion of his Spirit and *is the most precious of all the gifts he sends to us*.

~Jesus' spiritual mission became an open door for the "Christ mind" to enter this world. He did this, sending a portion of his spirit in the same way you send a portion of your spirit into the material realm~

Your spiritual being resides in the spiritual realm and the level it is at is according to your consciousness. Your consciousness' understanding allows you to be in the level where you have the same light you can receive. In other words you can receive more light as your understanding grows or your level of consciousness grows, but you reside in the level according to the light you can receive and *it is this light that determines your level of understanding.* This is why growing in the spiritual teachings is critical *in raising the light you can receive.* Raising the light is about you and you alone choosing to become more of the spiritual being you are. Jesus' level was at the Christ consciousness and the light of His spirit attained the title of the "light of the world" *because he had so much light in him.* We have a spiritual being residing in the spiritual realm and when we decide to embody, we first set up a plan and then we send a portion of our spirit into the world. *This is what Jesus did and he has left us with a part of his spiritual being. A continued light or portion of himself, which is called the Comforter.* He never left us alone and because his mission is for us to become full of the Christ consciousness he gave us a part of that consciousness to help us begin. The problem isn't in the gift *but in the receiving end.* It is available to us, ready and waiting to enlighten us but until we see the lies told around the life of Jesus, his life cannot give us the power to reclaim our identity and purpose.

People have been seeing Jesus as an idol, a Savior that will save them without them doing anything for themselves, for a very long time. The inner approach has been lived by *some* thru the years and some have called them mystics by religious people. They are people who don't work on the outward but the inward parts. Many Christians have persecuted them for this way of seeing salvation. Those who worked on the inward part understood *that the key of knowledge was there Christ Self,* the Spirit of truth that was within them. They knew from their own experience that what was within taught them many things, and brought much to their remembrance.

Many religious teachings reinforce that you cannot know the truth on your own, telling the people they need an outer scripture or church to teach it to them. This is one of the subtle lies that is told thru religion and it keeps people from going within and hearing the ***still small voice***. It keeps people trapped in believing they cannot save themselves but need the church to save them. ***It traps them from seeing beyond and learning that God has a continued revelation that He wants to share with all of us.*** Some churches allow people to read; study, and share but ultimately they tell them they need someone to explain it to them. This denial of your ability to know truth in your heart ***never came from the teachings of God or Jesus.*** Jesus came to show all of us that we could come to the Father, and learn of God and His Kingdom through our inner self. We do not need any person, or any institutions from outside of ourselves to be saved. We have everything we need for salvation within and the Spirit, the Comforter, is given to help us. The key to salvation is that we choose it for ourselves and we realize it is far more than just accepting Jesus died.

The true key to your salvation is that you are willing to understand the level of your consciousness and rise above the lower, carnal or ego mind you possess in this world.

~The true goal of your life is to ascend beyond the material world and enter the spiritual world, while you are still in embodiment~

I think we all can somewhat agree on this. The problem lies ***in how to do it.*** When I speak of the carnal mind or the ego, it was often referred to as the flesh and blood ***that could not inherit the kingdom.*** We have already established that the only way to the kingdom is ***in leaving behind the carnal mind, which is the lower level of consciousness.*** In Mark 4:34, "But without a parable spake he not unto them; and when they were alone, he expounded all things to his disciples." I think we can really see that Jesus was aware that people saw things at different levels of awareness or consciousness. ***Those to whom he spoke in parables could not understand a deeper spiritual meaning than what was told.*** But those he expounded all things to, were able to understand beyond the literal interpretation and they could not only understand what he said at a deeper level *but could also grow in understanding as in progressive revelation.* Keep in mind this was how it was in the days of Jesus but why do so many have the inability in today's time to understand the deeper message. The easiest way is to understand that religion has dominated our thoughts for so long in the stories it believes to be true *that the truth of the life of Jesus is still caught in the trap 2000 years ago.* Sometimes I envision Jesus is still in the bottle that holds a Genie and all of what He has tried to give in teachings and understandings, *simply remains trapped in that bottle.* Then I envision someone who is courageous, willing to open the bottle and let out the teachings and the life of Jesus is revealed. But so many have believed a lie for so long, that an idol of mass proportions is the very nature of the problem.

~We must be willing, one at a time, to take the bull by the horn and stop believing the lies. We must begin to stand up for Jesus and give him the honor that he earned.~

Give him the ability to see that his life was not in vain and allow him to watch a world that will hear his true message and empower their lives.

~Doesn't Jesus deserve to see the results of his incredible love and willingness of so long ago?~

By this I mean that we simply haven't pursued in changing what is written because we have this belief that the Bible is infallible, that the conformed teachings are the only interpretation, and that the teachings of the churches are infallible. Now that we know the overall problem, I want you to look at some of the basic teachings of the Christian Churches of Jesus and help you look beyond and *see a different Jesus.*

So why did the "only Son of God" became an official doctrine of the Christian Church? I think it is a little more complex than just people having a lower level of awareness or consciousness. Like anything in life when something catches on others jump on the bandwagon so to speak. The religions of the world have a motive to build their following. Then when you add the workings of the carnal mind and how it sees things and decides it will not take responsibility for anything, *it becomes the ultimate master for creating excuses and more lies to justify the first ones.* Look at history for a moment and you will see how humans are resistant to change. If humans saw for once that their own choices and *actions actually hurt themselves*, then *they would* change.

~As long as the soul identifies with the carnal mind, it doesn't realize that it really is only hurting itself.~

Jesus confronted often those who were not willing to hear his teachings of going within and changing their sense of identity. Jesus wanted people to be free of any outer institution or teaching that claimed they had to rely on it for their salvation. To make it clearer,

~...to the carnal mind, nothing is really wrong and nothing is really right but to the Christ mind there is an absolute standard for determining right or wrong.~

The Christ mind simply asks the question if something is from God or not and if it's not from God then it is wrong and needs to be changed right now. A Christed Being, when seeing something not of God, will simply leave it behind and just walk away. For the truth is when someone connects to their Christ consciousness they become more than willing to change by the deeper understanding to see what details can still be right and what are definitely wrong. They are willing to leave the old ways behind and embrace the higher understanding.

Jesus called his disciples and I am sure there were many he called but only 12 answered the call. Just think about the scenario of when he went to the fisherman of Galilee and said to leave their nets because he would make them fishers of men. I appreciated that they went but didn't quite understand that it was because they had a Christ consciousness

91

to some degree, and followed their inner understanding. They instantly recognized the Living Christ and with their free will they made a decision to leave their nets.

⁓Many times people don't want to change and they are comfortable remaining in ignorance.⁓

Sometimes fear grips them, because the doctrine they worship has caused them to not question. Jesus was a son of the living God and everyone could follow in his footsteps.

Another reason why Jesus was labeled the only Son of God is the ongoing battle on earth *for power*. The powerful of this world want to do everything for their own good. In the days of Jesus the Jewish authorities wanted him executed. It was simply a fear they had of him and they saw him as a threat to their power over the people. The power elite also don't like in religion that there is a God who rules. We are talking about government, kings and emperors when we talk of the power elite. *To them as long as God is supreme in the minds of the people they govern, they will always be second in command.* So this became a political power struggle with Jesus.

⁓We have Jesus trying to help the people believe they have the power within them to be god's and co-creators and then we have Jesus dealing with the rulers and emperors who want to rule the people.⁓

As I am attempting in this book to help you take hold of your life, *Jesus tried the very same thing. I stand by His life and tell you that unless you BE THE CHANGE on your own power, then this ongoing power elite will always have something over you.* The power elite would like nothing more than to just eliminate God and religion altogether but that is impossible *so they confuse it.* In politics I watch our President fighting the people in confusing battles. In his good will attempt to encourage our youth, he is put down as a criminal. WHAT

IS GOING ON? So confusing that I ask myself *what in the world is this about.* Even the media is questioning. It's about the power elite that are full of pride and would like nothing more than to destroy the potential for any truth to break thru or any *appearance of success* in our new president. Appearance of success would make those that didn't vote for him, wrong. But this is the very problem on earth.

~We conquer and divide in order to raise ourselves up.~

We want to prove right and wrong because that is how we get a good feeling about ourselves. I encourage you to see that we could actually find joy in another's success if we simply didn't have this insecurity in our beings of always needing to be right. Jesus showed us that Love is the greatest power on earth and loving another's contribution and hard work shouldn't be so hard.

~But pride and the ego keeps us in a catch 22 where we won't be happy in this world and we won't be happy if anyone tries to show us a better way.~

Step away from the picture and look at the things that don't need to be. Have a heart and give unto others what you want to receive. Is this for the good of the people or is it something greater at work? The same with Jesus, the same goes on in this world. *Until the spiritual people wake up and stand up and make known their light, the power elite and the dark forces at work in this world will confuse and destroy anything they can.* They also use science as a way of getting people to doubt the theory of a God. They believe that if you can't get people to let go of their belief in God, *you start to spread stories.* One of them is that there is only one church, meaning there is only one road to be saved. Because most people feel good when they feel better than others, this catches on and pretty soon you have many churches believing they are the only way. How can they all be the only way, you may ask? Then they set themselves up to be an authority in the one and only church and in turn teach the people that their teachings are infallible.

These understandings of how the power elite work and how they create many churches that are the only way to heaven, is very critical to understand and to see how deceiving it is. In order to understand Jesus true teachings, you have to recognize the wrongness of this way of the world. To understand the teachings of the "only" son of God, you need to understand why the churches created this to be the truth. Jesus came to bring the message that the only mediator between God and human beings is the Christ Consciousness.

~*The universal Christ Consciousness is the open door and no one can shut it.*~

So when someone attains their Christhood, they don't need a church or any authority to continue to grow. ***This is a major threat to churches that want your support and your obedience.*** It is a well-known fact in history that the development of the Christian church was designed to be a tool for gaining power. ***The Roman emperor Constantine decided to use the Christian church as a tool to unite his ailing empire under one religion.*** Eventually it became known as the Roman Catholic Church and as the only representative of God on earth. Believe it or not many of their forceful tactics were through militant means and this is where the doctrine that Jesus Christ was the only Son of God, came. So to wrap it up you need to understand that the true inner teachings of the life of Jesus *were not only taken away from us but were also replaced* by outer doctrines that went against all that Jesus lived and died for. In a nutshell Jesus' inner teachings declare that every human being has the potential to manifest Christhood. Jesus was not the only Son of God but simply an example to follow. Each of us are sons and daughter's who have the same potential to walk the earth as Christed Beings. A Christed being only recognizes the authority of God and is in alignment with God's will. A Christed being cannot be fooled into believing the lies of the world. You see the power elite had to kill Jesus to stop him because if they left him alive and others took upon themselves to be what Jesus came to teach us we could be, ***then they would have major problems. They would then have to deal with a multitude of***

beings that were co-creators and knew who they were spiritually. Leaving Jesus alive was a recipe for disaster and they would loose their power over the people. After getting rid of Jesus, **they had to make a determined effort to distort the true teachings.**

The religious world has cut and pasted much of his life to appear, as they want it to appear. They have put him on a pedestal so that you believe he is to be worshipped and he is someone that you can never match up to. If Jesus believed and taught this one truth then why did he say "Ye are gods" and "you can do greater things than I?" **They have taken away your power to believe you can take hold of your life** because they have told you that Jesus did everything for you and you don't have to do anything but **believe in him.** His life has become an empty vessel in which **there is nothing he can enable you to do but what he has done already.** This is wrong. Many religions just simply overemphasize that you are not worthy and you must remain obedient to Jesus. They keep you believing that all you can do is follow his footsteps and never become any more. **That saddest part of this teaching is that it cripples your own ability to think for yourself, experience life and really grow, as God needs you to grow.** If you asked your own child to do this would he ever be able to really live his own life? If you purposely crippled your child's ability to walk, could you live with yourself? The very nature of what the power elite does to people, reveals they don't respond from the heart. Would this philosophy work in our world? We cannot expect that just laying down our own will, and simply being obedient could ever produce growth in our world.

~Yet Christianity teaches that our relationship with Jesus is a done deal~

Meaning he did everything for us and we can't do anything but lay down our lives in submission to him. **This would logically mean, there is no power in the life of Jesus for you to take for yourself.** His love does continue to feed us but he wanted us to see his life as an example to live by so that we could become empowered to live our lives and grow into the co-creators, the Christed beings we are.

The pattern of our world in learning and growing as humans is very clear. We go to school much of our lives as children, we choose our occupation, our spouse, our geographical location and many other things throughout life but when it comes to religion and the purpose of the life of Jesus, it is supposedly one way and it remains unchangeable. Why? The answer is clear; ***this is not God's plan but man's interpretation.*** God proves in all of His creation that change is always on the horizon. God created us in His image and likeness and we are likened unto Him. He created, He had the power to use His imagination and free will and yet when Jesus came we are taught that all of that stopped and Jesus paid the price and we can't do anything else but just humbly submit to him. ***Wait a minute------this cannot be the truth.*** We not only could never grow beyond our limited walls we live in, and never become anymore than a past generation but we also couldn't become one with the Father. ***When you are one with someone, you both think similar ways and if we believe we are unworthy and can never do anything for our own salvation, then either we believe that God thinks He is unworthy or the only other option is to believe we are not one with the Father and never can be.*** If God is always becoming more, and we are to have the same mind as God, then we need to always become more. Thru the years I sat back and walked quietly in the religious world, but then I came to a point and I could no longer accept their theories. I stepped out of the box, and looked in from another angle and the whole world changed. I realized that all people want to live abundantly and enjoy life on earth but the only way they could do it, ***would be to put all the pieces together and see the greater masterpiece that Jesus came to show us.***

If in the days of Jesus, people only saw things according to the world's perception of life, science, etc, and if we only become obedient to those things then we will always see things this way because we are to remain the same, just obedient to what is right now understood in our eyes. The religious world often quotes that Jesus is the same yesterday, today and forever but this saying means simply that he hasn't changed *the fact that he still wants us to become more of who we are.* It isn't to be taken like they take it, as *a no change situation.* As I have already stated everything God created changes all the time. Even the pattern of life from the days that Jesus lived to now, reveal that enormous changes have occurred and we have a far different world than when he walked the earth. We are constantly changing in this world. Even nature never remains the same. Look at clouds, they appear different when we look at them at different angles and they are always changing. Watch them. Everything on the face of this earth changes on a constant basis, whether we see it or not. *So do you think that God really created man above all other of His creation and took away the power to constantly change and evolve and become more?* Do you feel that change is bad? Do you think God intended we just remain as clones of one another and never have the ability to be more?

Many contradictions of what the churches teach and what Jesus taught have discouraged countless people to simply walk away and have nothing to do with any of it. Religious people categorize these who walk away as those that either don't believe in God or just don't care. They often say these people are going to hell. *But isn't it hell believing a lie?* These people walk away because they have reached a higher understanding and can't ignore it. They may not have the answer they are currently looking for but they do know *they need to first be honest with themselves and no longer be willing to believe things that don't make sense.* To them they must find the answer and it isn't in the churches teachings and so being in a church that is disabled is like living in hell. The confusion is very frustrating. Some walk away and give up and others search. But the truth is we cannot put our head in the sand and ignore the obvious misconceptions of Jesus. *If you choose to believe only the teachings of the Christian churches then the life of Jesus does nothing to empower you to be more of who you are, because you simply bow to what he did and you acknowledge that this is all God wants you to do.* Jesus was not a unique individual *because he was the only one who could do what he did.*

> ***"Jesus was a unique individual because he showed us a path that all of us can follow, whereby we too can do the works that He did."***

Many Christians use the verse, "Jesus saith unto him, I am the way, the truth, and the life: no man cometh unto the Father, but by me." (John 14:6) to prove that Jesus is the only way to go to heaven. *The truth is that there is an inner meaning, as is true of many of Jesus' teachings.* Remember he said he talked one way to the multitude but another way to the disciples and this is because there was a deeper meaning and the people of the day were not able to grasp that understanding because of the level of consciousness they were at in understanding many things on earth. Religion teaches that Jesus is the only Son of God but *why would God only create one son*? Where do all the rest of us fit in?

> *~Do we believe that God sent his only son down to earth to show the rest of us what miserable sinners we are compared to Jesus' perfection?~*

If God created us, and if we are sinners by nature, then God must have created us as sinners. *What sense does that make that God would mock us by sending one son who was not created as a sinner?* Why would God want to make *us feel worse for the way He created us?* The religious world has made it very clear they see Jesus as an idol by the way they teach about him. They also make it very clear that they stand by their teachings no matter how they don't make sense. But how strange is it that Jesus himself was always reaching out to everyone and declared his oneness with all life.

> *~I feel that Jesus did everything he could to avoid being turned into an idol.~*

This is where my heart goes out to Jesus. It is very important to see him as he is and to let go of the false images that have been created around him. ***We must come to a point in our hearts of being able to really relate to Jesus without reservations.*** When we understand him as a friend that wants us to have the same victory as he did, it is then we will open our heart to receive the love Jesus has for us that is waiting to be embraced. ***The truth is that if we have reservations in our relationship with Jesus, we simply cannot receive the love he has for us, because we think we are unworthy of it.*** When those reservations fade away, we can receive Jesus' love, and it is truly more than you ever imagined.

Jesus' love is not based on conditions but is totally unconditional. Think about this statement. In religious teachings we are told to love Jesus because he came to earth and died for our sins. ***But if love is not based on conditions then we should not love him for this reason.*** We should not base our love for him because of what he has done for us. ***Our love for Jesus will be mirrored back to our soul in the most incredible way when we love him for who he is, which is a living presence of Love.*** The truth is that we must take Jesus down from the pedestal ***that makes him unapproachable to us.*** We must ***tear down the walls that the human ego has built*** between Jesus and us in an attempt to prevent us from following his example.

~It is time to cast down the idols of Jesus and finally see him as an elder brother who came to show us the narrow way, the way of unconditional love, the way to become the Christ~

I want to take a moment and explain something about the dualistic way of thinking. The reason that I feel it's important is to help you see how ***the mind divides our thinking into two opposites***, that actually can hinder your ability to re-look at anything in life. We are taking a very serious look at the life of Jesus and in doing so you might find your mind wanting to throw out the dirty water and at the same time throw out the Jesus you know. Don't allow your mind to take sides?

DORR TOWNSHIP LIBRARY
1804 SUNSET DR.
DORR, MI 49323

~There is a prison in your mind that the ego has kept you in bondage with.~

The prison is a "form" *of the way you think* and actually *builds walls around ideas* which in turn limits your ability *to expand* on in any given idea or truth. I have explained already that there is always MORE to learn about everything. *The ego traps your thinking to believe that one particular teaching is all there is to know.* It is subtle but when we allow ourselves to believe in duality, in opposites that oppose each other, such as black or white, right or wrong, good or bad, etc, *the result is that we lose our freedom of thought and our lives are turned into a struggle to maintain certain absolute beliefs.* We actually engage in a war in our minds and when someone opposes our beliefs we fight them to the death, so to speak. But when we reject the black and white thinking of the ego, *we actually free our minds from the struggle to defend outdated ideas and that is when we are open to see a higher understanding.* It is critical that you develop the mindset that is of the middle way, as Jesus came to show us. He spoke of having discernment, which simply means to have a *perception in the absence of judgment with a view to obtain spiritual direction and understanding.* Even with the Bible we have a belief that it is infallible and "all there is to know" but this isn't the truth. We need to give up the idea we hold to be the truth about the Bible, and know that it is not one hundred percent correct but we also need to *not* take on the belief it is worthless. *Go to the middle road and understand that the Bible is an incredible book that has much to teach us but feel free to develop a longing for a richer understanding and appreciation of it.* Remember that the Bible has timeless lessons of hardship, endurance, and history of how people have dealt with and overcome the human struggles. Many churches are trying to develop this kind of understanding and they are on the right track. As I write the words in this book I know I don't have the *"only way"* to understand everything and I don't have *"all there is to know"*, but if my words *inspire you to find more* of what God wants you to know, then I have helped you find the middle way and see that the problems of our pattern of thinking that created the situations of the world, cannot be the solution. *The patterns of how the problem came to be must be relooked at and together we will all become greater students from the lessons we have encountered on planet earth.* We are truly blessed to experience not only abundance but suffering because when we see things from the middle way we also see the solutions and in turn we draw closer to becoming the Christ, and seeing the change that needs to come. For me to help you put Jesus back into the picture of life, as it was to be, I need you to understand that it is possible to focus on specific aspects of Jesus' life *without compromising the overall message.* So when you read a teaching the best way to look at it is to see it as *something that will evolve over time and become More as your own level of understanding raises to a higher level. Be patient and in time you will understand at a higher level.* Jesus tried to help us understand the Holy Spirit as our comforter and our teacher. A Spirit has the ability to teach you all things and bring all things to your remembrance when you are ready to understand a higher teaching. With this better understood let's continue to learn more about Jesus.

Jesus came so that you might have life and this life is not just in taking his hand and acknowledging he died for you.

~*This life he wants you to have is to empower you to take hold of your own life and your own destination*~

He wants you to see you are more than what you are right now and that God lives within you and in order to become one with God's creation you must see that you must become one with God. You will never be above God but you will become a co-creator with God and have the same mind that God has and everything you do has the potential to help God become MORE, ever expanding, ever growing. Jesus is no more God than you are. *But the reality is that Jesus has God within him and so do you.* Do you know that the kingdom of God is already within you? Let me try to explain to you one of the most important parts of the life of Jesus as a man. His teaching was critical in helping you grasp who you really are *but when you teach someone that doesn't quite understand some of the fundamentals of the universe, you loose your ability to penetrate and they cannot build upon what you are trying to explain, because they are simply not ready to take it all in.* The Bible was written to help the people of the day in which Jesus walked with on the earth to understand things they needed to understand before he could take them further. The words were adapted to that understanding and that is why today we find the Bible is written in a certain way and yet our understanding is at a higher level and so the Bible doesn't answer all of our questions in a way that can help us. The Bible answers the questions for the people in the time it was written but today we see *there is more we need to know*. This is why many feel that Jesus had a deeper meaning. Our understanding in this day and age is far more advanced than 2000 years ago. If you take the way the religions want you to understand the life of Jesus and then you take word for word the scripture as it is written to help the people of that day, *this can be a recipe for "an illusion"*. Have you ever been to a circus and seen those mirrors that give a reflection that is so warped you hardly recognize yourself? You are not different and yet the illusion is that you are, when you stand in front of the mirror. Jesus said "I am What I Am" and that has never changed but how we understand his life, has changed. If you search the scriptures you will find many that are very hard to understand and to me this is proof that to fully understand Jesus we have to look beyond the literal meaning and we have to have a higher level of consciousness in order to understand. To have a higher level of consciousness we have to let go of the carnal mind, the ego, just as was explained in the bible days. We need to remember that he often taught at two different levels and then we need to ask ourselves what the deeper meaning might be.

A quicker understanding of the different levels of consciousness or understanding is found in re-looking at the Garden of Eden. When the scripture writes that they could eat of every tree of the garden but not the tree of good and evil, there is a deeper meaning of why this all took place. Since we know that Adam and Eve did not actually die, the death that God was talking about was not a physical death, but a spiritual death. *The "tree of the knowledge of good and evil" is a "symbol" for the duality consciousness* and not just a simple shift in consciousness. Consciousness is the level of their understanding and whether it is based on a human view or a spiritual view of life. Before Adam and Eve ate the fruit they saw themselves as connected to God but afterward *they had lost that direct connection.* Before they ate the fruit, they had a sense of identity as God's children, but afterward *they had lost that sense of identity.* We might say that their true sense of identity as spiritual beings had died, and they now had a sense of identity as mortal human beings. They simply *lost their ability to "see who they were"* as spiritual beings that came to this earth to become more of what they already were and they regressed and in turn lost their identity. *In order to regain that identity they would have to re-connect to who they really were as spiritual beings.* Jesus has made it clear that in order to enter the kingdom of God, we have to be spiritually reborn. What happened to Adam and Eve was they went through the opposite of a rebirth and *lost their connection to their spiritual identity.* Those who are spiritually dead can know only a false God, *an idol* that is created by the duality consciousness. *God cannot dwell in them because the ego keeps them separated from God.* Those who are trapped in the duality consciousness inevitably create a graven image of God. This image doesn't mean a statue but is a *mental image that springs from the duality consciousness.* The tree of good and evil is a thinking of black or white, right or wrong. *There is division in the mind and it affects ones ability to see things. A spiritual being sees the whole and there is no division. A spiritual being is not divided against itself.* So it is then *the ego that elevates this image to the status of infallibility*, and that is why people end up *worshiping their mental image* before the Living God.

> *~A graven image is a mental image that people refuse to change because they think it is complete and infallible~*

Yet God says that no mental image we could ever create could give us a complete understanding of God. The honest truth about Jesus is that he came to show us that there is *more to life* than being physically alive and that there is *a higher form of life than what most people experience.* We don't have to live a boring, mortal life in fear and we don't have to experience life as a struggle. We can find an entirely new way of looking at life that will truly give us the spiritually abundant life that Jesus enjoyed while on earth. *We can be more than human beings but in fact we can be spiritual beings walking the earth in human bodies.* When we are willing to be spiritual beings in human bodies, it is then that the Kingdom of God will come to earth, as the Second Coming of Christ. In understanding all of this we now can reach an interesting conclusion. When we are blinded by the duality consciousness of the ego, we see ourselves as mortal, human beings, and that we are "dead" in a spiritual sense. Jesus came to show us that there is an alternative to this state of consciousness.

We have already talked about how God created us with free will and the ability to create. We have covered the truth that we are created in the image and likeness of God, meaning we have a unique individuality. We also are aware we have spiritual teachers or parents that helped us with a plan in which we can grow from this lifetime by using our free will and creative potential. But the very important part to keep in mind is *that nothing is set in stone and when we come here we can deviate from the plan and essentially get totally lost in this human experience.* Life is a process through which our soul is constantly building it's sense of identity until you reach a point where you see your individualization of God and your ability to have full creative powers of God's. *You can potentially manifest the greatest abundance when you come to earth or you can fall into a lower state and loose all of your abilities.* The reason I am reminding you of who you are is that Jesus had the same experience. *He could go one of two ways and he choose the higher road and ultimately his life became representative of the Light of The World, God' light.*

In the days when Jesus walked the earth many had a very limited understanding of these things and so only a few had come to the full realization of their Christhood. To many Jesus *did appear to be far advanced* and it would have been easy for them to label him as the only Son of God. *When you look at how they viewed life, and then you saw the miracles and the wisdom Jesus brought, you can really understand with empathy that people saw him as an exception, as the only Son of God.* But the truth is it was from their viewpoint and because *their minds thought thru the carnal* they turned him into an idol to worship. So with that understanding you might wonder how the doctrine of the only Son of God became official in the churches. One reason is that the carnal mind has a tendency to create idols and because the carnal mind has a hard time later saying they made mistake or were wrong, they keep it as infallible truth. It becomes a road with no return in the minds of people with the carnal mind. *Human beings have a very deep resistance to change* and so no matter what, Jesus would remain the Only Son of God to the world.

Now for the critical question that is the bases of the life of Jesus as explained in the religious world. The question is Why do some Christians think Jesus has taken upon himself all the sins that could ever be committed? *So what we are saying is that Jesus has taken upon himself not only the sins that were committed up until he came, but also all of the sins that could possibly be committed after that time.* How could he possibly take on sins that have not yet been committed? Jesus was not caught up in the carnal mind and so how could this be possible and *furthermore how could people learn from this?* Jesus' whole life was as a teacher and his whole desire was to teach us by example. So how is this "an example"? Does this teach us to bear the burdens of everyone else? From my understanding Jesus was very clear that we are to pull the beam out of our *own* eyes. What I mean is that we can't save anyone but ourselves and only then we can be an example for others to take hold of their lives.

~Jesus was a spiritual teacher who desired so deeply to help humans learn their lessons and take up their bed and walk. The very essence of being a teacher is that you cannot learn someone's lesson for them~

People also have to understand that in learning the lesson they do this by *coming to an inner realization of the truth of that lesson.*

Like the saying, "You can lead a man to water but you cannot make him drink." So if he in fact died for all the sins that ever could be committed in the world and we are all freed by just going to him, *how is this going to strengthen our own ability to take back our lives and become enlightened by what we learned in the experience?* Well, we weren't able to experience the experience and make better choices and grow from them, because Jesus took care of it before that was necessary, *so how much wisdom can we learn?* We don't understand the results of our mistakes, so how will we be able to grow from them? None of this reasoning makes any sense if you believe that Jesus came to help us become empowered by our lives. But if you remove the ability for us to take hold of our lives and simply so nothing, then you can live with this reasoning. *For me, the dots didn't connect and the pieces of the puzzle didn't fit. Something seriously was missing and what was missing was the real truth about Jesus' life.*

Another major hindrance if Jesus would have taken the sins of the world on and removed them, is he also would have taken the opportunity to learn their lessons in life and a true teacher would never deprive his students of the value of the lesson. *Nowhere in scripture does Jesus say that he would take on all of the sins that could possibly be committed for all eternity.* That thought is put in your thinking by religious men who want you to see him that way. You may ask why would they want us to see Jesus that way? Because in seeing Jesus as the Savior of the world, we see him as a god and *our debt to him is so overwhelming that we can never do anything on our own. We see him, bow down to him, and sit at his feet, not able to ever be any more than just that. Is this what Jesus wanted?* Did he want to cripple us so that we could never be more than that? Did Jesus come to take away the spiritual being that we are? Did Jesus come to teach us we would never know how to live our lives unless someone tells us? Did Jesus come to make us *feel obligated* so that we would feel we could never match up to him? *The answer to all of these is NO!!!! ABSOLUTELY NOT!!!!!!!!!* Basically this belief cripples your own belief that you can do anything with your life. When we see Jesus this way, we loose the understanding that he could be our example and we loose our identity as spiritual beings who can become what Jesus wanted us to become, ONE with the Father. *In essence, this would have given a blank check to humankind and most would feel it wasn't important anymore how they live their lives.* Now if you think this is the truth then it would mean that if a person like Adolf Hitler confessed Christ on his deathbed, he would automatically be saved, even if he never did anything to admit his wrong or to change his way of living, but simply acknowledged Jesus as the son of God. If indeed you can commit evil acts and be saved by confessing Christ, then why did Jesus give the sermon on the mount and say, "But whoso shall offend one of these little ones which believe in me, it were better for him that a millstone were hanged about his neck, and that he were drowned in the depth of the sea." (Matt 18:6). *In this verse it seems to be clear that to Jesus salvation did depend on how people live their lives.* But if all that is required for salvation is that we confess Christ, *then all of Jesus' directions and warnings would seem to have been for naught.* So either Jesus didn't really understand that he is the key to salvation, or the idea that he has taken upon himself all future sins, is out of touch with his true teachings. The death on the cross was to reveal how in "manifesting the Christ Consciousness" we will atone for our sins and attain salvation, not through the outer person of Jesus but *through the inner "person" of the Christ consciousness, the Christ self.* Jesus is the Savior and can guarantee your salvation *only if you choose to follow in his footsteps and become the Christ.* Salvation is offered to everyone as a gift and the key to salvation *isn't the offering of the gift but the acceptance of the gift.* The gift is that you can be the Christ and have the mind of Christ within your being. Here again comes into the picture the need to exercise our free will. If a religion tries to keep people from using their free will to grow and learn and have a deeper understanding and know that God helps those who help themselves then it is only reasonable to see that God can't help those who are not willing to take hold of their lives and help themselves. In understanding all of this then how can *Jesus save them unless they are willing to do something with their own choices?* Free Will is designed so that individuals can have the ability to grow as they begin to see the need to exercise free choices. Free will is a very powerful tool that God wants us to take hold of so that we can eventually choose to have the mind of Christ be empowered within us. God gave you free will, so how can Jesus save you against your will? This is why humans must save themselves. We live and grow in a mechanized society and think we can achieve anything by pushing the right buttons. *Yet salvation isn't a matter of pushing buttons but a matter of choice, your choice.*

Remember God helps those who are willing to choose to help themselves. When we think that in times of trouble God will save us if we only ask, we need to remember the importance found in the story of Noah. *He was instructed to do something first on his own, build an ark.* God helps those *who understand they need to do something* to take hold of their lives. God is within us and therefore it is our choices that can transform our lives.

> *"Choose to understand that with free will choices we have the ability to see what needs to change in our lives and then make better choices and only then can our future change."*

The kingdom of God is within, and God is within us.

Many strict Christians focus on how to look or dress and yet when you talk to them they talk about the Inner Christ. Their lives reflect judgment on anyone that doesn't look like them but their lips say they are one with Christ. They are attached to certain outer doctrines and certain views of Jesus but when questioning them, they seem convinced they are not this way.

> *~The truth is that Jesus rebuked the way of the religious approach.~*

Jesus clearly wanted people to look beyond the letter of the law and *discover the "spirit" of the law.* He wanted them to look within and see an inner, spiritual or mystical approach to religion. Jesus forcefully denounced these kinds of religious teaching because a very important part of his mission was to help us free ourselves from the dogmatic approach to religion and see things from a more spiritual view. He wanted us to look beyond outer doctrines and interpretations and *go into our hearts and see what isn't written, see the heart of His Father, see a higher spiritual understanding by looking for the truth inside ourselves.* Most people that are religious are taught in the church that they cannot do things without someone higher giving them instructions and so they don't try. *Fear has them trapped* in believing they don't have what it takes or they shouldn't trust what is within them to help them. Jesus didn't fit into any religion because he knew that he wanted *the truth of his Father above all else.* I remember when leaving a very strict religion several years back that I had not believed like they did for some time. I stayed in hopes that I could help others but what I was doing *was hindering my own ability to see* with a yet deeper understanding. I realized I was compromising my own growth. I had to remove myself from the "box" of a limited belief system and simply jump ship. This was the best thing I ever did because it was then that I saw why.…

~Jesus never conformed to any religion. He knew it wasn't in His Father's best interest~

….and he would never let any earthly institution or doctrine prevent him from seeking God's plan in his life. In doing this, he became an example for us to follow. Jesus told us to seek truth and we will find it and *he wanted us to know that many of our questions are found, not in the written words, but in the heart* and mind of Christ, the Christ that lives within you to be your mentor. Many Christians think Jesus was in a special category, *yet he never said that he was the only one who could know truth.* He told us, "Seek and ye shall find." *If we were unable to find, why would Jesus tell us to seek?* He talked about the truth that will make us free and *if we were unable to find the truth, how could it set us free?* The problem in growing beyond our limited beliefs is that we still cling to those beliefs as everything and nothing more. We have lost belief in ourselves that we can take charge of our own destiny. *We have listened too long to the voices of religion and*

the men and women who say they serve God and yet discourage us from believing we are nothing more than puppets and we have nothing we can do to help ourselves. And if we only look for and accept, in our mind, those ideas that conform to those limited beliefs then we will never grow beyond that belief. It is critical to see the real Jesus because in seeing Him we realize ***how very much he loves us*** and wants us to be the sons and daughters of the living God.

Although Jesus clearly knew and respected the teachings of the Old Testament, he did not base his teachings on outer doctrines and interpretations, as so often the scribes and Pharisees. The reason for this was that Jesus knew the truth from within himself and ***he had internalized this truth*** and those that heard him knew he taught with authority and not as the scribes. So why do the ministers today base everything on the outer doctrine and often discourage you to find new teachings that add to the already truth from God. This is very important to understand because when our lives become one with our spiritual being, ***we become the Christ***. All of us need to be using the skill of going within and growing into more of the spiritual being we are. So if Jesus had simply taken the scripture of the Old Testament and that was what he based everything on, if Jesus had taught the outer doctrine he simply would not have been able to speak with authority. In the world's eyes they would have interpreted it as authority ***if they liked what they heard***.

> ***"The key to true God Given authority is when the truth is so internalized that it is the power of God within your being."***

Jesus demonstrated what ***could be done in your life***. This isn't a power to be great in the world but it is a power that is of oneness with your Father in heaven. When Jesus said, "The kingdom of God is within you," that is what he meant.

> ***~He did not say that the kingdom was only within him but he said it is within all of us~***

So we all have the potential to be the Christ and to do greater things than Jesus did. So what is the kingdom of God? *Is it really possible that by looking for the kingdom of God within ourselves, we can discover and attain contact with the same source of truth that Jesus tapped into?* Did Jesus perhaps mean that we all have the ability to find God's truth within ourselves? *If so, should we not be willing to look for truth the same place Jesus found it?* You may ask how do we find truth inside ourselves? I have in the past asked the same question but I realize more and more that what is within our being, whether it is the I AM THAT I AM Presence or Intuition, is already built into us and ready to be awakened. *There is a higher part of your mind that Jesus came to show us that is the Christ mind and it is the key to knowing the truth from within ourselves.* Remember the words of Paul and how he talked about the lower mind, the carnal mind and the natural man. He also talked about putting off the old man and putting on the new man. Was he really saying that we could rise above *the carnal mind, which cannot recognize truth*, and unite with the higher mind, which one with truth? Jesus came to demonstrate an ability that all people have. The potential to reach beyond how our lower mind sees our world today and really know God as he is.

> *"Jesus was saying that when we are willing to lose our life, the sense of life and identity based on the lower mind, we shall find a more spiritual life that is based on God's truth."*

I hope you can begin to see the pattern of the life of Jesus. I believe that all people have the potential to have a life of abundance and I firmly believe that one of the key elements in growing beyond the way we see life today in our lives it in taking hold, *with a firm grip*, of your life and your destiny. I also believe that the misunderstanding of what Jesus' life was about has hindered all of us. We have often thought we are helpless and are only to lay at the feet of Jesus and He will do the rest. *But this couldn't be farther from the truth.* It is totally up to us to take hold of our destiny and *that is what Jesus lived and died for.*

So many Christians have a fear-based approach to God and religion but ***Jesus' approach was based totally on love.*** I can't imagine Jesus being afraid of anything but because he was human, he had victory over his fears. Jesus wasn't afraid of God but ***loved God with all his heart and soul and mind.*** In the Old Testament times the Jewish nation had created an image of God as being an angry and judgmental God who was ready to punish people for the slightest transgression of His laws. ***But Jesus brought a very different and fresh view of his Father being a loving Father figure to all of mankind.*** However, after the time of Jesus, ***some Christian churches continued painting fear on the landscape of the mind of those who followed.*** Why? Was it a way to control people, I believe it was. Jesus did not have a fear-based approach to religion either.

> *~In fact it was his defiance and independence against what the religious world wanted the people to know, that got him killed.~*

So many times I have experienced ministers that will drive you to think you are going to hell if you think beyond their outer doctrine they preach. But Jesus went far beyond the Jewish doctrine and he revealed to us that this is needful in our growth. ***Jesus clearly loved God and he told us to love God with all our hearts, minds and souls. Fear and love are incompatible emotions and when you see that you want to get close to what you love and you want to get away from what you fear, that is when you know these two emotions are on two opposite sides of the spectrum.***

> ***"Remember perfect love CASTS OUT all fear."***

Many of us are aware of the constant talk of the second coming of Christ but what does this really mean. I have been trying to show you that Jesus preached an active approach to religion and we now have to consider that the second coming of Christ could be an event that depends ***on how we respond to the first coming of Christ.*** Let me explain. Let's go back to the days when Jesus walked on the earth. Why did the soldiers need Judas to point out Jesus among his disciples? *It was because the soldiers could not recognize the embodied Christ*. It seems likely that if the people were trapped in a lower state of consciousness, the carnal mind, they could not recognize the embodied Christ. As long as the majority of human beings are trapped in this lower state of consciousness, there might be no point in Christ coming again. For *who would recognize him* even if he walked among us? Think about the saying that it takes one to know one. *I believe that it is possible that the second coming of Christ cannot occur until a critical mass of people attain Christ consciousness and can recognize when Christ comes again.* In other words, the second coming of Christ might be an event *in which many Christed beings will walk the earth,* clearly recognizing the Christ in themselves and in each other. *It might be up to us to bring about the second coming by raising our consciousness and attaining Christ consciousness.*

So you see how each piece of the life of Jesus is a puzzle piece *when perfectly fit together reveals to you that you have the potential to be everything Jesus wanted you to believe you could be.* Jesus didn't come to bring peace, by not disturbing your limited beliefs. Jesus came to bring a sword and this means he wanted you to see that your understanding of who you are and what your potential to be, *has been crippled by the lies told about his life.* Jesus wanted you to know that your faith can move mountains and it is these *mountains that trap you in a limited understanding of which you are.* But you must begin by removing the mountains of false beliefs that cause you to doubt.

My hope is that if you could open your heart and hear the voice of Jesus that walked the earth so long ago and who is still talking to you today. *You will see that his life has the power to change everything about your life in a wonderful way and you will have a life of abundance.* Jesus says to fear not little flock, for it is the Father's good pleasure to give you *a direct experience of his inner kingdom*. Stop looking outside yourself and look within. My dear friends, we are the light of the world, and we need to go inside and turn on that light. As you begin to open your own understanding remember that

113

this knowledge has the ability to awaken all people but *you are only responsible for yourself.*

What I encourage you to do is to stay away from further arguing a point with anyone that might disagree with this new understanding you have. You can only change yourself and no amount of human argumentation will change anything for anyone.

~Arguing binds you to the earth and obedience binds you to heaven.~

Focus on your own growth and whether anyone agrees or believes these words, it's not important. *Make up your own mind to take hold of your life whether anyone else understands or not.* This power of your own determination in taking hold of your destiny is the beginning of being able to become the Christ. You must stand firm and not depend on anyone agreeing. When Jesus said what does it profit a man to gain the whole world and lose his soul, it really means that the things of this world whether they are material or opinions or whatever, *aren't going to help us if we walk away from the truth that is waiting for us to take hold of.* As you begin to understand the things that you can, at the level of understanding you are at, simply be patient and grow at your own pace. As you begin to see your eyes open, you will reach new levels of understanding and in turn you will be growing within. Begin to multiply your talents and take dominion over your *inner world and remember he who conquers self, conquers all.* When Jesus said you cannot serve two masters *he simply said you must follow the inner path or the outer path, it's that simple.* Remember again that a house divided against itself cannot stand. Your house is your mind and so it is critical to keep it together. When Jesus spoke about how hard it is for the rich man to enter heaven, do you wonder why? Many rich people and even just people so caught up in the things of this world, are simply too attached to their possessions, or goals or even their own ways of thinking. They are closed-minded and believe that their way will bring happiness on earth.

> ## *"It's not the possessions that are the problem but how they view the possessions and their attachments to them that is the real problem."*

It's not the riches that keep you out of heaven but how you attach to the riches. ***Furthermore all of it points to you having the lower level of consciousness, the ego or the carnal mind, and you cannot enter with this mind in you.*** For you see when anything is more important than God then it has the potential to take away from you the ability to draw close to God within. ***Your level of understanding or how you view life is what keeps you in a catch 22. This is why the key to salvation is totally your choice.*** You are the only one in control of your destiny and your choices are what will either help you or hurt you.

It is important to know that Jesus was just like any of us. He was born of a woman, had a childhood and an individual personality. He grew up like any other child. I am not trying to take away your ***imaginary image of him*** and take away the beauty of his life. What I want you to know is that his life can only be an example to you if you see him and can ***compare your own existence to his.*** Because the carnal mind can project a false image of God in saying he is an angry and judgmental God, ***they also can take away the human qualities of Jesus.*** When they take this away, it is then we elevate Jesus to a state where we cannot relate to him. Every soul was originally created with a distinct individuality. The soul has a very deep inner desire to preserve and develop that individuality. The inner desire is the driving force behind what people call the "survival instinct". ***Your spiritual survival instinct is a desire to preserve your true individuality so that it is not destroyed by any outside influence.*** Because of this survival instinct, no human being will want to put on Christhood if they believe that putting on Christhood ***means that you have to lose your individuality or personality.*** Therefore, it is very important for me to help you understand that ***you do not lose your individuality by putting on your Christhood.*** Because by putting on the new human of your Christhood, you will have to put off the old human of the carnal mind. In the beginning you might lose some of the characteristics that you are familiar with in your personality. Because the soul is very identified with the carnal mind, this might at first seem like a loss. But as soon as the soul begins to shift its sense of identity towards the Christ consciousness, that sense of loss will quickly disappear. *Jesus wanted us to see that we would not loose our true individuality by putting on the mind of Christ but instead we would find our God-given personality and be free from the prison of the false individuality that we think we are.* What's the secret to life? In reality, you are who you think you are and until you are willing to see things differently there will always be a gap between who you really are and who you think you are. *Jesus came to close that gap and he did this with his life.*

Another critical truth that must be looked at in order for you to take control of your life is found in the question about reincarnation. Many Christians strongly abhor the thought. Jesus was familiar with reincarnation but lets go back to historical facts. The concept of reincarnation has been part of religious life on this planet for as far back as we have recorded in history. *When Jesus walked the earth, there were many groups and sects in Israel that believed in reincarnation.* In fact it is well known fact that Mary, his mother, *practiced in a religion known as the Essenes and they believed strongly in reincarnation.* Now if you just look at this fact and then you connect the dots of Mary with the Catholic Church and Jesus in early Christianity, you see that their background was strongly influenced by this teaching. If it was indeed well known by the community about Mary and her strong belief in reincarnation *then why did the Catholic Church worship Mary as almost a god?* Something doesn't make sense, again and *this pattern in religion is what often causes many to walk away altogether*. Consider in scripture how Jesus healed a man who was blind from birth. After the healing, Jesus disciples asked Jesus: "Who did sin, this man or his parents?" Obviously the disciples must have believed that it was possible for this man to have brought his blindness upon himself. *Yet the man was BORN blind and so when could he have possibly sinned?* Some reason that he must have sinned in the womb but does that really make any sense? *How could an unborn child commit a sin so serious that it warranted the punishment of blindness?* Would a just and loving God ever impose such a horrible punishment? Would a better explanation be that the man had sinned in a previous lifetime and was born as a result of the actions he committed in that life? Think about it. Now consider another scripture in the Bible. Jesus stated very clearly that John the Baptist was indeed Elijah come again. If John was Elijah, how could he have come again? John did not suddenly appear as the result of some kind of miracle but John was conceived and born by a woman like any other child. I believe that Jesus was telling us plain and clear that *John the Baptist was the reincarnation of the prophet Elijah.* I also believe that Jesus came on a very important mission to help people see that their lives can become the living Christ in embodiment and in doing this I feel very strongly that it would seem only right that other prophets descended at the same time to help him in his ministry. John the Baptist was a part of that mission to help Jesus and he helped lay the foundation for what Jesus came to do. God enlists many who are ascended to help when help is needed and there were more.

If you dig into the historical records of the early church you will find that between the third and fifth century, the Roman Catholic Church issued a number of documents that effectively banned the idea of reincarnation as heresy. *The fact that the church made a determined effort to ban it means that it was truly a part of early Christianity.* Now why was there so much opposition to reincarnation? Remember how there is an outer reason of Jesus being the "only" Son of God and an inner reason, *so in the same token it must be the same with reincarnation.* Let's look at this for a moment. Keep in mind all that we have learned thus far about the carnal or closed mind. The inner reason for rejecting reincarnation is the carnal mind and *its complete refusal to take accountability for anything.* As long as a person thinks carnally, that person is most likely seeking for ways to justify his or her actions. Now let's remember the Universal Law of Karma. Even the Bible teaches, you reap what you sow. If you accept this teaching which most people in Christianity do, then you simply know that every act has consequences. But how much do you really understand this and could this have been one reason people rejected reincarnation. The carnal mind does have a "way out" of this dilemma of *being responsible for your actions*. Most people experience that they can commit a wrong act and avoid suffering the consequences when no one finds out about it or if they can't prove the act was committed by you. To the carnal mind, it appears they got away with what they did and when this happens *they totally believe they have avoided the consequences of their actions*. The carnal mind thinks this is a perfectly logical line of reasoning and yet when confronted with the idea of reincarnation they absolutely stand by it as a lie. *The very idea of reincarnation is that you can never escape the consequences of your actions* and *that you might be able to hide a wrong act from other human beings so that you do not suffer any consequences of the act in this lifetime is how people justify the way they live.* But the truth is that you can never hide anything from God and you will inevitably suffer the consequences of your actions. If you do not feel these consequences in this lifetime, you will feel them in a future lifetime. *The truth is that the concept of reincarnation is a severe blow to the carnal mind's reasoning that it is possible to escape the consequences of your actions.* So now you understand how in our carnal way or closed way of seeing things, *we actually take away the power awaiting within to transform.* The carnal sees a certain way and with the help of religion in its false interpretation of the life of Jesus, *we can easily loose the "knowing" that we have control over our lives. The truth is that when you face the truth about life, it is then that you can see how everything can help you in becoming what you need to become.* What I am trying to make you see here is that many people fall prey to a psychological mechanism that *is set in motion for them to ignore, reject, or explain away the concept of reincarnation*.

Now let's look at an outer reason for banning reincarnation. It is a historical fact that one of the people who were instrumental in having the church ban the idea of reincarnation was the wife of the Roman emperor Justinian. Her name was Theodora and she didn't like the idea that *she could be punished for her actions in a future life.* So with *great influence she insisted the Roman Catholic Church remove all traces of reincarnation from Christianity.* This is a very good example how the rich and powerful, the power elite, can try to manipulate the world. The truth is *it never changed God's laws and it never changed the reality* but what it did do was confuse the world for way too long. *The ironic part of this is that the rich and powerful used their power to control and in turn it took control away from their lives and the lives of all of us when we choose to see it this way.* In hurting others, they also hurt themselves and created a downward spiral in which they also couldn't take power of their lives. The truth is human ego reasoning and not their real selves powered them. You see, even though they are the reason for some of the major conflicts, and they are responsible of taking the precious life of Jesus down an illusionary road where his message is lost, they too have paid by the karma they sent out. They sent out lies by allowing the ego to rule and they in turn have paid dearly. It's not about making others pay for the false roads they created and in turn we walked down. *What is important is we UNDERSTAND and then WE MAKE BETTER CHOICES, today, right now.* We cannot undo or change anything of the past but let us go with courage, and give power back to the life of Jesus. I have come to be His voice. I know Him very well and I know that He loves you and needs you to take a stand for your life and in turn you are taking a stand for His. BE THE CHANGE!!!

Beyond the personal concern of reincarnation there is another reason why they do not want people to believe. The idea of reincarnation states that you can be punished for your actions in a future lifetime but on the other side of coin is that you have more than one lifetime to work out your salvation. *This is an idea that really doesn't sit well to the powerful that want to use religion to gain absolute power over the people.* It is a well-known fact that many an organized religion claims that it has the only path to salvation and if the people feel they only have this lifetime to secure their salvation *then they are most likely to follow the outer church out of fear.* But if you see that you have more than one chance to qualify for salvation, then the urgency goes away. You may say, well then someone will just put it off and never make a choice to search for salvation. That is possible but **keep in mind that fear doesn't reap a real and honest desire, either.**

> **"If a person is so fearful and makes choices based on fear, then those choices are no better than if they made no decision at all."**

What Jesus wanted to help us understand is that our individual presence, our soul has come to earth to become one with the Father. Many people take many lifetimes to understand what it is that will help them become the spiritual beings they are. The ultimate desire of the Father is that no matter how many lifetimes we take, **He loves us unconditionally and wants us to become one with Him.** He doesn't want us to suffer but He wants us to know He understands our need to grow in our own time. **This is how powerful His love is.** Life is a journey and each experience we have is there to help us grow and learn the deeper meaning about it. Each experience, no matter how difficult, is there to help us move **out of the way of reasoning that is common to the world,** the carnal mind. God wants us to **see beyond our limited understanding** and He knows that if we could see beyond and see the **unconditional love from Him**, we wouldn't want to waste our lives doing things that do not help us but only hurt us.

We are all on a journey together and how we affect one another can hurt us or help us. When we go back to the story of the man born blind because maybe something in another lifetime caused him to have to walk thru this, **we need to not automatically think that God is always punishing when these kinds of things happen.**

> **"Above all of the beliefs you have, you need to remember that God is not capable of punishing nor is he able to be angry."**

He firmly stands by the laws he created of Karma and Free Will and the reason He created them was **because He wanted us to see they were give to become the power for our own ability to change and** *take hold of our lives. He didn't put those laws into affect because he was angry or judgmental. He put them into affect because of His deep and lasting UNCONDITIONAL LOVE that has always been and always will be.* The blind man was receiving something from his own hands and yet this was not to destroy him but it had the potential to enrich his journey by his experience in the affliction. Life on earth is a series of lessons and when we pass one lesson with the right attitude and with what we can learn for our spiritual being, then we move into a higher level of understanding.

Do you ever wonder why children that are stricken with cancer have so much love? Not all but many can teach us to put aside our own afflictions and see beyond this life. Are you now asking what they did in another life that caused the cancer? *Sometimes it's better to not always try to get too hung up in the whys but try to see the value in what can make you a better person.* We can think or imagine the "whys" but if we choose to get so involved in trying to figure it out, *we will loose sight of our goal.* We also will become emotionally involved and this usually takes us down the wrong road. Like I said we are all on a journey together. Life isn't just about you but about the oneness of mankind. Life has the opportunity waiting to see how you can not only change yourself and become more spiritual but you also can help others take the courage to do the same.

The concept of reincarnation can explain many of the questions that Christians so far have been unable to answer.

~Many of the outer teachings of Jesus do not contain the keys to his inner teachings.~

Because of this, Jesus is very aware that many unanswered questions cause doubt and anger and even resentment towards his Father. The truth is that Christianity has held up a goal for Christians but there is not *a defined path to reaching it and yet most long to have eternal life.*

"The teachings of individual Christhood have been removed and yet this is the only key to eternal life."

Reincarnation is also a way to explain much heartache in life. Think about a severely handicapped child and if you do not believe in reincarnation then you might believe that God wanted the child to be born that way. So then you ask WHY would God want that if they were only given one lifetime. How unfair? What happens to those who cannot make choices? When you consider that the church emphasized God as a punishing God, then you are led to conclude that God is punishing this soul. And then you ask yourself if God were just and loving then why would he want to punish a soul who had not even had the opportunity to sin? When you accept the concept of reincarnation, you see an explanation very clearly. ***This is where understanding will calm your fears and help you to take control over what you can do in this lifetime.*** Every human being has lived before and the conditions you experience in this life are the effects of causes that you personally set in motion in previous lifetimes. In it's purest form, the concept of reincarnation ***does not include the idea of punishment.*** Let me explain.

When God created the world, he commanded that light come first. Light is energy and everything in this world is a form of energy. At the same token everything you do is with the energy of God. Because God has given you free will, ***you can decide what to do with God's energy.*** It is your choice and your choice will help you grow one way or another. ***But at the same time it wouldn't make a whole lot of sense if God created a universe in which a person with free will could do anything they wanted regardless of the consequences it had for them or others.*** So God created the law of cause and effect and this law states that what you send out into the universe will return unto you. It is really an ***impersonal law*** just like gravity. In other words in the law of gravity, if you jump out of an airplane without a parachute, you will fall to the earth and die.

~Your death is not the punishment of God but a result of your choice.~

In the same token, if you put your hand on hot coals, you will get burnt. *It's not because you are bad or because God wants to hurt you but simply because your actions are your responsibility* and with this law of cause and effect you can take hold of making better choices. In other words you are..

~NOT A VICTIM OF CIRCUMSTANCES OR OF THIS LIFE~

..but your experiences are the result of choices that you made either in this life or another. You can curl up and die or you can decide that you will get thru each circumstance, learn the lesson and grow into the spiritual being you need to become. It's your choice. If you want to feel sorry for yourself, then you will go nowhere. *Feeling sorry for yourself only keeps you in a stuck situation.* Look at the truth of what you are dealing with, look for ways to make better choices, look how you can grow from everything and decide to use this opportunity to become a better person. The law of cause and effect is simply the law of Karma or what Jesus spoke when he said you reap what you sow. *In reality this law is simply a substitute teacher when you have lost your Spiritual teacher in your life.* You lost it only because you have chosen to see more carnally in this life. Again it's critical to have the higher mindset. The law of Karma as we will refer to it, is simply a mirror that reflects back to you what you send out. If you send out hatred, you will receive hatred in return. If you send out love you will receive love in return. God wants us to come to him and in doing this sometimes we have to resolve certain issues we are plagued with. We can't escape the consequences of our choices but sometimes we don't receive the consequences until another lifetime and this is because *God has mercy. Sometimes it would just be too overwhelming if it returned in the same lifetime.* You see the truth is *God loves us very,*

very much and the delay of karma reveals his mercy and grace. It's very important to let go of the lie that God is an angry and judgmental God and wants to punish you for everything you do wrong. The honest truth is that God is a loving and merciful God who only wants to see you grow in your Christhood. God has only one desire in all of this and that is to see you learn your lessons in life. By delaying the return of the consequences of your actions, God opens up the possibility that if you truly learn your lesson, and *abandon the state of consciousness that caused you to commit a wrong action, then you do not have to suffer the consequences of that act. GOD DOESN'T WANT TO PUNISH YOU, BUT WANTS YOU TO LEARN, AND GROW AND MOVE CLOSER TO ATTAINING ONENESS WITH HIM.* And if you don't learn your lesson, *then God will allow the universe to return the energy you have sent out and you can then receive a second opportunity to learn even if it is the hard way.* The important thing to remember is that you are in control of your life and if you want good things to come to you then you need to send good things out. If you want your world to change you must first *BE THE CHANGE.* And *when Jesus came to bring the keys to knowledge he wanted those keys to be tools for you to use so that you can attain an abundant life.* Take time to consider that Jesus was far more than a Son of God, *He was your mentor, your teacher, and your comforter and above all he was the best friend you could possibly have.*

The power of the life of Jesus is that he truly is the way, the truth, and the life and his life is your example. As you look at the many false beliefs of why Jesus lived and died, I hope you can begin to see that there is far more to him than we have been led to believe. Because he lived so long ago, we have a tendency to rely on what is written but the truth behind all of our own identities is found in understanding *that we must begin to trust what is within us to tell us more of everything in life.* All I have tried to do is just simply help you put to rest some misconceptions and to look beyond the limited beliefs you have of his life.

Don't ever again take a persons word and believe that it is the whole story but ask yourself if maybe there is more or maybe the way we see something is thru our own interpretation. What I'm saying is that **words alone do not do justice to a life**. Many men have lived lives of great influence and the words of others have written their story but how many stories written are really all there is to the life? **Jesus wanted us to see the power within us and to trust that there is far more we can learn by just going within and allowing the God within our being to lead us and to teach us.** This takes faith, and it takes courage to let go of opinions, and judgments and be able to look beyond what is said and what is written. The **courage** it takes to do this **is the prerequisite** that you need to also take control of your life and your destiny. What I'm saying is that you will not loose anything by simply using the courage to step outside the box of what you believe is all there is to know about life, because that so called experiment, or exercise, will be the very thing you need when it is time to use the same principle to slowly take back control over your life. **Jesus' example is the most profound path to Christhood but if you see him as an idol, or someone so far above you, then you cannot see him as an example.** If you feel you are nothing in his sight, if you feel so unworthy and so worthless, then you cannot walk beside him. **Not because he won't let you but because you won't be able to in your own mind.** You will always feel worthless. Do you really want to know the power to take hold of your life? Do you really want to stop all the suffering you feel on earth? If you do, then take one more step, step outside the box of limited beliefs you have carried, and **go back into your life with a new perspective.** The truth is you are what you think you are, and you will always do what you have always done unless you decide right now to take one step in another direction. The road of life is long and it becomes weary many times. If we can keep a belief in our hearts, even when we can hardly lift our heads from the tears, then we have the ability to see like the eagle sees. For the eagles eyes see far beyond this life.

Remember that when Jesus came 2,000 years ago, he came to show a higher state of consciousness. The true message **Jesus came to bring was that every human being has the potential to attain the Christ consciousness, even without becoming a member of a Christian church.** But the religions of the world all seem to have a **common** *distorted truth of Jesus' message.* They claim that the key to salvation is the outer religion and automatic salvation is only achieved by being a member of the right church and by blindly believing it's doctrines. They believe if they do this then God has to save them. Yet God is not a respecter of persons or the institutions created by people. *The truth is the truth and Jesus wants it clear.* No church can guarantee your salvation because *the key to salvation is the Christ Consciousness. And the key to attaining the Christ Consciousness is found inside you.* Jesus made a very loud exclamation that the Kingdom of God is within *which simply means that the key to salvation is not found in any outer religion or teaching.* What I am trying to clarify here one more time, *is that you can never allow your search for truth to be confined to an outer framework, no matter what claims are made by the leaders of that belief system.* I will say again as I have already said,

"If someone claims a monopoly on "truth", they demonstrate by their words that they do not know truth."

If you truly want to find who you are as a spiritual person and you are a seeker of truth, why would you want to follow people who demonstrate that they have not found truth? *How can they possibly help you find what they do not have?* They can't. Your journey begins with your decision to pull the beam out of your own eyes and begin to walk a path in which you can learn and grow one step at a time.

I love Jesus more than life and I feel that I need to tell you that *He longs for you to hear the truth of why he came to earth, lived and died.* Hear ye Him, and begin a new relationship by putting away the foolish teachings of the past. I know we are all capable of simply walking away from the things that truly hurt our growth. Let's not fight about the past, but *just understand that it became what it became for a certain length of time* but today is new and we can begin again. *Let's learn from the lies by seeing them as an understanding of how powerful the carnal, ego mind is and how blinding it is when the power elite chooses to be the only voice in this world.* We have a voice;

we who are spiritual and ***we need to now make our voice known.*** The only reason the power elite and lies of the Carnal mind continue is because the spiritual beings that inhabit the earth have chosen to remain silent. ***WAKE UP AND KNOW YE ARE GODS.*** Speak and you will be heard. ***It is time for us, who have remained silent to be a voice of the most wonderful and loving God and one of his very special son's who came to show us the pattern in which we can become the Christ.***

RELIGION, THE BIBLE AND SALVATION

I wondered how easy it would be to explain religion. Let me explain something in a backwards way. Because we seek religion to assure us of our salvation, religion is a choice in which we hope God will save us. But the greatest threat to our salvation *is actually religion*. Religion is basically an ***outer form*** that is often fear-based to set up guidelines or rules to follow and instills a picture of an external God who is outside the inner kingdom, what is within all of us. It causes us to search for God somewhere outside ourselves and that is how we choose our religion. The truth is religion denies God in many ways because it teaches that God is somewhere outside of your inner self and is separate from you. Religion usually teaches that you cannot find God on your own and so you need a religion. Many religions also set up an impossible picture for how perfect human beings should be by bringing in a picture of some human being that is acceptable in the eyes of God. Most use Jesus but many have others to reinforce this same general idea. They want you to know that in order to get into the kingdom of Heaven you must be like these examples, which actually is against what Jesus stated in that the Kingdom of God is within. ***So religion has set up a way in which we can enter the kingdom but Jesus said we don't need to look for it because it is within us.*** It's rather confusing to say the least.

Most religions then encourage a person to mold themselves after the image of the one they lift up to be the "perfect" being that God will accept. *They actually violate the first two commandments in creating an Idol that you are to mirror after.* But you don't recognize this to be so. So you try your best to fit the mold. *The interesting part is that you have to be fooled that this is the truth because in all reality no human being could ever live up to becoming a clone to another being.* You are led to believe that, let's say Jesus, is the idol you are to pattern your life after and so only by becoming a duplicate, with no individuality, can you enter the kingdom which by the way, in truth, is not outside yourself. If you really step back and see how ridiculous this is *you wonder how so many people believe it.* They are like the blind leading the blind. So what religion is essentially saying is that there is only one way to heaven and it is in following a mechanical way in which you strive to become a clone to Jesus, because God doesn't accept any other person accept Jesus. This actually leads us to spend a lifetime in striving for the outer righteousness that was the righteousness of the Scribes and Pharisees and *was the very thing Jesus despised*. How on earth could this be so confused? How can religion teach something that is *against what Jesus taught* and yet lift him up as an Idol, *which he never wanted*, so that we could never match up to him. There is no way into the so-called kingdom that man has defined thru the method he has made.

Let's think about entering the Kingdom of God for a moment. If God is in everything and is omnipresent then you are never be separate from God. You cannot enter the Kingdom because *YOU ARE in the kingdom of Heaven* or you are outside in how your level of consciousness is. It's your level of Consciousness that separates you from God. God is already where you are, because God is in you.

~*The illusion is in your mind that you are separated from God's kingdom.*~

This is how the mind traps your understanding in a dualistic battle of in or out, right or wrong, good or bad, etc. *Your mind has come to believe that in order to be saved, it must live up to an outer teaching but in reality the outer teaching disables your own ability to create and to know who you really are as a spiritual being.* In other words the outer mind is trying to force you to believe in an outer path to salvation. At a deeper level you know that this won't lead to salvation and so you rebel against the rules of a religion. This is where you become a house divided against yourself. The only way to become one, to become whole is to really understand the truth. *If you don't, you become your own worst enemy.* Religion is one the most argumentative subjects in our world. I believe it is because of how we become trapped in our own mind, in a place called no-man's land. *We argue with others in an effort to convince ourselves or to assure ourselves that we are right.* That is why people try to force his or her religion down someone else's throat. *They are actually manifesting a house divided against itself in the own being.* In Revelation the people are referred to as lukewarm, neither hot nor cold and I think this is a wonderful way to explain the trap we find our minds in. Our outer mind has believed according to religious explanations and is trying to force something upon our inner soul, which by the way has an inner knowing of what the truth is. *So the core of your being is rebelling because it knows it is not God's will.*

"As long as you continue to be a house divided against itself and remain trapped in duality, you cannot move forward or backward."

You are neither fully alive nor fully dead. This is where it is your choice to take ownership, to choose this day whom you will serve, God or mammon.

"If you don't take ownership of your own will, the free will God gave you and is protected to remain yours by the Universal Law of Free Will, then you will never know your divine plan."

I like to think about it as choosing life *but in choosing life you must take ownership of what is yours*. We will talk about identity and claiming who you are as yours. For now it is critical to know that in religion, there are different paths. The earthly concept is often to control the people and that is because of the need for power and influence and to prove they are the only right way. This is because of the need for the EGO or the carnal mind to be right. This is proof that when religions think they are the only right way, they reveal they reason with the carnal mind and not the mind of the Christ Consciousness. People want to know God and when you mix business with your identity, *you are asking for trouble. I am sure Jesus is thoroughly disgusted with how the religions of the world have taken His Good name, His pure motives, and twisted everything to fit their outer ideas of the interpretation of God's salvation for man.* Take back your life and only then you can have the power to choose your own free will choices.

Let's go a little deeper in understanding the complexities of why religion is so much a part of life on earth. *We have a memory, an inner knowing that transcends all outer teachings or scriptures and we know that God is good*. So because of this "knowing", we expect that religion and their leaders, who claim to represent God on Earth, are sincerely striving to live the truth. But when we see different behavior that often takes no consideration for the people who are trying to find God and live for Him, and often the religious people show behavior that is clearly not good, many people then loose their faith in the religion. And sometimes they loose all faith in God. The truth is whether the religions are blindly following their leaders or misguiding innocent people for their own gain, they are contributing to confusion and ultimately they contribute to their own demise.

~The greatest crime that can be committed in this world is in destroying a person's relationship with God. I speak this with a loud voice.~

132

If religion destroys our ability to see God in our own experience then it has blinded us to our ability to become the creation God Created us for.

God is beyond religion and so the first thing I would like you to do is **separate God from religion** so that we can get to know God and so that **your religion will no longer have power in shattering your personal relationship with God.** We need to understand that most of us carry our identity as an inseparable part of our religion. Keep in mind that the more religious someone is, **the more they see the outer religion as an essential and inseparable part of their identity.** They feel that if the outer religion were proven wrong, part of their identity would be lost. No one can bear the thought of loosing his or her identity. This was why Paul spoke so much on dying to oneself and yet dying isn't in leaving the earth but in leaving behind beliefs that hinder you from growing beyond what you currently know, and that hinder you from finding your spiritual identity. So if you can believe that you are more than your religion and that God is more than religion, **then you can clearly see that your identity is not threatened by looking at your religion.** It's possible if you were raised in a strict religion and yet inside you have a deep conviction of what the real truth is, you may have been sent to this earth at this particular time in history to help raise religion **above the consciousness of duality thinking so that the earth can see it's original purpose.** It's possible that if this is your mission and you refuse to break free of things that you know are wrong, you will keep yourself from fulfilling your divine plan.

So what was the original purpose for religion on the earth? Let's look at the first recorded story in the Bible. In the Garden of Eden did you ever read anything that states that Adam and Even went to church every Sunday. It doesn't even say there was a church in the Garden and **so I have wonder if they even had a religion.** Why didn't they have a religion if this is so important to God, as man reasons? I would have to say they didn't have religion because they walked and talked with God or a direct spiritual teacher. If you have a direct spiritual teacher why would you need an outer religion to serve as an intermediary between you and the spiritual realm? ***Keep in mind that religion often preaches that we cannot know God without an intermediary.*** Some religions consider Jesus as that intermediary and yet many strict ones go one step further and say that the people cannot know Jesus without a teacher, meaning without their ministers. All of this is a lie and it keeps you from reaching out to the source, namely God or a spiritual teacher. So we might say that the Garden of Eden needed no church because it was a church, ***it was an environment where most beings lived their religion every moment.*** But it seems that planet Earth is a place where most have lost contact with their spiritual teachers and their higher selves which is what holds the blueprint of who you are as a spiritual being. If you have lost contact with our higher self then you are a house divided against itself ***because to know your higher self you must know what is within you.*** When people do not have direct contact they simply walk in a closed circle that leads them into a downward, self-reinforcing spiral where they cannot grow and become MORE. Becoming More of who you were when you came to earth, is why you chose to come to earth, the first place. ***We are spiritual beings that are growing in each lifetime we embody and each lifetime has the potential to help us become closer to oneness with God.*** When we come to earth we have laid out a plan with a spiritual teacher before we came, with things we want to overcome, we want to learn and we want to grow from. We came here to achieve a greater sense of oneness with our creator. So if religion hinders our growth and we are aware of it's crippling power over us then we must exercise our free will to overcome and have victory. We must take hold of our destiny.

~*Many times religion has become a replacement for our spiritual teacher.*~

But only our original spiritual teacher that helped us formulate the plan we choose before coming, can help us achieve the things we wanted to achieve and ***furthermore take us beyond what we planned.*** Anytime a plan is made, remember that when achievements come to pass there is always more that can manifest if we keep on the path. In other words, in our Father's house there are many mansions and we want in each lifetime to grow closer to God and yet the plan we came with is only the beginning of what we can do. Like anything, when your motive is pure and unconditional love becomes the driving force, so much more can grow from each step we take.

Let's try to understand the purpose of religion. We have been brought up to believe that the role of religion is to save us and many times the religion we follow teaches us that only members of the right religion will be saved. However, the true role of religion is to serve as an intermediary between you and the real saviors of mankind, the spiritual teachers of the Ascended Host who can help people save themselves. You may ask who are the Ascended Host? Let me explain who they are. There is a spiritual realm above and beyond the material universe and in this spiritual realm are a large number of spiritual beings that serve as the spiritual teachers for humankind. They have been called by many different names in the course of humanity but I will refer to them as the Ascended Host. ***The role of the Ascended Host is to raise the consciousness of our unascended brothers and sisters until they reach a higher state of consciousness, which I will call the Christ Consciousness.*** Even greater, their role is to anchor this consciousness thru those that are ***willing to be in embodiment and still become the living Christ on planet earth*** and thereby raise the vibration of the entire planet until it becomes spiritualized.

What is true religion? Some, who walk a certain way, eventually come to the understanding that there just can't be "one way" to God. In their hearts they see many good people, with hearts full of love for all, and they ask themselves from within, how can these people be condemned to hell if they are not walking the way I do.

~We can go on blindly believing that whatever religion we are in is the only way but that doesn't mean it's the truth.~

It's only the truth in our own eyes, in our way of seeing things. This is where our minds can take certain words or actions and apply those, as all there is to know. The truth is the truth and so what is the truth? God holds the truth in His knowing and we want to understand what that is. If we have to put aside all our beliefs and all our indoctrination, then lets do that and see what we can see. Let's give ourselves a chance to open our hearts and see beyond what we currently see. If you could take all your experiences in life, and then understand the real truth about you, about religion, about God, and about all that live on planet earth, don't you think *the truth would set you free*? If you could have all the tools to help you understand the truth about your life, *would you want to have them?* Let's take some time and try to really understand the purpose of religion from the mind God. Let's take a moment, step away from all that you have believed to be true or the whole picture and re-look at the purpose of life on planet earth. If you just look at the life of Jesus you will remember that he was in opposition to the religious authorities of his day.

~He came to set people free from those who say you can find God only through an outer religion.~

But the people have turned Jesus' teachings about the inner path to God, into another outer religion. Remember that the Sabbath was made to help man, not for man to help the Sabbath.

~Religion was meant as a tool for your soul's liberation, not as a trap for your mind.~

Jesus made it clear that his house was a house of prayer, but the world has made it a den of thieves, by selling their wares of *dead doctrines that are void of the LIVING SPIRIT OF TRUTH.* Yes the truth is living and not written in a book form only. Keep in mind that God is an unlimited, infinite Being, and God doesn't have human needs. *Religion was not created for God's sake but for your sake. So don't use religion to worship God, use it to find God.* Love is an attractive force, not a binding force. Contrary to what so many religious people say, God's love is given freely to all who are open to receiving it and there are *not* strings attached. In heaven it is not make up of religious fanatics, but a universal brotherhood of love.

So is there only one true religion in this world? Let's talk for a moment. The answer is yes and no. There is only one true religion, but that religion is the universal, inner religion of God. On planet earth you will find many true religions that teach the living elements of the universal path. Expressing God's truth is found in a universal path in which many religions teach a particular version of the truth of God. Understanding God and his truth is simply beyond words and no one religion could possibly give you a complete understanding. We read in the scriptures that if everything that Jesus said or did should be written down, the world itself could not contain the books that should be written. The truth is the statement applies to the truth of God, not the life of Jesus, because Jesus came so that we might have life and more abundantly and the only way to life is knowing God. So in other words Jesus came to help us get to know more of Our Father. God created this entire world of form, a world that is so vast that no human being could possibly grasp the greatest of God's creation. So if one were to write down a complete description of all that God is, planet earth simply could not contain the books that should be written. But even a deeper understanding is that it would not be possible to express in "human words" the totality of God's being *because the inner mysteries of God simply cannot be expressed through words.*

The concept of one true religion is something that is placed on planet earth through the human consciousness or the lower mind. It did not originate in Heaven, *but it originated in the mind of man. This is where beliefs that were never intended can actually create an image that is reflected and becomes real to man.* I know many people can argue that their religion is the only way *but no amount of a human argumentation can change the reality of God.* God is not mocked and is no respecter of persons.

Let me talk about a true prophet who was called Muhammad. Muhammad received teaching from Archangel Michael and yet it was *never the intent* to turn the spiritual teachings of Islam into a warring culture. Mohammed was a man, and as any other prophet, he had to raise his consciousness so that he was able to serve as a prophet. Because of people and how they easily take one person and build idolatry around them, they often assume that a true prophet is speaking the direct word of God and that some higher force predestined his entire life. *In order for Muhammad to raise his consciousness, he had to go through the process of spiritual growth. Not everyone can achieve the higher understanding because not everyone sees his or her potential.* He had to *make decisions* to raise his consciousness, and as a part of the process he had to be willing to leave behind some of his former beliefs. *This was a process that was entirely based on his willingness to utilize God given "free will".* While Muhammad raised his consciousness, he didn't let go of all of his beliefs in the things that were based on his culture. *This affected the teachings that were delivered through him and this was partly responsible for the fact that Islam became a warring religion.* After Muhammad was gone, man added more to the fire, so to speak and this wasn't Muhammad's fault. The same can be said of Christianity. Jesus came to bring a clear message and because He didn't allow Culture to influence his message, because He stepped away from the many problems that influenced man, He left a clear message of an inner path but much has been added to Christianity and has distorted the truth of God. This was not Jesus' fault.

So what is the common link between the world's religions? To bring human beings closer to God by helping them to get regain the memory of their true identity and their relationship with God. *True religion is meant to help humans rediscover their identity through inner, intuitive or mystical experiences so that they internalize and fully accept who they are.* True religion is meant to help people attain such experiences and ultimately a direct communion with their God. But because many religions deny, by not teaching the importance for people to talk and walk with God on their own, this causes religion to become another obstacle. It's not meant to be but it is oftentimes. When you understand this it makes the picture clear in that the only way to see a link between the true faiths of the world is for people to adopt a mystical or spiritual approach to religion. As long as people are caught in the carnal mind, they will be more concerned about promoting the so-called uniqueness *of their own religion* instead of promoting the universal elements behind all religions. So the only real solution to the conflicts on planet earth in the religious realm *is that people must take hold of their own lives and begin to rise to a higher state of consciousness, which many call the Christ Consciousness for simplicity.* You don't have to call it that but it simply is having the mind of Christ or the higher mind. So in a nutshell the common link between all true religions is *a universal path that gradually leads people to attain a higher state of consciousness* and overcomes conflicts and the sense of separation that springs from the carnal mind. You might ask what are the true religions and all I can say is that a true religion is one in which they strive to awaken people to a universal path so that there creates a oneness, in which each person can begin to find out who they are and grow, reconnecting to the spiritual being they already are but have lost identity with. All true religions will live the truth and as Jesus said, *"The truth will set them free."*

So if you personally desire to see peaceful coexistence between the world's religions then you must begin with yourself and make an effort *to live the universal path.* Nothing else will ever bring peace among religious people. Most of us can agree that the conflict of religion is the major cause of all wars. Martin Luther King, Jr. left us with a profound understanding of peace when he wrote these words, *"The non-violent approach does not immediately change the heart of the oppressor. It first does something to the hearts and souls of those committed to it. It gives them a new self-respect; it calls up resources of strength and courage that they did not know they had. Finally it teaches the opponent and so stirs his conscience that reconciliation becomes a reality."* When you choose the non-violent approach to anything, the first change comes *within you.* Your choice has empowered change on your heart and only until we change ourselves from within, can we experience change in our world. When anyone tries to lure you into an argument or conflict and even adds gifts to the formula, you can simply *pass,* when accepting them. This is to help you understand that you cannot change anyone but when you take upon yourself to *become an instrument of grace* no matter what life brings your way; you become the change *by becoming more peaceful from within*. The power of change is more real to you than ever before. *When we commit ourselves to having a peaceful heart, it is then that we gain courage and a new strength we have never known before.* Peace cannot become our reality through the carnal mind, even if we cleverly disguise it as being good and tolerant of others. When someone sends you anger and hostility and you don't respond to it or in essence you don't receive it, *then it won't affect you*. Buddha encountered a man who was determined to change Buddha's reputation of a peaceful and nonviolent man. So the man put Buddha to a test and was rude and obnoxious for three days. He found criticism and fault with everything Buddha did and through constant verbal abuse hoped to get Buddha to react and prove his point. But Buddha responded with love and kindness instead. The man got angry and asked Buddha how he could remain so peaceful and kind through all the cruel accusations. Buddha said, *"If someone offers you a gift, and you do not accept that gift, to whom does the gift belong?"* What Buddha meant was that if someone offers you a gift of anger and hostility and you do not accept it, *then it still belongs to the giver.* Why choose to be angry or upset over something that does not belong to you? *Peace comes from within and when you choose to live your life in peace, then nothing should disturb it, unless you choose to allow it to enter in.* Deep inside of our inner being we need to come to terms with the beauty of having oneness with God and all of humanity. We are one with God and God is in us, *why would we want to be divided from Him and from each other?* If God is in us and all of us are one with Him *then the greatest experience is to find the universal oneness with all of Creation.* Others have written that both Buddha and Jesus would raise the level of consciousness of those around them, by just their presence. The highest vibration of light can only come *through willing individuals that come to earth to bring it through their lives.* Each of us can do this.

~IT IS GOD'S WILL THAT WE WOULD ALL DESIRE TO BECOME THE LIGHT OF THE WORLD.~

I have been told many times that when I walk into a room, light and peace become so powerful. It humbles me and also makes me aware that God is working through me and *can work through anyone who is willing*. I believe with all my heart Dr. Martin Luther King, Jr. had the same ability. So many who have walked the earth have had this. To bring the light of God to any situation is symbolic of how becoming the Light of the World, is an individual choice that can change life on planet earth for all eternity.

So if no religion could possibly give an accurate description of God, then doesn't it seem likely that the only way to know God is *by looking beyond the outer teachings and doctrines found in any religion?* The truth is that the *only way to know God is to discover the universal, inner path behind the outer religion.* This was something that constantly kept coming in to my mind, even as I walked in a very strict religion that looked down on reading anything other than the Bible. The Bible should be read with your heart and not your intellect. Keep in mind that *the scriptures are a guide for the people that lived in those times.* They were written to help them in how they specifically understood *at that time and in today's time they are outdated*. When I say outdated I want you to remember that explanations are always adapted to the understanding in the culture and in the time period. If you were to tell the same story to a child of 6 yrs old and also to a 40 yr old person, wouldn't the story be told so that *each could understand* it? If you were to travel back into time and explain our technology in today's world to someone in the 13th Century, would you find yourself speaking in very simplistic words and explanations? Wouldn't you have to leave some things out of the story in either case? The truth is, it's told *for understanding* and so variations must apply *if the ultimate goal is to "understand"*. So if you look at the Bible and the ability to understand at that time, you will realize that God wanted things to be *written for understanding of the time period.*

In understanding the *"incompleteness"* of the Scriptures I want to share with you how our human mind perceives things. When a teaching is brought to us *it is a foundation of more to come.* However we see the teaching thru the carnal mind, which takes it word for word and *creates*

an infallible wall around it. Our mind perceives through the illusion that this is all there is and then you add how the teaching is written for the time in which the people lived and through the language they understood and last but not least through the level of understanding they had, and all of this spells "incompleteness" for us in our day and age. However when it was written it helped the people of those times to understand, it served the purpose. They key is to realize that there is always more to know.

~When you know God always wants to bring us higher in understanding then you see the scriptures for what they are. They are to provide a foundation to build upon and not all there is to know.~

This is when you become open to learning more. When you see the scriptures in their true light ***then you cease to argue over every little thing and prove a point.*** When you understand you are part of the WHOLE and all are learning to understand more, you begin to share thoughts and not think that how you see things is the only way to see it. ***You begin to work together and in turn you grow together.*** When the threat and fear of not being perfect and knowing everything leaves, you can breathe and growth becomes quicker. ***You let down your guard and become teachable.*** This understanding of scripture can help you really take hold of your life and bring about the understanding of your divine plan.

~Many times it is fear that keeps us from ever becoming more~.

Don't be afraid to know that the Bible doesn't have everything in it but you can learn more by going within and the ***Living Word will teach you.***

Let's look at the Bible as one literary piece in our world. ***We consider the Bible to be the most important book ever written.***

The language of the Bible when written is not the language most of us read. Interpretations in other languages can give us access to accumulated wisdom and experience but it also can create a picture that becomes concrete and *never any more* than what is written by whatever language has interpreted it. So interpretation can be good and can be bad. How does God see we can get past all the arguments we hold onto, in scripture? There is only one way to heal from all the problems we have of the Bible. Step out of the picture, read the words as they are written and begin to understand that *there is far more than dead, concrete words written so long ago to people that had a limited understanding of life.* See that beyond the written word, there is a living word that Jesus tried *desperately to emphasize.* The living word comes to each person thru the perception they hold in their mind of everything in the material universe and the memory they still have of the spiritual realm. The Living Word is individualized and the belief that one man or minister or religions are the only ones that can interpret it and deliver it to the people *is a lie.* God's word is Living and the Bible was to serve as a foundation *but not as an idol, set in stone that can never be any more.* If you believe that what God had men write so long ago, is all that God has to reveal to us, *then you believe God is a dead God, never changing, never revealing more.* God is *"Living"* and even in His creation He proves He is living by creating the same pattern, of everything always changing, always becoming more. *Today we understand things at a higher level and therefore the scriptures are outdated in how they can convey the "whole" truth to us.* They aren't enough and in many ways *they leave gaps in the whole story.* It's like they are past the expiration date and so this is why Jesus spoke about the *Living Word before he left this earth.* It was as if He knew there would come a time *soon* that the Living Word would convey what is necessary when people rose in the ability to comprehend at a higher level of consciousness. The words written have an understanding but they are *to open a door for the heart to receive a living word, which is a higher understanding.*

The *living word is also individualized* and because of this you must keep in mind that each of us understand at different levels. *Don't get upset if you have a totally different take on a teaching.* It's good when we don't see the same in a teaching because it helps bring more to the Whole of mankind. You might ask how? When we have different divine plans, different abilities to understand and we see thru the lenses of our experiences in life, *we are going to have a different view on what the teaching means to us. We have been so trained in religion to learn a certain interpretation, that we have lost our ability to allow the Living Word to teach us.* We have lost the essential skill we need, to begin to grow to a higher understanding. The truth is God has used each teaching to bring about growth in all of us. No one sees it the exact same way. The problem with humans is we get an idea that the way we interpret something is the only way to see it. This is the dualistic mindset, the carnal or ego way of seeing things. What if you were standing under a night sky with 4 friends and a meteor shower occurred. All of you saw it as it happened. It was amazing and the most incredible sight you had ever seen. But if you were to separately talk to each of your 4 friends and even give your own take on what you saw, *you would find 5 different views of the experience.* Each had seen something uniquely for themselves, as if God had prepared a feast at each of their tables and what they saw was what God knew they would need, to grow. Are they all wrong? Not hardly. Just think instead of one view of the incredible meteor shower you now have 5 views and *the beauty of the experience is now multiplied. Why can't we see our differences in each other as a blessing?* Why can't we understand God has individualized us because *He wants us to see there is more to every experience* and every teaching given? If we could put aside our need to always be right, and to always feel superior in our opinion, *we would actually experience the freedom God wants us to have by seeing the vast beauty when nothing is held back.* The picture of anything is given, but the differences in perception *leaves open a door of unimaginable possibilities.* Do you know that when you simply let go of pride and open your heart, the love and the beauty of all of God's creation will be unimaginable and *you will never be the same?* God wants individualization and He wants to speak *to you and to your needs.* Because He longs for you to grow and become More as a spiritual being. He knows that you must have a unique understanding because **YOU ARE SPECIAL** and have a special divine plan. This is critical so you don't try to persuade everyone around you to see things the way you do. *God wants individualization because this is the pattern of God himself.* He wants individual interpretation so that we can begin to allow Him to speak to us and help us achieve the understanding that will *help us become MORE* of the spiritual being we have the potential to be. If you can see that God is always becoming more and that God created us to add MORE to who He was, and to the Whole of creation, *then you will know it was NOT God's plan that you live within the confines of a doctrine that keeps you from becoming any more than you are.* It doesn't make sense. Even in nature, change is constant. God created man in his image and *His image is an ever expanding, ever growing Spirit and so are we.* This is why religion can hinder our growth.

When I was in the strict religion, I saw over and over that the words they hung onto were the "written" words and yet I saw for myself, *there had to be a greater understanding.* I began to separately explore the greater understanding, the Living word. I stayed for 26 years but the religion was very confining and the ministers worked on keeping walls around so that what you can and cannot do became a prison in which growth wasn't possible. I stayed and kept growing and when I left it was hard on so many. They missed the deeper part of those words written, because I always shared the Living Word that was spoken to me in my heart. Others left after me. The truth is, it wasn't me that opened the door of understanding *but the Living words, the greater understanding of the words written were what they craved.* To me in leaving, and watching them miss what I brought (the Living Word), I had proof that my choice was right. I knew beyond any doubt that I made a decision that would create enormous understanding for me very soon. The written word is not confined as all of the truth. Many times people use the written word as weapons *to defeat, to belittle, and to humiliate their fellow man. But how can we believe that God or Jesus meant this to happen.* Jesus and His Father represent unconditional love and they want people to know there is more than the

145

outer words of a doctrine; they want them to put them in their hearts and apply them to bring more love into the world. God gives us spiritual truth and yet the greatest fault of man is they then turn them into *religious, infallible doctrines that become idols unto themselves.* A good religious doctrine is related to truth just as the moon is related to the sun. *It can reflect but never contain.* It is said that man shall not live by bread alone, but by every word that proceeds out of the mouth of God.

~God's word is the Living Word and it can never be contained by any outer doctrine.~

Listen with your heart and apply with love for your brothers and sisters. Jesus was in the book called the Bible. The Bible is a great masterpiece of information *but don't confine Jesus to the Bible*, because he and His Father *are much greater than any book.* The truth is we need the outer doctrine of the Bible and we need the inner doctrine found in the heart, which is the Living Word, in order to make it home.

~Religion wasn't meant to give people the absolute truth.~

Religion is given to people who are with a lower state of consciousness with the hope of getting them *out of that frame of mind.* In other words those who think their religion is the only way *have actually gone deeper into the lower state of consciousness. The only one who can solve this problem is YOU and not God.* When Jesus said my Yoke is easy, he was telling you He was an easy Master to follow, that is if you are willing to leave everything else behind. Leave behind the doctrines that trap you into believing you know everything and there is nothing else to know. Leave behind the doctrines that say, this is the final word.

There is one TRUTH, but many religions. Why? Even Pilate asked, "What is Truth?" *The only true religion is the one that Jesus taught* of *"unconditional love" found in the heart of all who want it.* Love attracts more love and doesn't hold you prisoner to only give it to certain people.

> *~Jesus gave love to all people and there were no strings attached. It was free and always flowing.~*

We don't need outer religions and Jesus made that clear. In all actuality Jesus wanted us to know of a Universal Path of Spiritual oneness and *not another religion.* To know God we know that *God doesn't need religion* but is a self-contained spiritual being.

> *~God doesn't need to be worshiped and definitely doesn't need or want to be admired.~*

God is not proud and arrogant but God is loving and gentle, not willing that anyone suffer. He also doesn't need to be feared. *When someone needs to be feared it's because they have a power struggle going on within them.* Do you really think God wants you to fear Him? Absolutely not! God doesn't bring forth a particular religion *because He needs that religion.* God brings forth a particular religion *because a particular group of people needs that religion.* The truth is that this planet has an enormous amount of many different groups of people and if God could formulate one religion that would appeal to all people, it would be impossible. An outer religion is given by God in an attempt to appeal to a specific group of people living at a particular time. Sometimes a religion is *meant to be short-lived* and other times God hopes that the religion will take on the ability for people to grow beyond and eventually become a living word. *God never intended that any religion would be the "only way" or even suppress all other people's growth if they are on a different path.*

One of the most meaningless conflicts of human kind is that over religion. All true religion that is inspired from above has only one purpose. *To serve as a stepladder that will help people ascend to the heavenly kingdom.* The key to entering God's kingdom is found *in overcoming any sense of separation or division from God.* When people use religion to divide and create more separation from others, they are inevitably using the carnal mind *in a direct opposite to the purposes of God and also in direct opposition to what Jesus lived for. Religious conflict always works against God's reason for bringing forth religion on this planet.* If you consider yourself to be a spiritual person you need to respect God's law of Free will and allow people the right to grow and understand more of who they are and what God stands for. *You need to inspire them to follow their heart and intuition and don't try to force them to follow your religion.* Like I said before *no outer religion has the ability to save you* so don't spend endless hours trying to convince someone else that your religion will save him or her. Only the oneness with God will bring salvation to you and in order to achieve that you must begin to grow *as freely as a tree planted in an open meadow.* Begin to expand your understanding and allow what is within you to council with you, guide you, and ultimately challenge the beliefs that have kept you in your own prison in your mind.

When Jesus told the disciples to go out into the world and make all people his disciples, he didn't want all people to become members of a particular outer Christian church. Jesus demonstrated an inner, mystical path to God and he wanted all people to follow that inner path. The inner path is not determined by any one religion and *you can follow the inner path whether or not you are in a religion of any kind*. I am not saying there is anything wrong with outer religions because not everyone *is ready* to follow the inner path. This is why staying in the religion of your choice *might be best for now* because it can gradually lead you to discover the inner mysteries of God. Staying in a church can serve as a foundation that *will stabilize you until you are able to go beyond religion* and learn more of who God is and what purpose there is for mankind. This was what happened to me. I stayed and helped people and when the time came for me to leave, I simply walked away. I learned a lot but I no longer could grow in the religion because I knew that some of the teachings were entrapping my mindset, and I couldn't grow beyond their limited view. As I said before, sometimes God allows outer religions to continue on for the purpose of using it only as a stepping-stone. An outer religion and its doctrines must never become a mental prison that keeps your mind trapped where you cannot look beyond the teachings.

In heaven there are no divisions and so the true inner religion is a universal religion in which all people understand they are all created from God's substance, all created from the same source.

~The divisions found on earth DID NOT COME FROM GOD but from the carnal mind and its sense of separation.~

The carnal mind **cannot see unity behind diversity** and so the differences must inevitably lead to division and conflict. The carnal mind seeks to determine that one person is better than another person or that one church is better than another church.

~A TRUE CHURCH is the church that leads people to discover the inner path of Christhood.~

In heaven, people are not divided as Catholics, Protestants, Buddhists, Jews, Muslims or Taoists but are just simply God's co-creators, God's Children, God's Creation. How can I tell you how *simple* being in God's family really is? All it takes is a willingness *to be a part* of His wonderful Kingdom. It's not about rules and regulations. It's not about being a perfect specimen in human form. How do we as humans get things so messed up? Why have we believed for so long that God is judgmental and waiting to put us in a fiery hell? *We have wasted precious time when we could be loving our Father, and appreciating everything He has done for all of us.* Remember that in Unconditional Love they're IS NO FEAR, so why do the religions of the world include a fear of God if we don't match up to *their idea* of obedience? The answer is that they are fearful they are wrong and so they try to control others in fear to make it appear they have the only right way. No matter how you cut it, anyone that tries to get you to do something with a fear tactic, does not serve the Loving Way of Our Creator. There is NO FEAR IN LOVE!!!!! In Heaven it's about pure love and oneness and *a joy to be in the Father's presence.* In heaven you will find only sons and daughters of God, *because once you are there it really doesn't matter which path you followed to get there.* Once you step through the straight and narrow gate, you leave all the outer human divisions behind.

Let's look at religion thru Jesus for a moment. Jesus came as *a* Son of God, *not the only Son of God.* Jesus came because he had an unconditional love for all humans and longed for each to anchor them on the universal spiritual path *that transcends all religions.* He didn't have a particular loyalty to a particular religion but loved all people. People often referred to Jesus as a carpenter from Nazareth. In the world of carpentry, a carpenter has a select amount of tools to shape the wood. They are simply tools used but the carpenter doesn't worship the tools and has no particular loyalty to them either. And if the tools get dull, he simply sharpens them. And if they can't be sharpened then he gets new tools. The same way a carpenter sees the tools, *so do those in the Ascended Host see religion. A religious organization is simply a tool that is used in an attempt to cut through the density of the lower consciousness, or better said, the lower level of understanding God and His Realm.* If the teachings of a religious organization become useless, then another organization takes its place in the same attempt a carpenter would be willing to sharpen the tools. And thru the years we have seen many religions or organizations become useless, no longer able to grow or be renewed and they simply are left behind and a new one is started. *Let me make something clear. If anyone engages in religious conflict then they are not true followers of Jesus. There is nothing sadder than those who justify killing in the name of God.* This justification is not to please God and *God is not going to thank you.* This justification to kill someone in the name of God can only come from the carnal mind and how reasoning takes place. The same goes if you persecute others for their efforts in finding God.

~Do not Judge someone else for being willing to search for God, no matter what religion they go to.~

This kind of mindset comes from a lower sense of understanding or consciousness. And it is the very mindset that killed Jesus and has created all the religious wars. *It has absolutely nothing to do with what God approves of.* So if you really are a follower of Jesus and learning to be an example as Jesus was, *then make peace with your brothers and sisters who follow a religion that is different from your own.* If you cannot or *will not* make peace with your brothers and sisters *then how could you possible hope to make peace with God?* And if you have not made peace with God, *then how could you possibly hope to enter his kingdom.*

Humans have a tendency to become attached to things quickly and they often attach to religion. They insist that the organization *must be infallible, and they do not want it to change.* Many times when change begins to happen in a religion that has appeared to be the same for so long, it is God's way of saying, *it's coming to an end and you must search for ME.* God never intended that a religion that creates it's own following *be more important to follow than God Himself.* That is why many religions change or simply cease to exist. They reason by thinking that if something is perfect, people think it should not have to change. This is how humans elevate religion to an idol, *just like they did with Jesus,* and such people are literally doing what was seen in the time of Moses, *dancing around the Golden Calf instead of seeking a Living Word, a Living truth.*

So let's get back to *why anyone would choose religion.* They choose religion because *deep inside they know there is a God and they have a belief that they are more than human beings.* We have talked about the inner and outer path in life. The outer approach to finding answers such as in a church or a doctrine or belief system has several limitations. If you accept that your church or belief, as *"complete" then how do you deal with questions that are not answered by them about the spiritual side of life.* As this happens, and even if you don't want to admit it, it has already occurred in your life, it often leads you to a feeling that God simply doesn't make sense. And so if you accept an outer doctrine as "infallible", then all different or conflicting doctrines, you will label as false. This alone causes you conflict between groups of religious people. But it also causes a deep division within you and whether you admit it or not, it affects your faith. The unanswered questions in the Bible will be given to you if you first focus on going within and learning the deeper understandings of everything. It will take time and when you finally find that answer you wanted, you will notice you have changed so much and feel so close to God, that the question that always seemed a mystery, isn't really so important. You have moved way beyond and now understand things at such a higher level.

The inner approach to spirituality is the only way to keep growing and to continually build upon *a greater sense of knowing* of who you are and why you are here. In this day and age we find many people losing faith in a particular religion or even in religion in general. *This doesn't mean they don't care about the spiritual side of life* but it means they have grown disappointed and are not finding answers to questions that will help them grow.

The way to finding the answers to life is to go within yourself. Jesus was very clear that the kingdom of God was within and what he was trying to demonstrate is that what is within you, namely a part of God, has the answers *and has the ability to find more answers.* Religion has the potential to become *a journey of self-discovery and discovery of God and His great kingdom.* To go on this journey you *don't have to abandon your religion, just keep in mind that your religion SERVES AS A FOUNDATION, or a stepping-stone, for your personal quest for answers.*

"The outer religion MUST NEVER BECOME A CAGE that prevents you from looking for answers within your heart."

The purpose of the journey of discovery is to attain a higher understanding, to keep in mind *the journey is ongoing* and remember that it is not an ultimate or absolute understanding.

In today's world there is constant need for more understanding and we are more than ever aware that change is inevitable. So if we take the teaching of Jesus formulated 2,000 years ago for the people of that day to understand, as **all there is to know** then we will never grow much further. We know that humankind is engaged in a process of increasing our understanding of life and so the teachings so long ago will not satisfy our longings. There is an alternative to our lack in today's world. We need to go within and believe **that what is within a man is that part of him that is brought from the spiritual world when he came to earth to fulfill his mission.** What is within a man is an inner understanding of life as it really is. If we could see **that what is within each of us has the power to change our world and our perception of our world, we will become the change and our world will never again be the same.** We have the capability to rise higher than ever before and to become a planet of great abundance in which all people will enjoy life on earth. What is within each individual is a greater understanding of life as it is but also there is power in the individual perception of life and what can be. What I am saying is that the key to change in our world is **tapping into what is within**, and then allowing it to become our teacher so that we will not only understand life but **we will have the capability to enhance God's love and creative abilities unlike we ever dreamed possible.** What is within our own being is God and our spiritual memory of all we know when we are in the spiritual realm. In religion they fight against you accepting an inner approach to spirituality. Follow God and not religion and accept Jesus' teaching of the inner approach to spirituality.

~He lived and died to teach you the truth, don't let His message be in vain.~

The Bible is a book of Love, a personal love letter from God to all of us. The Bible is God encouraging us to **understand the bigger picture** and to learn from the struggles of the ego and understand they are lessons so that we can become what Gods want us to become.

~God wants us to grow beyond human circumstances and see the spiritual beings we are.~

The Bible is a good example in understanding that no doctrine could ever capture the fullness of God Almighty.

~To know that fullness, you must use an outer doctrine only as a ladder.~

Realize that although you can't climb without the ladder, the ladder itself doesn't reach into Heaven. Jesus never wanted spiritual teachers to limit their teaching to doctrines but instead he wanted them to help guide people to a greater understanding of God, His plans for mankind and the purpose for their lives.

~I learned that in religion no matter how many times you try to define the outer doctrine, you could never change the reality of the Living Word of God.~

The way that "seems right" into a man is the belief of strictly following an outer doctrine instead of looking *for the inner understanding*. So many people from different religions argue over how to interpret this or that passage in scripture. But to discover the true inner meaning requires you to go into your heart. I will talk much about the Christ Consciousness, the Mind of Christ and for now keep in mind the words of Jesus that except your righteousness shall exceed the righteousness of the scribes and Pharisees, you shall not enter the kingdom. Just having the knowledge of scripture is no substitute for having the living word thru the mind of Christ.

Thru the ages many devout spiritual people have become so attached to the Bible that they are not willing to consider any other spiritual teachings. They have become so attached that they **aren't open to a Living Word** because they only focus on the written word in the Bible. If Jesus or any other Spiritual Teacher is to communicate the Living

Word ***they have to have hearts and minds open*** to the possibility that God can communicate through other teachings. This is a critical part that stops many sincere people from going any further in their growth. So, Is the Bible the Word of God? Let's try to re-look at what the Bible consists of. We can know that the Bible is complex and has incredible teachings. Like anything ever written and re-published for as long as the Bible has been, things can be lost. If you go back to orthodox Christians and materialistic scientists, you find that is where the origins of the Bible start. The Old Testament comes from an ancient oral tradition that has been told and retold over many generations. If you just take this into account it is easy to understand the possibilities of loosing, distorting or adding things. ***And even further of how interpretations can honestly be different because people in those days saw life different than we do today.*** That only makes sense and is logical ***but a lot of reasoning I have noticed is based on illogical explanations and people will believe whatever their minister or church says without questioning.*** This is why much of the trouble begins with us. ***We must stand up and look at things with open hearts.*** However, parts of the Old Testament did indeed originate as a result of divine inspiration. In understanding how religion is often changed to suit the purposes of the leaders, the same has happened with the Word of God. We can deny this but in doing that we deny an open mind to More of what we can learn. This is where the Living Word must take hold. It is not my purpose to tell you what is true and what isn't. But I want you to open up to the possibility that all of what is in the Bible ***isn't all there is to know.*** Also, that some of the stories may only contain fragments of what was meant to be told. Some of the meanings behind the stories may be lost because they were given to people of a different level of understanding. Taking everything word for word is going to get you into false teaching because you are going to believe it as it is written. For instance the hair, if you feel everyone that cut's their hair is going to hell, then you are taking a written word and not applying the living word. ***The living word opens your heart to apply things in perspective and to teach you more.*** It also keeps you from getting stuck and not growing beyond what is written. The Old Testament serves to tell much of historical records of a certain group of people. *You will notice that the whole time Jesus lived He never wrote down His teachings. I ask myself why? If Jesus meant for the Written word to be left as a powerful testament of the truth, then why didn't He specifically write everything down, Himself, so that no mistakes could be made.* In my heart I believe the reason was because of His belief that a written doctrine could eventually be distorted and would loose their true message. *Maybe another reason is because if He brought forth an official written doctrine when He was still bringing forth the Living Word, then when He died we would hold to the words written instead of seeing the value of a continual Living Word that would serve as our guide, even after His death.* He actually was *setting up a pattern* to how we could continue on the path of greater enlightenment. Those that wrote the Bible left out many things of Jesus' life, including many teachings. Maybe in some ways they were attempting to preserve a historical account of some of the highlights of the life of Jesus and in turn it would be able to guide the Christian Movement. That is ok but if you lean *only* on the written word and never allow God to speak to you through the Living word then the Bible is the only thing you will know. *That wasn't the intention and that was probably why Jesus avoided making the effort to write everything down himself.* The hidden message in not writing down all of His teachings so that it would be accurately told was that the written word is fallible and you can never learn everything there is to learn by the words written. *There is much arguing among religions even with a written word.* The only way to resolve disputes among the different groups is through the Living Word and the Christ Consciousness. When people are consumed with the carnal mind where they create division among each other, no written record, no matter how authoritative it might seem, could ever resolve the disputes and differences between people. The problem is the carnal mind and it stands in the way of creating a oneness. I believe that the original gospel writers had a certain measure of Christ Consciousness and most were inspired writers.

To understand the Bible better, we must have a better understanding of what is meant by the expression the "Word of God". Nothing is impossible with God and so *He can speak audible words* to us. However they are rare occurrences. Most of the time God has delivered the *Living Word through a person* who has raised their consciousness to the level of the Christ consciousness. This is where a person becomes the open door through which the Living Word enters the world. Many people have been this and it wasn't just Jesus or his apostles. In understanding the Living Word that comes through an individual, it's important to understand that *words becomes individualized and are affected by the mind and personality of the individual* who serves as the open door. When I say affected I mean through the presentation they give of the words and through the reception of others in receiving what is said. Even today, just look at how people judge others in politics. The person might have incredible ideas but if their personality or their looks, people don't like, they cast out. Humans are the quickest to judge and the harshest. Think of religious groups. *Their judgment goes deeper than their venomous words. It comes from their heart and reveals the condition of their heart.* A heart that condemns others to hell because they don't belong to "their" religion surely can't convince you they are full of unconditional love, could they? I mean let's reason together. Many people feel it's there way or no way and they will argue until they die. Jesus faced the problems too. Many didn't like him because of outer appearance, stature, and how he talked and whom he hung out with. *Jesus wasn't as accepted as you might think by the "Christians" of the time*. In fact it was the religious scrutiny that brought about his death. The condemnation of him desiring people to find for themselves God and not rely on churches was the very issue that killed him. **As for the messenger Jesus was he was judged also by his personality**. He was no different. He didn't walk around with an angelic halo over his head. He was a man that came as a messenger and most people; *even religious people didn't recognize him*.

The Word of God can be delivered in many different ways that are all valid and *all support the universal truth from which they came*. In order to move past that the Bible is the only Word of God, we must try to understand that it was only one version and not the only possible version. Another fact you must keep in mind is that throughout history there have been people selected to be an open door in delivering the word of God but they were not able to be a pure instrument. In other words some of their spiritual teachings that were definitely inspired by God still contained some false ideas or concepts. ***The truth is a teaching inspired by God, given through a human messenger holds the possibility that some of God's original message can be lost in the process of bringing it to the material world.***

I believe that the New Testament in its original form was to a large degree inspired by God and so we have a wonderful reason to call it the Word of God. But through the 2,000 years that have passed since the original Gospels were written, I have a feeling that only fragments of what was meant to be useful ***for many generations to come***, are there. I also believe what I have already stated, that a lesson thru scripture taught to the people 2,000 years ago was taught ***according to their understanding***. It was simplified and ***Jesus could not reveal a higher understanding because they simply didn't have the ability to understand it***. Not that they weren't intellectual but they were at a certain level of Consciousness or awareness. Like I said earlier, what if you traveled back in time to the 13th Century and told of all you knew in technology. You would be labeled crazy and they would have no clue as to what in the world you were talking about. This is critical in every part of this book.

~The level of Consciousness is what helps you to become more.~

Many religious people that stick to dead doctrines don't allow themselves to become the true messengers they have the ability to become. They won't deviate from the written word and so it's just plain and simple, they will only know the written word. God would like the religious people that have a deep love for truth, ***to come forward and take a new approach*** by understanding they can be instruments of change just like Jesus. ***When he came to earth Jesus taught many things that were never revealed before.*** Many had relied on Old Testament doctrine but Jesus was a vessel to bring a whole new outlook on everything. Jesus became the living word in order to do this. ***What makes you think that You haven't been called also?*** Jesus is our example and we can be a messenger today by bringing forth new teachings. The Ascended Host has many new teachings waiting but they can only bring it forth through those in embodiment that are willing. Today we have the ability to understand with a greater depth and we can still hear God and the higher teaching but only thru the Living Word. The word spoken to us individually to what is within, to our Higher Self.

Don't believe for one minute that the New Testament is everything there is to know. Then you read the claim that if all Jesus did and said should be written down, the world itself could not contain the books that should be written. ***This alone tells us that even the original scriptures did not contain Jesus' entire message.*** How much clearer does this have to be? Now take a step further and ask yourself if Jesus lived his life, died, and rose again, why wouldn't he want to tell us more of His Father's kingdom than what is recorded in the present-day Gospels? ***I can hardly believe that what was written was all that Jesus ever cared to share.*** Knowing the love He had for all of mankind, He would have been a continued guiding light and the Bible would not contain the new things He wanted to share. I wonder how Jesus feels about the Bible. I wonder if He feels the words written have become a hindrance ***because many don't open their hearts to learn more.*** Many feel that this is the final word on the matter but ***that can't be.*** If God were a transcending being that is constantly becoming **MORE** and He reveals in nature that everything is changing and becoming more, ***then why would the most important communication between Him and man be stopped by a "final" word?*** No this is NOT the final word and so we need to be open to new messages. I wonder what He thinks that so many Christian cling to the written word and to a particular interpretation, closing their minds and hearts to the Living Word which I believe He delivers daily to those willing to listen. Jesus lived to show us how to live and He ***opened the door*** for us to have a greater revelation of His Father. He didn't open the door and then close it. Let's be real! He opened the door and the only way it can close ***is when we close***

it because we have this belief that we know all there is to know and we are the only ones that have it. *You see it is in our minds that we hinder our own growth.* But more than that *He set the stage for us to be willing to accept* MORE *through a Living revelation that would be ongoing, by not writing down His teachings, himself.* He set the stage for us to continue to accept the Living Word so we could grow more and more and not become stagnant.

~TO BECOME STAGNANT MEANS DEATH.~

Yes in kindness many took the time to remember His life and write down what was revealed to them and we can thank them for this. The same goes for my time in writing what I write and the many other writers who have written books thru the years. *We all are a part of the change but our words are not the "final" word.* Anything you read you need to look at it for yourself, determine within if it can be valuable to help *you grow*, use it to help yourself become more and then remember that *there is more to learn and there is never a final word.* Even nature teaches that humans, plants, animals, the earth and the atmosphere are, all changing constantly. Nothing remains the same. This is God's purpose for growth and God wants you to see this is the pattern, the foundation of all of life. It is an opportunity to grow more. If you carry a belief in your heart that the word of God is all that God has to say on the matter, then you will continue in life never becoming any more than what you are spiritually. But if you are willing to see that God wants you to know more because He wants you to become one with Him, then you will reach heights of enlightenment you never thought possible. Don't fear you will lose your life or your salvation *because your salvation depends on you becoming more.* I will talk about salvation next. So when Jesus said, "I will be with you always" *he meant he would continually speak to us and would never be done teaching us. He never intended to leave us alone in a dark world where all we had, as a guiding rod was a set of written words that only produced fragments of His incredible life and teachings.*

Jesus is our friend, the truest kind and He desired to give us *an ongoing support of comfort and understanding through the Living Word,* which He was the embodiment of. Jesus said, "I have many things to say unto you, but you cannot bear them now." The reason they could not bear them now, at the time it was written was their level of consciousness. This is proof that he knew they might not understand now but one day they would and *to me that is another open door for More to come of God's teachings.* Like a child can only understand at a certain level yet when they mature they understand and can receive more teachings. The same goes spiritually. Just by looking at the natural things in our lives *in how we grow and transcend on a "normal basis",* and then look at nature, the same pattern is in the spiritual understanding and growth process. If we can begin to go within and find some of our answers, we will be encouraged and strengthened to know that *we are able to become all we need to become by going to God within us.* This alone will take away a lot of our fears. It will help us to see that God is within us and He is still speaking today. We will begin to know *we are not alone and never have been.* God will help us as we help ourselves and the more we walk and grow accustomed to the mind of Christ, the better we become in being our own guide. Today we can bear more, simply because humans have a greater willingness to see beyond the written scriptures but also because we have a higher level of understanding. We have grown up in a world where high-tech and higher teachings of energy, and theories of science have taught our minds to expand our awareness. It's just the nature of the time in which we live. *Jesus made that statement because he knew one day there would come a time when they could bear more or understand more.* Just think of the computer world alone. I have three sons and they are computer savvy because they have learned the technology the same as we learned math in school. They have learned and grown up in a world that has a higher understanding. *It's not about intelligence when I talk of a higher understanding but it's about our ability to take in the information and make sense of it.*

The computer world is a great example of how it has changed our world and how it has become so much easier thru the years. The technology of computers hasn't always been easy but in fact it was like a foreign language. It was incredibly promising but it was hard to figure many times. In the beginning it revealed a door open to the greatest abilities we could imagine but it wasn't all known and it wasn't set in stone. We can be thankful it wasn't set in stone and that is because growth can only become something beyond our wildest imagination *when we keep it always becoming more*. In other words knowledge is power only when we keep moving to learn more. But thru a greater understanding of how computers work and a number of people who have taken what they knew and learned easier ways to do things, and *built upon the foundation* of the technology learned, they have made it possible for all of us to enjoy the use and excitement of computers, videos, and game consoles and even more than you ever imagined. Keep in mind that only in the last 100 years has this kind of advancement in technology become so great. It's because when we are ready for a greater understanding, we grow quickly and the vast applications of our knowledge multiply our abundance. This is proof how in spirituality and a higher understanding, the Golden Age, The Age of Aquarius will happen soon. A spiritual person, who gathers the understanding of teachings of the past, and becomes an open door for new teachings, can be a change in the world as great as we ever imagined. In turn the new teachings become easier to understand and therefore they are applied at a new level and the path to Abundant life becomes so incredibly simple to understand. The computer world became the tool of the future and everyone could use it because some individuals *became open to a new understanding of the same technology.* With that they built upon it new ideas and new possibilities. The same goes for the spiritual world. We have tools. We have what is within us, we have the Ascended Host ready and willing to open new doors of understanding and to bring forth new teachings, and we have a God that loves us and believes in us more than you will ever know. As you take a moment and look out into the world, notice that many writers, actors, politicians, businessmen, average people and even presidents have an open heart and an inspiring motivation *to take the "bull by the horn" and BECOME THE CHANGE.* No matter who you are, YOU can make an incredible difference in our world by just taking hold of your life. Because when you take hold of your life you inspire others by your courage. You start the change needed for this planet at this time in earth's existence, by pulling the beam out of your own eye so that you can take the next step and each step after.

"YOUR LIFE AND YOUR HEART'S WILLINGNESS IS WHAT GOD NEEDS OF YOU."

Don't be afraid to look at things differently. Remember if you are afraid, you can always go back to the way you saw it before.

Again I will bring up the question, Why do so many that claim they follow Jesus in such a reverent way, reject that there might be more teachings than what is in the Bible? A lot of the reason has nothing to do with their love for God but they have been told by religion that if they wander away from what they are told is all there is, they will die. *Fear keeps them from becoming more.* People are born with their spiritual identity and everyone has the potential to reconnect with that identity. But the reason you find the most reverent people strictly adhering to teachings of a religion is *because they fear for their salvation.* So in a nutshell, it's truly an eye opener that some people seriously believe that the teachings Jesus gave so long ago represent the highest teachings that God could ever bring forth on this planet.

~The fear of being lost or not being saved is what drives humans to find a way in which they can be saved.~

This is what causes us to find a religion in which we can quell that fear. We all see things thru our level of consciousness. And the religion we choose to be our path is chosen *to the best of our ability or the best of our conscious awareness.* We are all trying to have the *best possible outcome.* Through many years of being in an exclusive religion that thought they were the only way heaven, I found times when I believed them, maybe because *I wanted to believe them,* but deep down it just didn't seem right. The part of me that believed was the ego and the part of me that questioned it, was *my spiritual self that wanted me to know the truth.* The spiritual self is who you were before you came in this embodiment. But you loose your connection when you come to earth. It is God's will that you reconnect to the spiritual self, find the reason why you came, do the plan you came to do, and *then become MORE.* This is how you attain a higher level in the spiritual realm and this is the goal each time you become embodied. This is why the key to growing is found in your ability to reconnect to your higher self, your spiritual being that holds the blueprint you specifically laid out before you came into this embodiment, has the answers to your many questions.

Let's talk about what salvation really is. So many people think that salvation is a walk, over which they have little or no influence, accept to choose the path *in which they can find it.* They think it can happen through grace or some kind of miracle *if they are good enough and obedient enough.* Their level of spiritual understanding determines choosing the path, in which they think they can find it. Many have been raised in a religion and that is where they gravitate. It's understandable and yet God hopes *that at some point you are willing to look beyond the religion* and believe *there is more to understand about salvation.* And at some point you are open to greater understandings of what salvation really is. Because of the universal Law of Free Will, *we cannot be saved against our own will.* Yes, God gracefully gives us the ability to become one with Him but grace is *NOT the action that saves us.* If you are to be saved, you must decide that you are willing to be saved or worthy to be saved. To feel worthy of being saved requires you to see yourself as a co-creator of God and *not a hopeless sinner that can never be anymore than a sinner.* This *decision* creates "a vehicle" in which can you travel to a higher level of consciousness. In other words the first step to becoming MORE is in *your own decision*; your Free Will choice begins the process. *Neither God nor Jesus can or will make that decision for you. It is your choice.* William Shakespeare was one of the spiritual messengers sent forth in his time and he wrote many plays. One was "Hamlet" and in a scene there was a line that became famous. "TO BE OR NOT TO BE: that was the question."

This is where all things on earth have a message. Here was an author, a writer, who made an incredible contribution to the world through his writings. They were spiritual messages with deeper meanings that he put forth in his lifetime. The deeper meaning in this statement *is that you must choose whether to be who you are or not to be who you are.*

So what does it take to be saved? If you are willing to see that there is a spiritual side to life, then you will automatically come to the conclusion that there is a definite difference between this world of form and the spiritual world. In today's time more than ever people are at a higher level of consciousness. They understand far more than in the times of Jesus. They are more open to variables and they are more willing to see beyond the dogmatic teachings of the past. People from all religions have come to feel deep inside that there is a universal belief of the difference between the spiritual world and material world. They also share the belief that Earth is not the permanent home for human beings. *Many feel that the goal in life is to ascend beyond the material world and enter the spiritual world.* Humans also have a deep inner knowing that before they can enter the spiritual world, they must fulfill certain requirements.

If you just look at our world today and all of the many horrible things that take place on this planet, you will come to *your own conclusion* that what is happening on planet earth *would not be tolerated in the spiritual world.* You also may come to the understanding that how people treat each other, in the wrong ways on planet earth, *would not be tolerated in the spiritual world.*

Before I go further I want to explain what the difference between heaven and hell is *so that you can remove the "fear" you carry.* The fear you carry keeps you in a state of believing the "limited beliefs" you have, because you want to be saved and so you feel if you walk away from those beliefs you will surely go to hell. This is where "salvation" takes control over you and you cannot see the truth. When I say, Walk away; what I am trying to prepare you for is that in order to really understand salvation, you might need to step away so you can receive a higher teaching. If you don't physically leave them, then mentally leave them but this might create a fear inside. When I came to the conclusion that I could no longer believe the teachings of a certain church, I felt as if I was jumping off a cliff, and I had to tell myself that I wouldn't die and God would help me no matter what. ***But I needed to step away because I could no longer believe and accept their teachings.*** It was a ***fear in me*** that had been a part of my psyche for so long. The difference in heaven and hell or heaven and earth, is in an energy vibration. I haven't talked much about this but in order to understand you need to have this foundational truth in the back of your mind ***so that you can better understand salvation.***

Everything is made from energy and that energy is vibration. There are different levels of vibration. There are three main levels. The level that all human beings can detect with the physical senses is what we might call the material world. This level is made from energies that vibrate within a certain frequency spectrum. A second level is the spiritual realm, which is made of energies that vibrate at higher frequencies than the energies found in the material realm. There is really more than three but for simple clarification, let just use three. So the third is the ultimate vibration, which is the level of the creator. Because we live in the world at this time, and you already have a lot of common knowledge of energy, this is not hard for you to grasp. This is where the teachings of Jesus can reach beyond what was written in the Bible in today's world but ***this wasn't possible in the days Jesus lived*** and that is why the Bible isn't clear to us today. ***Like He said, there is much more He has to share when we are ready to understand.*** We are ready because we have risen in our level of consciousness. Not all of us but many of us. So let's go on. Heaven is not literally located in the direction of the sky. Heaven is made from vibrations that exist in the same space as the vibrations of the material realm. In other words, in the space that exists around us, there are many levels of vibration and in order to enter them we must obtain that higher understanding. We obtain that by going beyond what we know and growing more aware of the spiritual teachings. The room in which you are sitting is being penetrated by radio waves of different frequencies. ***Because the waves have different frequencies, they can coexist in the same space.*** That is why there are places found on planet earth that many people can actually feel a higher vibration than others. This exists because there are localized areas where the vibration has been raised to such a level that the gap between the material and the spiritual worlds has become non-existent. This is where people are already experiencing the peace of heaven even though still in there physical body, but they don't see it because their level of consciousness is tuned into a lower vibration, which is the material realm. ***Seeing is believing but you don't see it, even though it is right before your eyes because of your level of understanding.*** In order to see, you must be willing to step outside of the box of current beliefs and begin to walk, learning, and growing and that is when you will reach a higher level of consciousness or understanding.

~Hell is simply a realm made from energies that are lower than the energies in the material realm.~

There are definitely places on Earth that are so low in vibration that it seems to the person of a lower vibration to be Hell on Earth. Heaven and Hell exists in our understanding of life and in order to feel the love from heaven we have to take hold of our lives and raise our level of consciousness. What scientists call energy in today's world is really consciousness. In the Gospel of John it says that in the beginning was the Word and that everything was created out of the Word. What is the "Word", you may ask. ***The Word is the universal Christ Consciousness or the universal Christ Mind.*** This is what Jesus became after living on earth for a time. Jesus was a son of God and not the only son. Jesus was our example and he became the example of the Christ consciousness by learning and growing. This state of consciousness was the first element of creation and so we can easily refer it as the only begotten Son of the Father. Keep in mind that in the days of Jesus, the people had no understanding of energy and so Jesus couldn't explain it to them ***and that is why it is not written in the Bible.*** This is another example of why you must be open to More that Jesus has to share. The universal Christ Consciousness is the basic substance from which everything else is created. The Christ Consciousness is embodied in everything and that is why everyone has the potential to follow in the steps of Jesus and become a Christed Being. *My point is that Heaven, Earth and Hell are at different states of consciousness and those states are perceived within each human being according to their own level at which they see things.* God created the spiritual realm and everything in it is in perfect alignment with the laws and the original vision of God. God also created Earth and because humans have free will, they have descended into a lower state of consciousness and forgotten their spiritual origin. So it is understandable that everything on earth is not in alignment with the laws and the vision of God. This is where you need to really understand that *God never created Hell.* If you believe God did create hell then you are holding on to an image of Hell that was created in a lower consciousness. In the times of Jesus when the Bible was written, the people did not have an understanding of energy and *so there was no simple way to correctly explain Hell.* Think about it. Could you have explained it? Hell is a level of vibration *where God's light and presence cannot enter* but it is in the minds where people live in their level of consciousness. Heaven and Earth are real, but Hell is simply a figment of a warped imagination. So you might ask, then why is it such a strong force in religion? *Hell does exist in the mind and it has a temporary reality if a person chooses to live at that level of consciousness* and that person will literally be magnetized to Hell after it leaves the physical body. So going to Hell is a real possibility for a human soul *but hell is the state of conscious understanding and literally without having a higher understanding you do feel miserable and cannot be close to God.* So it is hell because you are a spiritual being first, and you are made to be a co-creator of God and your fulfillment, your joy is in being one with God. So it is Hell. But what I am trying to say through all of this is people need to accept that an angry God does not send souls to Hell as a punishment.

~Souls literally send themselves to Hell by lowering their state of consciousness and by keeping it that way by their own choice.~

The only way to raise your consciousness or awareness is to make the choice to do so. You are in control of your destiny. It is your state of consciousness that determines whether your soul is *magnetized to the vibrations of the spiritual realm or the vibrations of Hell*. Hell has often been used in religion to generate *"fear"* among the followers and *the intention is to scare people into following the outer rules and doctrines without questioning church authorities.* This is common practice in the underlying persuasion to convince people to follow "their" way. In many religions that promote violence or force the fear of going to Hell scares the followers into submitting to games of power and control. When you understand that hell is by your choice because when *you choose to not grow in having a better understanding that is what you achieve.* Hell is separation from God and because you are a spiritual being, it is almost like a person slowly suffocating but still gets some oxygen. It's a slow death and you feel you are in hell. You naturally want to feed off of God's love and if you are separated then you are slowly dying. The beautiful part of understanding all of this is finding out that *you can* prevent it and *you can* rise, not only to your calling *but also above and beyond*. That is why life is journey and not a destination. If there was a final word, a final destination, then once you get there, there is nowhere else to go. The truth is Our Father has many mansions and once you achieve the higher understanding you continue to achieve more and more according to your willingness. *What you give, you receive, you reap what you sow and so if want to keep going and becoming more of the spiritual being, then your free will allows you to do this.* You are empowered when you know the truth. This is my intent. *I want to empower you to be all you can* and in turn you will empower those around you, to do the same. Believe it or not when so many people realize this power they will rise and they will bring the level of awareness higher on planet earth. This is how the Kingdom of God comes to earth. This is why taking the beam out of your own eye allows you to BE THE CHANGE. *You are one single life and can make a difference like you never thought possible*, and you don't have to be famous. In all actuality you, being anonymous will give you more freedom. But if you are famous then you have *a special*

task to penetrate where no one can. You can influence at higher levels with your example. Keep a pure heart and stay on the path leaving the ego behind.

In understanding Heaven and Hell, you are now given breathing room to listen to what salvation truly is. You are now given time to grow and not to just hear my words but be open to hear MORE of other spiritual teachers. My words ***can only open the door*** for you to become MORE. And my intention is to clearly state that what I share isn't all there is to know. The purpose of my words are to open a door within your individual being of awareness so that you will trust what is within you to be a guide in which you can ***use this book as a stepping stone*** to more teachings given in the future. Never take anything "as all there is". Even those in the Ascended Host are learning more. You can help them by opening the door so they can know they can help you on planet earth. Create a relationship of working together with them. ***They would love it.*** They cannot interfere with free will and ***so you must ask them to help*** and in turn they realize that they can do what they long to do and that is to help planet earth rise in vibration to a higher level of understanding. We are one, whether on earth or in heaven and when we see the value in the help we can give one another and leave behind pride or jealousy because someone else seems to have a higher understanding, we can all become a force of unconditional love and become one with the Father. When we are willing to take these steps ***the potential for all beings to rise and really do the Father's will is beyond what we ever imagined and the joy we will experience will not be likened unto anything we have ever felt.***

So let's return to understanding Salvation. Keeping in mind what we have learned about differences in vibration, you need to know that you do have the capacity to ascend to the spiritual world. But before you can enter our Father's Kingdom, you must meet certain requirements. The key requirement is that you must rise above the lower consciousness of the carnal mind or how you see things in the lower level of consciousness. So the atrocities you see taking place on this planet, and many other actions that people do not necessarily consider to be wrong, are the results of the lower state of consciousness. Jesus said "flesh and blood hath not revealed it unto thee" when talking to Simon Barjona in Matthew 16. What he was saying is that the lower consciousness simply cannot inherit the kingdom. The only way that you could possibly ascend into our Father's Kingdom is by leaving behind the lower state of consciousness, the carnal mind. *The vibrations of the carnal mind can never cross the threshold and enter the straight and narrow gate that leads to our Father's Kingdom.* Even if these vibrations are disguises as one might call "human goodness", they still cannot enter our Father's Kingdom. *You cannot enter the kingdom by becoming a good human being. In the eyes of God, there is no such thing as a good, or perfect, human being.* You can enter the kingdom only by overcoming the sense of identity that causes you to believe that you are a mortal human being who is separated from God. By putting off the old human of mortality and putting on the new human, which is your higher self or the spiritual being you are.

~In other words to put it very clearly the only way into the Father's kingdom is by putting on the Mind of the Christ Consciousness.~

This is the way you will unite with your higher self. Your sense of identity must be built on the Rock of Christ and not on the shifting sands of the lower consciousness.

This is where when you really understand what salvation is and how to attain it, *you open up within, an essential truth* and you begin to have a whole new look on what life is about as a human being. You get a clear picture that the ascension to the spiritual world is achieved by raising your level of consciousness. You also see that it is a gradual process, which Jesus would like you to refer to as the spiritual path.

"This is where you put off the old man, the lower consciousness and put on the new man, the Christ Consciousness."

So let's put away the old belief that salvation is an outer process over which you have no control. ***Salvation is not about waiting for an outer savior who has come to do all the work for you.*** Salvation is not about just saying a prayer and then you are saved. The outer savior does exist but only for the purpose of helping you to understand and ***begin*** the process. ***The outer savior serves as an open door through which God can give you a morsel of the universal Christ Consciousness.*** This morsel is the leaven to raise the whole loaf of your consciousness. Remember the parable about the sower whose seeds fall on barren ground. A savior comes, gives you a morsel of the Christ consciousness and yet you must make a free will choice to accept that Christ consciousness in order to have salvation. ***Jesus offered us help but he didn't say we had nothing to do to achieve it.*** Even when he healed the sick and lame, they usually had to do something to receive the healing. Jesus leads us to living waters but ***no one can make you drink.*** Free Will is for you to take hold of your life. You know very well that if you make life easy for someone to live a certain way, they may appear to be doing well but the power lies in giving them an opportunity to make their life how they want it and on their own. ***Jesus gave his life as an example, he gave us the ability to rise and he wanted to help us with our burdens but we must take hold of our lives.*** In taking hold of your life doesn't mean you just hold it in a napkin as the parable says and keep it safe. ***No, in taking hold of your life, it means you become active in choosing your path and with each turn you take, you learn and grow and become more.*** If it is a bad choice then you will know and you will make a better choice in the future.

> ***~The goal is the Christ Consciousness and whatever level you achieve before you die, God will honor it and when you become in embodiment again you will have the opportunity to rise higher.~***

The truth is that the lower consciousness has a very deep belief that there is an easy way out or quick fix or a form of automatic salvation.

This is where religion has distorted the truth. Along with that they claim Jesus as the Only Son of God and that by simply believing on him and declaring him as their Lord and Savior, you will automatically be saved. *I believe Jesus wants the record straight because he never came to say all you have to do is believe on him and you will saved.* That would *totally take away your ability* to become MORE and to be a co-creator because you could not exercise your own ability to pull the beam out of your own and *begin transcending. It would mock the Universal Law of Free Will and mock that you were made in the image of God where you are also a co-creator.* If anything comes to easy, there is a price, and *Jesus definitely did NOT come to hurt humanities ability to be self-sufficient.* Salvation is a gift to every human being from God and yet the key to receiving it is not the offering of the gift, *but the acceptance of the gift.* Without accepting the gift, God cannot save you. In other words, your salvation does not ultimately depend on your outer actions in this world but on your state of consciousness. Of course, what you do in this world is a reflection of your state of consciousness, but the point is that it is by reforming your consciousness, not your outer actions, that you can qualify for eternal life. *Remember that there are levels of energy vibration and in order to enter a certain vibration you have to be able to accept it, to enter into it.*

So what is the path to achieve salvation? It has several steps and it is a process that starts with your choice. It's not instant and it's not a miracle. In the Law of Moses the people of the time were at a very low state of consciousness and in order to keep them from wandering there were a set of laws established. In some ways their level of consciousness was simply not mature and so simple laws but clearly written were important so they didn't misinterpret them. It was to help them *not go lower* in consciousness. But even that was a challenge and so Fear of punishment came into play. It wasn't God that was going to punish them and *God is not an angry God as many have often claimed.* The truth is that by another Law of the universe, the Law of Karma, it is clear that God doesn't punish humans *but humans punish themselves by their choices.* The Law of Moses was to help the people of that time from self-destructive behavior and so it focused on outer behavior *to keep them in a somewhat "teachable" state*. When Jesus came and his mission started things had changed enough that he could bring forth a higher law, which was mostly the Sermon on the Mount. I feel that the Law of Moses tried to change people's outer behavior but the Sermon on the Mount focused on the inner behavior, what was within man. Jesus took outer acts like adultery and killing and applied an understanding of changing *what caused you to do such acts*. He was challenging what was within you and in turn he was helping you to be your own guide to enlightenment. When you change your heart and remedy why you do what you do, you raise your awareness a little at a time. He was trying to connect the meaning and *show people the power of understanding something at a higher level*, so that they would see clearly why they needed to change to attain the mind of Christ. It was difficult in those days.

Decide for yourself to be saved and remember it takes a process of time. Make the decision to come up higher. You cannot serve two masters. *You cannot enter a house as long as you are running away from that house*. If you run away from the *understanding* that you must be willing to attain a new level of consciousness then you cannot move forward by walking backwards. As was said in the Bible, you cannot follow me as long as you are kicking against the pricks. If you are unhappy with your life and you feel that life is a continuous stream of suffering but you are *not willing to make the decision that you alone can make* that will start you on a path of abundant life and where you can escape the suffering, *then nothing can be done until you are willing.* The situation is just that simple. Your salvation depends on your willingness to accept what it takes to have it and to be ready to start on the road that will totally change your life.

Let's look at it another way. The Bible states we are saved by grace and it is a gift from God. Keep in mind that a gift has two aspects. *One is that the gift is offered and the other is that the gift must be received.* This opens the potential that while the gift is offered to all, not everyone might want the gift. God's grace rains on the just and the unjust, yet only the just are able to receive it. So what does it mean to be just? Think of life on earth as lessons in a classroom. If Jesus pays our debts without requiring us to change the consciousness that cause us to create the debt, then how will we learn our lessons. Jesus wanted us to stop sinning and the only way we can do this is if we change our level of consciousness or awareness or understanding. The action is created by something deeper inside and so *in order to stop the action you must change what it was that caused the action.* This is the deeper part of us that needs to change in order to raise our level of consciousness. God forgives sins when we are reborn into a new sense of identity. Grace is a state of consciousness that is given freely to all. However you cannot receive grace until you are willing to leave behind the carnal mind, or the duality consciousness and loose the mortal sense of life. So you cannot obtain salvation with an outward work such as a prayer or just accepting Jesus gift but *you must change from within*, change your level of consciousness. So the bottom line is that Jesus did not come to offer us a mechanical way to salvation.

~Jesus' way is an inner way that goes through a personal transformation and a spiritual rebirth.~

The works needed are simply inner changes within your understanding and awareness, and it begins with pulling the beam out of your own eye. When you do the work that is required to purify your heart, soul, and mind, that is when you find nothing but love and that is when you are able to receive the gift of salvation. It simply takes inner works, changing yourself from the carnal and ego mind that keeps you in a lower vibrational consciousness to bring you to the point where you are able to receive the gift of grace. Jesus wants us to do more than simply follow him. He wants us to walk the path he walked, namely the path of attaining a new identity that gives us a sense of oneness with God. Those that are trapped in the duality consciousness of the ego cannot understand the path of oneness. *The main effect of the ego is that it blinds us where we simply do not see a need to change, and that is why we cannot see the beam in our own eyes.* Our egos want to keep us separated from God and so it is easier to believe we

175

are not worthy to be one with God and that only Jesus can attain this oneness. Many religions teach this and believe that Jesus is beyond their reach and is an idol above the rest of us. However, ***this is where overcoming the duality consciousness is critical in the next step of making a choice to come up higher.*** When we overcome the duality consciousness, we realize that Jesus did not see himself above us or anyone else and of course he doesn't want anyone to see him that way. He wants us to believe we can do the same. He wants to empower us by his life's example. He wants us to attain the inner knowing that we can have the same oneness with the Father and this is what he came to teach us.

WHO ARE YOU

"All that we are is the result of what we have thought. The mind is everything. What we think we become"-Buddha-

When Buddha made this statement, he knew where the power of man was. It wasn't in taking force over others, it wasn't in government, it wasn't in what money can buy, *but the power of man lies within a man himself.* To know who you are you must come to this understanding. What you see you are in this life of yours is very inaccurate. You see only the outward identity and although this means something in your life right now, at this time in history, *it doesn't tell you who you are spiritually.* Although where you live, who you know, your name, your status, and your occupation have importance in this life, it is a little deceiving. Because who you really are *is more than this life*, and your identity as defined by all these things, is *only your identity "in this life".* Think about it this way. Your name does not tell anything about the real you, the spiritual you. It only gives a name to your face. *Who you really are is what is inside and even more it is about the spiritual you, the part of you that is all of what you think, believe, and what motivates you.*

Let me share my story first so that maybe you will understand how important it is for you to see who you are. I am not going to tell you every detail because my point is to help you see how to tap into the real intuitive knowing of who you are. I have always had a deep love for everyone and I was always able to see the future of someone's life and help him or her on his or her journey by my own caring ways. To see the future in anyone or even in the world is a gift but *any gift should be used wisely.* When I met someone or just knew them, I could see into their soul and know who they were and what they came to do in life. I didn't have the ability to see every detail of their future but I saw the potential. I never really understood why I saw what I saw and didn't identify with being able to see the future until 10 years ago. But through out my life *I always knew what someone needed before they needed it* and I provided it for them before they even knew their need. It was as if my soul connected through a greater oneness with them. The problem I would encounter was with people that were somewhat resistant to the spiritual plan they came with. In other words I would do something for someone before they even knew they needed it and they would turn on me. I had a lot of people thru the years either love me or hate me. Yet I kept loving them no matter what and this just made them madder. It wasn't because I wanted them to be mad that I kept giving but it was because I kept believing in them, when they didn't even know themselves. But they treated me different because of my light I gave off. I stood for the light of God and they didn't like the light. Everyone is on there own journey and so to protect myself from the pain of rejection, I just helped them and didn't expect anything in return. I kept being who I was and kept my light and my love flowing thru my being but *something in me didn't understand what was happening.* Sometimes I just felt so alone and so hurt. I actually had given up on my life and really didn't care anymore of living. It wasn't like I wanted to end it but I just *didn't want to live it* anymore. One day I came in contact with a friend and that day I changed into a determined effort to find out who I was. And so it did hurt when people rejected my love and it caused me to wonder, "Who I Was?" It wasn't like any situation would explain their behavior but it seemed that people were very resistant to my light and love. As years past I realized who I was and that I was a spiritual being with a God Flame that I came to bring. I came to bring light and love and it was resisted by those that I had chosen to accompany me in my journey. We all set out on a path and sometimes by the choices we make, like religion, we walk with certain people. I had chosen a religion that was very strict. But ***I was supposed to be in that religion for that period of time.*** When I finally left it, the people seemed to express the same thing. We miss your smile, your laughter and your love for us. They missed my light and my genuine love. The minister told them they had to separate from me because it was said I was lost and going to hell *"according to the doctrine"* they believed. But the truth is ***my life intersected with theirs for a time and a reason.*** All of our journeys are different in detail but the overall reason for why we go through what we go thru is the same. ***We are all Spiritual Beings with a divine plan that will bring us optimal growth in this lifetime.*** Our lives intersect with others for a chance to grow. Each has his or her own lesson plan and so we cannot force anything on anyone. My gifts that I came with, the ability to see the future, ***would be to give people the hope that what they are currently going through won't last*** and so much beauty is waiting if they keep faithful in staying true to finding their greater purpose in life. I also had a gift of seeing the spiritual being someone is in the higher realm. This explained why, even when they hurt me, I loved them. I loved them, and ***I saw who they really were*** and not who their earthly identity had defined them as. I saw their potential and their purpose but how could I tell them that? So I just loved them and tried to help them. Many would mock or hurt me but it didn't change what I saw and the possibilities their lives could manifest if they only knew the truth. I never gave up hope but sometimes the pain and struggle they created toward me, caused me to just walk away in peace. ***Here is good example of how a spiritual being on earth has gifts but they can't reveal what they know because people would be driven farther from them.*** In my heart I knew I had to just remain silent but I would give all my love to help them possibly wake up and know who they were. If my love never woke them up, then there was nothing more I could do. Jesus had many spiritual gifts but simply kept them inside. However, He loved and gave what he could and hoped it would help awaken them.

It's not about being perfect or doing everything right but ***it's about hearing the voice within***, the intuitive voice of what is within, and allowing it to guide you. Learning that you have everything you need inside, and beginning to hear the inner voice as if it links you to your divine plan, ***is your greatest teacher.*** Whoever you are, and whatever gifts you have, use them wisely and ***lovingly*** to help others accomplish their divine plan. There are people that will read this book or books like it, gain access to the power of their lives and then use it for their own gain in life. ***They will have their season but they cannot last.***

~Living for selfish desires runs a course and then you are left further away from who you are. ~

You become your own worst enemy. You may have your abundance ***because you took it by force***, but it won't last long. ***The truth is that what you do to others will be done to you.*** If you send out selfish motives and desires into the cosmic mirror and ***you try to take abundance by force***, it will be returned unto you ***in the same way***. What you took from others will be taken from you not because those you hurt will do it in vengeance but because it's the law of the Universe. It is a Law God set in motion to guide us and to keep us in the quest of finding our purpose.

~Our own actions become our teacher.~

If someone does return unto you what you wrongfully did to them, in an attempt for vengeance then they will also have karma return to them. ***It is in your best interest on the path of finding out who you are to live honestly and with love for others so that you do not create more to deal with along the way.*** I have found who I am and I am another spiritual being, ***just like you*** but I have such a sense of joy ***in knowing the plan of my life*** and the ability I have to help others and myself. My name isn't important and the gifts I have are ***given to me*** to help others but ***not because*** I am anymore special than you.

~Who you are is the most important bit of knowledge you can obtain at this point.~

Once you know who you are, **you will give who you are back to God** so that you can fulfill your divine plan. What you sent out you will receive back in abundance. **This is the power of your identity.**

I hope that I can help YOU find the real you inside. Think of yourself right now, on a journey. You have come to this earth in an effort to heal brokenness from past lives, to overcome struggles of the past and to help you, as a spiritual being, **reconnect and go beyond what you were when you first arrived.** You are on a journey and the experiences that you have encountered in this life are lessons to learn by. When you learn the lesson, you move into new lessons. Your life is ultimately set up by you and your spiritual teacher to accomplish what will enable you to become MORE of who you currently are right now in the spiritual sense.

Think of it as school, or college, if you want. **Who you are is a SPIRITUAL BEING who has come to earth in an effort to be challenged** and in those challenges you have the potential to grow. **The growth comes when confronting the struggles and taking active control over the solution, not by force but by learning what it is you need to learn and allowing the circumstances to make you a better person.**

Active control over your life doesn't mean you interfere with the lives of others. People that take from others whether it is money or privacy are actually people that have taken another road **farther away from where they need to be. You don't serve yourself any good in harming the lives of others.** In all actuality you take away enormous freedom **from yourself and you make another road for yourself in which you must go down** and oftentimes it is hard to find your way back. I will not walk softly on this matter!

~Anyone who thinks in order to take control over their own life, they must harm others or be a force to take what they want, has a lot to learn.~

They need to learn you reap what you sow, and when you hurt others, you fling so many obstacles at yourself and in turn **the harm is more to you**. Is that what you want? Wasn't your intention to have a better life but in taking from others you have a worse life? ***Do you think for one minute that God gave man free will, so that he could freely harm others and themselves?*** Well, God gave you free will so that if you choose to betray trust from another, intentionally set up harm for innocent people all for monetary gain, then you can do that. ***But what you reap will be something that will take you down a road in which your difficulties in life will multiply.*** The results of your choices **are your fault** and no one else. You make wrong choices and you must feel them return to you. It takes you down a road of lower consciousness in which you put your mind in a thinking pattern **that is centered on your self.** You were **not** created to be self-centered **but you have every right to choose this road**. As I said, **it's your choice**. But let's say you betrayed the loving trust of someone that offered you an opportunity to grow in a profession. Let's say that you saw a profit in doing something and you tried to take abundance for yourself but this act betrayed them. You not only have to overcome this horrible act but you also have to set your mind on a higher understanding.

"You have to rise above the action that brought you there but you also need to rise above that mindset."

Abundant life **isn't** in taking what you want and it isn't in hurting those that put their trust in you because you saw a way to profit from them. Abundant life comes from an honest, loving soul who is trying to not only grow in their own life but also become more of who they are now and help others become more. It is a connected journey in which your life intersects with others and all can grow from it. You'd be surprised if you really saw how much you would gain if you did something in love and never betrayed someone's trust in you. *The abundance that would return to you in doing right and staying true to your promises will be greater than anything you receive by taking it by force.*

So as I said many people have simply forgotten their spiritual origin and that loss of memory is the only real problem on planet earth.

"If you knew who you were and understood how important you are to God, you wouldn't waste a lifetime with things that only take you away from all God has promised."

If we are who we think we are and yet we don't have the full understanding of who we really are, *then who we think we are and who we really are will not be the same.* You are a spiritual being and you have come to this earth to experience life here so that *your spiritual growth can be increased.* Like I said you are a spiritual being and the purpose of finding out your true identity is to *reconnect to why you forgot* who you were and why you came to this earth.

When you came to earth, you came thru your parents, and this connects you to a country, a religion, a family tree, and with all this you begin to have certain beliefs. The beliefs you have can be a *mixture of all you have experienced* in this life. The bottom line is that, who man says your are, in this life isn't all of who you are spiritually. This is really critical in understanding your true identity. Your beliefs are often influenced by all of these things. You can be very independent and have totally rejected the beliefs of your family but somewhere deep inside they still have an influence in you. Take for example. Your family is strongly Jewish and the traditions they follow are woven in every aspect of your family and their approval of you. Let's say, you know you are Jewish but you don't feel obligated to follow their traditions and therefore you choose to do things differently. The family gives you a hard time, finds ways to belittle you and when circumstances arise they put you in a place of guilt. But you keep true to yourself and thru the process of time you make a statement by choices in your life, that you will be who you are.

It is very important to understand that you must stand up for your life and take control over your life. It's also important to understand that you respect others and their choices. But when I say somewhere deep inside they still have an influence over you, I want you to hear what I am referring to. The voices within our minds are often what we tell ourselves of what *we think* defines us. In an effort to overcome strong influences by family we justify why we do what we do. We might be strong in keeping true to our choices but we also tell ourselves self-defeating statements in our mind. For instance we might say, "I won't let anyone control me as they have controlled me in the past", "I am sick of them telling me how to live my life", "Who are they to tell me how to live", "I can do what I want and they have no control over me". All of these statements *may be the strength you lean on in your "assurance" of your choices.* You will notice that they are statements **of a fight to justify your rights**.

~The attitude behind the statements you make have as much importance as the statement themselves.~

So if you take back your "right", in defiance, you will have to also deal with the *defiance in your heart. This is where the power of change is based on the heart.*

~The heart is the key to the kingdom of God.~

The heart is what saves us or doesn't save us.

"Why we do what we do is what has the power."

In other words the action appears to have power as an *outward show* but what is inside defines why you do what you do and *that is what defines the real power of your being.* So what I am trying to explain is that taking control of your life is setting boundaries and seeing that those boundaries **are your conscious decision** and can in fact enable you to become who you really are "spiritually".

Setting boundaries *in defiance* won't reap a heart of love and understanding and therefore won't really have much ability to further your growth in a healthy way. *Unconditional love includes love for yourself and love for your family even if they don't agree and that is when you open a door that can change your life and help others change their lives.* Doing things with a loving heart and knowing that this love begins *with loving yourself* is what has the potential to change your world.

I am not talking about forcing change when I say BE THE CHANGE. I am talking about *truly being a loving force* of unconditional love for all people, with respect for their own ideas and thru that the changes *you make* will begin to help others in their lives.

~An attitude of gratitude but a voice of independence is what will literally change your life into a life of abundance.~

The foundation with which you need to build your sense of identity is *based on you truly loving yourself unconditionally.* When you step back and look at the path you have walked remember that Rome wasn't built in a day and all that we need to learn doesn't come quickly. It is through trial and error, times of loss, times of victory and when you look at life from a distant shore, you realize how quickly time passes and *you see that you really did do what you could with what understanding you had at the time.* If we knew better we would do better. *But knowing better often comes from the trials of life.* Like I said life is a journey and we are learning as we are walking. It is my hope that as you continue reading you will continue growing. Jesus said in your patience, posses ye your soul but never let your patience become indulgence or procrastination. Simply understand that in learning things, it takes time and while you are learning, you are still trying to really understand the "whole picture".

When living in this world we often take on an inner desire to have what we want right now. We find that in our desperation and in the pain we feel of loss, we want everything now and if it doesn't come soon we will hit the road and find it in another place or even worse we try to take what we want by force. This is why you need to make up your mind and remember that you have lived this way for so long and now in your quest to truly find happiness and fulfillment you must adhere to the fact that *it's going to take some time*. You must stick to this even if you feel anxious enough to take things by force. During this time you can easily go back and forth from understanding to not understanding. This happens because your mind is *adjusting* to a new level of understanding. Your mind is taking in new things and *sometimes when the teachings are overwhelming it takes time to adjust*. You will adjust and each time you will find that you are able to understand even more things that in turn raises your level of understanding. *Just love yourself and know that you are going to learn the truth about the importance of your special life on earth, in due time*.

Believe you will find the truth and then watch the pages unfold as a new chapter begins to awaken you to your purpose. If you have read up to this point and are eager to learn more, you need to understand that thru your acceptance you are accepting that you do have a specific place at this time on planet earth that can bring more of God's kingdom to earth. That acceptance is a message from within that can encourage you to take the next step.

"God's victory is nothing more and nothing less than your acceptance of your divine identity."

Accept who you are as important in God's eyes and begin the journey.

One very important part of life on earth is death. I feel in understanding what death really is it will help you eliminate some of the fears you carry with you in living. When you don't understand what "death" really is you never can live because you are always in a fear state to some degree. Even if you appear to be well adjusted and adventurous you still might have internal fears that don't allow you to really live. I'm not talking about someone who respects cautious living but I am talking about *an internal fear of the unknown*. What do you think about when you see a loved one in a casket? Do you wonder where they are? Death is movement from one realm to another. *Death is not death but a change in how your presence is manifested.* Your inner soul simply moves from the body it was given in *this lifetime* to another realm, the spiritual realm that has many levels. Death is simply the end of this current embodiment and can open a door for a new chance of another embodiment. This is a choice made by the soul and whether it wants to engage in more growth. Don't fear death for in all actuality it is a relief for many to be done with this life and move on to another.

In understanding who you are you need to address the relationships you encounter in this life, *as tools to learn by*. As a friend, who is a doctor, once said, *look at it for what it is and don't read into it and don't make it into more than it really is.* We learn that in a lifetime we take on many misconceptions about ourselves and the problems we encounter through the experiences we go through. When I say this, it's important to not immediately blame those you interacted with, and *don't blame yourself as the total cause.* I am not saying, don't take responsibility but I am saying don't begin self-talk to yourself of failure or how you did this wrong or that. *This kind of self-talk only strengthens a deep belief in you of feeling unworthy and not in control of your life.* So don't start that, either. This is where bringing up problems can lead to more problems. This is where professionals who are to guide you and help you overcome what you are dealing with, *can only do so much in your healing.* They get you to open up and then it opens a can of worms. This is only helpful when you take hold of your life and get past it. *But if it adds more fuel to the fires you deal with already, then your problems become greater.* That is not all bad, because sometimes we have to stir up the pot *in order to get to all the ingredients that created the problem.* But what you do with what you know becomes either a strength or a weakness. *Instead of moving away from all that hinders you, you enhance the problem and it becomes a bonfire.* The same doctor made a statement to me once when he knew, that I allow myself to take struggles and take blame and then wander down "another road" I have to deal with, and he simply said

"Don't go there, we love you and don't want to loose you." What he is saying is don't wander off the path of your potential to heal. This statement simply says, look at the problem for **what it is**, **don't add more fuel to the fire**, but just look at it, grow in understanding and move on. The solution to the problem is found when you change what you can in yourself and leave the rest. Build on the qualities that help you become more and if you need to fix things that hinder the Whole, then fix them. Fix them or leave them, whichever is most suitable **but don't dwell on them**.

~Dwelling in one place too long will cause you to sink and loose sight of the greater picture.~

Find what you can learn, and move on. Don't try to change others. Don't emotionally think about it any more. Look around and see the rest of your life and focus on the beauty, not the problems.

~The problems can only teach you when you learn the lesson and MOVE ON.~

We add more problems to our plate by our interpretation and our ways we have incorporated in our thinking and in turn we create more of life's struggles. The way a man thinks can help a woman regain balance to her life and visa versa. Many women get frustrated with the "cut and dry" ways a man has in dealing with a problem. But I believe that God made it this way so that "each of our extremes" in doing things can help us return to balance. The way a woman does something is one extreme and the way a man does something is another extreme, **if you want to look at it that way.** What I see is a beauty that can only be attained by each of us embracing our differences, not fighting to make the other the way we are, and **creating a balanced union. This is how all things work on earth,** through a balanced union. Men and Women and their differences are "not" to create a war but are to create a beautiful understanding that God has presented to us in our relationships and is an answer to all our problems on planet earth. A man does this very thing. He looks at it in simple terms, he looks over the ways to solve it, and he offers a solution. ***The answer is in bringing "balance" in all scenarios.*** Let's take an example. A woman gets mad, because she wants to talk about it but her talking is ***only*** good for her if she can lay it aside and see the solution. However, many times it never gets laid aside, ***it is a broken record,*** and it only becomes one more brick on the wall she is building to present a case in which she wants to resurrect a picture of her troubles. Men empathize but want to move on to better things. ***This is where the combination is a perfect fit when they understand the need for balance.*** Each side of God, the masculine and the feminine are a balanced union by bringing out the best in each. I don't have all the solutions but being a woman and really watching myself go thru some of these things and trying to understand what the real problems is, I am learning that because women have been asked take on roles that are not normally theirs they have become angry and have lost the nurturing side of them. We can't change the world and what we need to do to live in it, but ***we can go within and regain the love and compassion we, as women, have thrived on since our creation.***

Lay the cards on the table and look at everything from a non-attached perspective. Step out of the "picture" and look at it from a non-emotional state of mind. The experiences that we encounter are what can teach us. What determines what we need to learn is the "pattern of our thinking" in our reaction to every experience.

> ***"So if you keep having the same feelings come up in your mind when something goes wrong, this is like an arrow pointing out something you must get past."***

When the same things keep happening as a result of relationships, it's because there is something that needs to be understood and "removed" or "transcended" from how "you" see it. To transcend something you must see your feelings as real and validate them to yourself how you might feel this way, ***but transcend by going beyond what you see and***

189

using the experience and the emotions that follow to see the deeper meaning behind it. To transcend means to grow and to go beyond your limited understanding and know this has a key in the beginning of your healing. This is where you and you alone hold the key to a better life. *No spouse, no doctor, and no friend can change the way you feel about something.* They can try but you and you alone hold the power to change how you see things and what you feel inside. *How "you" see things isn't to condemn you further but to help you transcend to a better view of your life.* The reason you see things a certain way is because something in your being, you cannot heal from, hinders your growth. And so, how you see things is the first part of how you can find a way to begin your healing.

Through the years I have watched the differences of men and women and how these differences are a perfect fit but the reason they often start out good and soon fail is because *they see their way is the only way* to see something. Again this is the ego. This is where balance must enter into the equation. *God never wanted us to see one way as the only way in anything* and so do you think he wanted this in the relationship between men and women. Absolutely not. Men are independent by nature. Men are much more simplistic in living in the NOW. They don't dwell on things like women do and they don't go into the deeper reasons of things. *It's just not them. Simple as that.* It *doesn't* mean they are shallow and it *doesn't* mean they are heartless; it's just the way they are made. It doesn't mean they don't care or they don't love you, it's just their nature. Don't add more to it and don't begin to add more to the story. *They care in different ways than women care, but it's the same caring and the same effort to show it.* But women are conditioned to be the "pleasers" in a relationship. But in reality, men also see themselves as the "pleasers" in a relationship. They want desperately to make you happy. This is their makeup. When a man's efforts to please you, fails, they try with something else until they realize nothing pleases you. Women want to feel their man cares but oftentimes what a man does *as a wholehearted effort to show he cares*, fails thru a women's eyes and then they women say they don't care. Through years women's roles have gone from being strong at home to becoming sole providers and taking on the role of men. They have appeared to be very strong in the view of the world. Many are very strong. ***But there is a part of the "female" that remains female.*** So if a woman is asked to be strong and hold the position of a man as the provider and as both parents and still give the children the feminine nurturing, she can do this because women easily wear many hats. But if she finds a man that can help her, she will return to the natural state of being taken care of by the man. However, in returning to that natural state, she might in fact regress for a time into a needy state and this is because she has lost her identity as a woman. She was asked to live the role of a man and when she returns to the role God gave her as the woman, she is confused. This is because the roles of men and women are so mixed up and ***often require each of us to loose who we are so we can make the best of our world.*** The key is to return to balance. This is where a man can help her return to feeling it's OK to feel these things and he can give her what she needs to feel fulfilled. When a man gives his love to help her heal, ***she needs to allow him to "feel he has helped her".*** I call this the breathing in and out of the masculine and feminine sides of God. This breathing in and out, like we naturally breathe in our body, is what creates wholeness, healing, and balance. The key to healing is found in understanding the problems, but the real healing comes when we allow our partner to help us and ***feel like we have moved on, transcended and now have a future of greater blessing.*** This is why letting go of the past, letting it truly die, must be done.

~Only when your story changes, does your life change.~

When you remember what you are as female and male and what makes you the beautiful person you are, you also have the ability to return to the real you.

Another point I want to bring up is this of self-help ideas. There is nothing wrong with them. I have specifically found myself trying to fix relationships just like you might have. I am older and have grown by being an observer of my own struggles. There are a lot of wonderful books that narrow in on specifics in fixing relationships. They often give you rules to abide by or things to do. Nothing is wrong with this but *if you stick closely to their rules then you take away your own creativity and you hinder your growth by just following those rules.* You set yourself up to just be a follower. The truth is you are a co-creator of God. You have the ability to do great things but if you set yourself up as a follower, *you disable your greater potential.* And if you deviate from their rules after you have tried to follow them and then you find failure in your relationship again, you feel another sense of failure. Take ideas as just that, and then don't be so strict as to follow them to a "T" but use those ideas they present as a guide. *The important thing is that you keep in mind to not loose your sense of independence, or your sense of identity.* This is critical. This is why any good solution can be ok for some, but for others create more problems. The problems they create are that you loose your sense of who you are as an individual spiritual being that has the ability to co-create with God. This is where teachers can hurt the student.

~A true teacher gives you ideas but wants you to exercise your own creativity and think for yourself.~

Teachers or ideas can set you in a pattern of understanding the ideas behind them but you must creatively adapt the solution by really understanding the problems you deal with and *be willing to find your own solution.* The reason that this is so critical is because if you stick to a certain belief system or set of rules as the only solution, you lock yourself into this and *get quickly lost when it doesn't work.* When you get lost again, and begin to feel like this doesn't work either, you take on the feeling of failure again and hopelessness is returned to you. In all actuality you are not back at "square one" but actually because you now have lost confidence that your life will ever change, *you are even further back.* Use author's ideas, teacher's philosophies, doctor's suggestions and courses you might take as *"tools" to grow with.* Understand that no "one" solution fixes all problems. Be willing *to not put so much into one way of doing things but be flexible to new ideas* as you utilize the tools they give you. Like they say, Don't put all your eggs in one basket. Keep in mind there are other tools in the toolbox *that you might not see right now* but *in order to see them you must believe they are there* and not put all your trust in the tools you are working with right now. Many times I say, that there is more to your story than what you currently see and that is because *our vision is based on our understanding right now.* But as you walk the walk, you begin to understand more and in turn you begin to see more of who you are and the beauty of your life. If you are going to really see who you are then you need to be willing to take the first step and begin the journey. Be willing to take the tools given to you but keep in mind that because God wants you to know change is inevitable and nothing stays the same, you must remember that one solution might not fix your problem *but it might help you see how something else can help. All steps lead to another step and so on the path of life remember there is always another step that you can count on being there when it seems you have come to a dead end.* Open your mind to possibilities by not locking yourself into one way of doing something. Be flexible, accept new ideas, and learn to think for yourself. *Challenging situations in your life are there because you need to see you are more than just finding a solution to "this" problem.* Maybe the problem is given only to help you with a greater problem you believe about yourself. The greater problem might simply be that you have lost your belief in your ability to take control of your life and when you take back control, the problems that plagued you are quickly resolved. If change is inevitable and if God wants you to always believe there is more to learn and grow from, *then one way of doing something can never be suitable for all situations.* Be flexible and keep an open mind. You may know that on paper something looks like it will work but if applied to your situation it may not be the answer, then don't set yourself up for failure. When new ideas come, when suggestions are presented, keep in mind that you can try them but *if they don't work, then it is in your hands to believe there are other solutions.* When we deal with problems in life, we need to be flexible in knowing that *in our journey to find the solution* we can learn valuable things totally off that subject, about ourselves. In the journey of self-discovery we set out in the beginning with specific goals and with questions to answer but in the journey we find many valuable encounters of things *we never considered to be something we needed to find. But those things are added blessings, like the icing on the cake. The greatest part is that we find the journey was far greater in revelation than when we arrived at the destination.*

All of those who present ideas to us as solutions to our problems have the potential to get you to a better understanding of your life. Some people use religion to guide them in fixing their problems. Religion is not all bad. It can help you re-establish a *platform* where you can find yourself at a new beginning point. But religion often has a tendency to make you believe, again, that this is the only way. You are in charge of your healing. This is where you can go through a lifetime of counseling and not get too far. You must take control of the wheel, and when I say this, I mean you are in the drivers seat and only you can heal yourself. *The doctors you go to can only help you if you are willing to take control.* This is why many people who go to counselors or doctors, and see minimal progress, give up and stop going. The truth is that the reason there is minimal progress is because *you haven't understood how much control you have over your own healing.* You can only see change in your life when you are willing to make the change. No doctor can do anything for you unless you do it for yourself. Many times the professionals *are incredible at what they do* but people can't heal because they feel the professional should heal them and because of this belief alone they often get in deeper when a new problem arises. They are convinced that in paying for help, this doctor will help them and fix them and their life. *No one can fix you, but yourself. Doctors are there to guide you and assist you in how you change your own life.* You must understand *they are there to assist you in your healing.* Their greatest reward is to see you grow and heal. So if it is self-help books, or a class, or a counselor or doctor, or a religious belief that you rely on, keep in mind that all of these tools are to help you get in touch with what is within you or the real you. They are "tools" to help but not to lock you into some pattern of doing something.

To summarize how relationships are critical in helping you find the real you. I want to leave you with the understanding that relationships and our struggles with them exist because there is something we lack that holds us back from seeing the beautiful person we really are.

~Any struggle in life is not to take you down, is not to cause you to give up, but any struggle is like a new door that swung open, that has something to teach you about you.~

It's not all-bad stuff but in all actuality when difficult struggles emerge they are giving you a chance to see yourself and to see how much God loves you and how much he wants you to rise above something. **They are opportunities in disguise**. They may appear in dark clothing, they may be surrounded by difficult obstacles but with all the help out there today, and all the encouragement in our world through so much available, we have more than ever, a chance to grow and become more than what we currently see of ourselves. The truth is that we now live in an age that is unlike any age ever before in the history of earth. Our conscious level of understanding is so incredibly open, that we literally can change our world by simply changing ourselves. Don't see struggles as a door shut, with no way out.

~See struggles as a door swung open in which something wonderful is waiting to emerge once you see you must take back the control over your mind and your life.~

Don't let struggles cause you to tell yourself negative lies but let the same struggles, remind you that God has just presented a new challenge **so you can become MORE of who you currently are right now**.

In order to change anything you must first be willing to **detach from your so called reality** and this detaching is only an "avenue" that can give you opportunity to stop making life so hard on yourself and begin to grow.

~Detaching isn't intended to loose who you are on this earth right now. It is about finding the real you.~

Sometimes in life we have to let go of what has defined us in the past or gives identity to who we appear to be on this earth. Are you open to the possibility that there is a better way to live? Are you willing to detach from things that have kept you from understanding life in a higher way? Jesus said that He came that we might have life and more abundantly and this has never changed. What has changed is how we believe this can really be our reality. ***What has changed is that we have lost the inner knowing that we do have a purpose*** and the reality is we can re-attach to all that we are in God's eyes. My hope is that you will walk with me and maybe thru this walk ***you will see for yourself*** that life doesn't have to be dominated by suffering and human limitations that come as a result of how we see ourselves and what we choose in life to be the path we walk. I hope that you can see the power of your choices and how you can make different and therefore better choices. What is your goal in life? If it is to gain thru wealth and status and attain an earthly treasure here, then you will continue to live as you have in the past until you decide that there is more to life on earth than these things. But if you are ready to see differently that life is more than what you attain here on a temporary basis then you are ready to know the secret to life on earth. Wherever you are in your understanding I hope that you will take my hand and walk for a while. ***I want you to know that it is possible for anyone to rise above the human life we live and attain the spirituality of abundant life while still alive on earth.***

So how is, ***"Who you think you are"*** so separated from ***"who God knows you are"***? Keep in mind that it is ***your own doubts,*** about who you are that divided you against who you really are. It is your interpretation of who you are and it is your belief that has formulated an illusion that this is "the real you" that has separated you from the reality. Remember in mathematics that 1 x 1 is always one. You are one with God and ***you cannot ever be separate no matter how many times you multiply it.*** The same goes with who you are spiritually. You are one with the living God who lives and loves abundantly. No matter how many times you divide your beliefs and interpret your separation from God, you will always remain one with God. ***The truth is that you***

have never lost any of God's presence within you, no matter what you have done on this earth. You never lost any of the spiritual plan you came to this earth to fulfill.

⁓*It's never too late to begin again.*⁓

Nothing is lost and you have everything to gain when you find out who you really are. The only thing that has changed *is your belief that you hold in your mind* of who you are and that belief has divided you into two parts or in many cases you have allowed so many divisions within that you simply have allowed yourself enormous confusion. Oneness with God is the only way to abundant life and so in order to truly find happiness and abundant life you must return within, to this oneness *that is and always has been available to you.* A house divided against itself simply cannot stand and *the enemies that are the greatest are in your household.* Keep in mind that your house is your mind. So, one of the keys to eliminating the separation you have of who you think you are and who you really are is found in changing your beliefs within your mind and coming to an inner realization that you are a spiritual being that has a plan from God to manifest God's kingdom on this earth. Another very important gift God gave all humans was the ability to use something that would help them grow freely as a human being, and ultimately a spiritual being that could eventually help God with the ability to co-create. This is called *"Free Will"*. Free will has the ability for you to create your life experience as you see that you want it. With Free Will you can create something that has little use to the original plan you came with. With free will you can actually create an inner perception of yourself that can easily be somewhat out of touch with the reality of all the God given talents he gave you. In other words Free Will given to all human beings can help you ultimately be a co-creator with God and bring the kingdom of God to earth or *it can totally destroy all you can potentially be if you keep making choices based on the belief that the experience on earth and all you can gain for yourself, all you can control to come into being is all that is important to life.* God wants you to choose and when you choose to live solely for this life God still wants you to exercise free will. God is a God of love and mercy and he knows that your choices ultimately bring empowerment to you and this is very important to God.

You see God truly desires that all humans use the gifts they are given, and become independent co-creators. ***God is not a God of anger, revenge and punishment as the religions of the world have defined him. He is quite the opposite.*** He encourages you to love unconditionally all people and each one that has come thru the ages has given the same consistent message. Why do humans insist that God is anything other than this love that his servants have purposely emphasized in their lives? What God would be so two faced and send his servants to present one message and then be so different in how he feels? Oneness is straight across the board and God has consistently brought the same message to this earth all these years.

So back to free will and your ability to create anything you want to be in your life. This can be a dangerous freedom but God has faith that you will use it and learn from it as you walk thru life. So if you use free will to create a world of gain for you and in turn you hurt so many, then God has given you the permission to do as you wish. Even though it wasn't what God intended you to do with free will, it is still important because it allows you to exercise this skill and ***eventually understand the importance of exercising free choices.*** But you may ask why God would give permission to hurt others. God doesn't want anyone hurt but when humans understand that their own works and the reason behind those works are what is responsible for pain and suffering on this earth, then they will see that they are part of a oneness, part of the "whole" and when you hurt another, you hurt yourself. Karma, or you reap what you sow is critical in understanding. This is another of God's laws he laid out to help us desire to know who we really are and why are we here. Karma only punishes to save us. God gave us this law so we wouldn't self-destruct and ***we would pay attention*** to how our choices are affecting others and us. With these two laws, Free Will, and Karma, ***we can exercise the ability to become independent and yet be able to mature and see the bigger picture.*** We ultimately need to have a perception of ourselves in alignment with God. You notice I am not saying *exactly as God wants us* to be, *but in alignment*. God doesn't want a bunch of clones or robots but wants you to think "on your own" so you can eventually add to the whole of mankind. God wants you to use the part of Him *within you* to become an individual co-creator with Him so that when you connect to this spiritual being you really are, you will bring more of the Kingdom of God to earth. With free will you have the freedom to create your own worldview and your own sense of identity. So many people often struggling in life whether financially or health wise or even just being alone feel they are created a certain way or are victims of a particular condition or circumstances. In other words they believe that how they feel inside or where they live or how they live, *is a result of factors beyond their control, and it was forced upon them from without*, and now their only option is to live with it or to some people they take it by force to create a better life and hurt people along the way. The is a lie and one of the most dangerous lies found on planet earth.

~The lie is that human beings are victims of forces beyond their control instead of authors of their own destiny.~

If you choose to believe this about anything in your life, then you set yourself up to remain a victim and *you simply cannot grow spiritually as long as you see yourself as a victim.* You can only grow by recognizing that you do have the power to change your situation and the recognition can only come when you accept *that your situation is the result of your soul's past choices. Only by accepting this do you become empowered to change your situation.* In knowing that the power of choice is in your hands in making better choices in the future is the key to resolving the false beliefs and psychological wounds that caused you to make limiting choices in the past. My hope is that you let go of this and really find the ability to use the free will God wants you to use. *With free will you can easily create an illusion that God is separate from you and the world as a whole.* Please understand that when God gave you freedoms, He knew that you might wander off the track of what is real but *its only temporary and you can return* by connecting to the God within your being. For now please understand that any illusion exists only inside your mind and it will continue to exist as long as you allow it. All of the problems on earth are simply due to the fact that humans have forgotten their true identity. To begin to change the illusions and see the reality you must first accept that you are a spiritual being *"first and foremost"* and you are having an earthly experience right now.

Another awareness you need to take into account is this *"knowing"* that is deep inside of you. What I mean, is a realization in which you have a *"hitting the ground experience"* where you realize that something in your understanding *isn't quite right*. You also realize that there is so much more to your identity and what you are capable of doing in life. So there is both a feeling of something more and *a feeling that you have been doing things in a way that isn't so beneficial to the overall possibilities of your life.* How *you respond* to this experience can either bring wholeness to your being or a division in your being. Your ultimate goal is to eventually bring balance to your understanding and in turn you will heal your own heart. But you may ask how can I bring the balance I need to make my life easier than it has been?

~Balance is made thru understanding what factors in life have created imbalance.~

Anytime we are open to an understanding that changes how we have seen things in the past, *we are also opening a beautiful passageway where new growth can accelerate and our understanding of many things opens up.* So the beginning of walking a new path that can bring balance to your life comes as you begin to *open up your heart and your mind* and remember to not fear when it feels that all you have once believed no longer seems real and true. *Not everything in your life and the way you have done things has to be tossed aside. But when an awakening occurs we often respond to it in extremes.* In other words we think in our mind that it is all bad or all good but what I ask you to try and do from this point forward is to find a happy medium. *Life is not about extremes but about bringing balance and when we bring balance we eliminate the emotional feelings of desperation and fear that go along with thinking that all you have done is so wrong.* As growth will sometimes cause pain it is important to remember that little saying, *"No Pain, No Gain."* To remember that saying helps you to know that pain is to bring something to your attention so that you can re-look at it and see things differently and when you allow this you have said you are willing to re-look at your life and sift thru what is unnecessary and add the things that can bring you into balance. *It is a challenge that comes to you by the need for you to move past something that is hindering your growth.* All of us have a journey to take. In that journey we are challenged with various obstacles that have the power to help us see more of the purpose of our lives. *Pain is not all bad and is only temporary.* Keep in mind when experiencing pain over situations you feel responsible for, that it only lasts for a very short time and there is a reward in understanding things, awaiting you.

Try to keep in mind that no matter how painful an experience is, that *there is a reason why you walked down that road* and why you feel the pain you do. *You needed to come full circle in understanding something that is critical to move past and when you understand and come to peace with yourself, only then can you grow.* Also keep in mind that the things you have struggled with are tools given specifically to you from someone in the Spiritual realm trying to help you grow. *These tools can help you go beyond your own current limitations in how you see life* and help you learn how you can see the bigger picture. The problems actually are to wake us up and help us see there is more to our life. Remember how it feels when you are in a deep sleep and you are at peace for that moment in time and someone comes into your room and shakes you awake. *Do you not feel angry or disturbed or even violated?* Weren't you at peace and now you have to wake up to the reality of life and the responsibilities waiting for you and doesn't that alone disturb you? Yes, it does and *it is hard sometimes to wake up and face life. But if you remain asleep to the problems waiting to be addressed by you and you alone, then even your sleep will change and you will find a time come when you no longer can sleep deep.*

Address problems by waking up to there reality can only bring more abundant life in the future and can help you find the greatest joy God has waiting for you. If only you could see something coming, if only you would have stopped smoking or drinking, if only you didn't do this or that. *The "if only's" are there after things went from bad to worse. But what if someone could wake you up to prevent you from ever saying, "if only".* Wisdom is available and a wise man responds to something before he goes down so many roads that he no longer can see how he can return to a peaceful life.

The beginning of being able to understand the truth of who you are is when you realize that no matter what mistakes you might have made in the past, no matter how life's circumstances have hurt you or caused you to struggle with and no matter what you have in the past believed that life was about, *it is entirely possible for you to rise above your limited belief and obtain a clear view of who you are as a spiritual being.*

~We are not defined by our circumstances~

You came from God and God put a part of Him in you. This is where the belief that God is somewhere else, is wrong. Through religion we are taught we have to find God and put Him in our lives, but God is already within us and we cannot loose Him even if we wanted to. God never leaves us alone. In other words we cannot loose God *but we can loose our ability to connect with God.* When we feel so alone and wonder where God is, it is simply because *we have closed the door on Him* and we no longer see that He is still inside waiting for us to come to Him. *God never went anywhere, for it is us and our beliefs that have changed* and they change because as we see circumstances in life become difficult we automatically think God left us. Each time you go thru this kind of experience where you feel God is not with you, you build a wall, *a brick at a time* and *when that wall becomes solid and impassible you can convince yourself you truly are alone.* You have built brick by brick a wall that you yourself have erected and it appears in all reality to you that you truly are alone and so it will take courage to admit that this is where you begin. To prevent this in the future, don't believe God is somewhere outside yourself, and don't believe you are unworthy of His help and His love because if you believe that, *then you are saying that God Himself is unworthy because God is already within you and you are a part of God.* If you have built a wall, then I encourage taking each brick down one by one, and *re-look at what made you put that brick up.* To get past this we must have faith that the difficulties in life are not to destroy us *but to teach us* and when we understand this, we know God will not leave us, but instead is ready to help us. The truth is *we just don't see the value in the difficulties* and therefore we start seeing things from an earthly point of view. When we see things this way we want to keep a sense of self worth no matter what and so in order to eliminate the pain of what we don't understand *we simply put up a wall so we don't have to look at it.* This wall is erected by us to help us survive and continue to live. It is not intentionally to get us off the correct path but *is a way in which we honestly believe will help us keep going in this world.* When enough walls are erected we become boxed in and in that box we use what is left in our belief system to reason ourselves out of any forthcoming problems. Many times we simply find ourselves so limited in what we can or cannot do and when this happens we simply stop growing. We become robots to our beliefs and whether we still have faith in our beliefs or not, we can't go too far in changing things. When these things take place, sometimes the only option is to break out of the box. But *this creates fear and a feeling that is so overwhelming in which we just don't know what to do.* Desperation, fear, loneliness, and even anger take hold and that is when we loose it. What do we loose? Well, it's different for all people but it can be anywhere from just not interested in life anymore to taking yours or others lives. As you look at why you do what you do, *have an understanding heart towards yourself in how you got to where you are today. Don't be so hard on yourself.* Remember we all can find ourselves in these kinds of situations and the most important part of understanding is having a love for yourself in which you believe *that you got into this and you will get out of it. Unconditional love for you is number one on the list of things to do.*

So when life's difficulties come flying at us *we automatically think we have done something wrong and this perspective is one of the many that hinders our ability to see things in a way that can help us grow and understand ourselves.* When you see something go wrong, and you blame yourself when it wasn't your fault you have created a lie to yourself and *that lie can grow.* Just like the lies we tell others and we find ourselves telling more lies to convince others of the first lie we told them. *The same goes with how you lie to yourself.* If you think taking all the blame on yourself is the answer to re-connecting to the real spiritual being you already are, then you will have to walk down that road until you are convinced otherwise. It is lies that have hurt our oneness on earth and only the truth of who we are and why we are here and our ability to be one with God will heal this world and bring abundant life to all people. When you automatically blame yourself when life gets very hard, you spend your whole time trying to reason, to rethink what you could have done. But what if you kept an open mind and when life dealt you blows so hard that they knocked you to your knees, *you asked yourself what you could learn from it.* The power of the "blow" would be gone. Be honest with yourself and to others and that is when understanding can take place. Sometimes life is hard not *because we have necessarily done something wrong but because there is something critical we have to learn before we can move to an even deeper understanding.* Life is much like a ladder where each step leads to the next step until we eventually reach the top.

I feel many of us also take deep responsibility and carry guilt with us for a lifetime over our children, our spouses, and our family in general. In order to not let the circumstances of our loved ones personally take us off our own road of growth we must first understand their real relationship to us. Take for instance our children. We become so responsible for them as we raise them and when something goes wrong or they have difficult times *we blame ourselves and many times we can't go on in life.* We feel that we have failed them or that our lives have hurt them. We feel an overwhelming responsibility to make things right for them. The truth is that your child is not *your* child. You do not have any ownership over the soul of your child. Your child is a completely separate individual, and as your child has an absolute God-given right to exercise free will according to his or her own understanding they will in turn reap the consequences of their choices. Your child was given to you from God and was brought to earth ***thru your being***. But your child is a child of God's. When you have a possessive attitude toward your child, you will seek to control their choices and you might even seek to prevent them from experiencing the consequences of their choices, which is ***their free will*** given to them by God. Just because God gave you this child to be put into your life at this given time in human history, you do not own this child. God asks you to raise them, protect them as seems necessary ***but also to give them the same freedoms God gave you to experience life.*** Our children and their wrongs in life ***are not to destroy our freedoms nor are they to diminish our own need to find our spiritual plan***. This is where understanding "who we are" is critical. We are all brothers and sisters, we are all God's children and we all have the ability to become co-creators of God. So as you look at your child try to understand the benefit of overcoming this kind of ownership of your child. ***Try to see that having a possessive love is not only damaging to their growth but also is very damaging to your own growth.*** As parents we want to protect our children but if your protection is actually not allowing them to learn and grow from their choices then you are only hurting them. ***You hurt yourself because you have this limited belief that you must control their lives*** and therefore this belief creates a lot fear, unhappiness and frustration in you. What you need to do is embrace the unconditional love of God and then you will not seek to control the child ***but you will then desire to educate and direct them.*** As a mother of 4 children, I found myself trying to teach my children the results of their choices early in life but sometimes it was awfully hard to see that their choices were going to be very difficult to face. All parents feel that in protecting their children they are loving them. Yes, they are loving them but it takes a greater love ***to allow someone to learn from their choices.*** I found that as I practiced allowing them to choose when it wasn't life threatening, I could also be there when they had to experience difficult times and guide them ***not only thru everything*** but also share with them my experiences and encourage them to learn what they need and then think about how they might choose differently next time. But if my fear was greater than my self-confidence that their freedom was good as long as it didn't endanger them, then I couldn't help them while they faced the consequences. *I realized that fear had to go first*. Roseanne Cash once said, *"The key to change ... is to let go of fear"*. When I let go of fear and saw the value in doing it different, I felt I could breath and as I experienced the times of their growth, I felt so thankful to God that His ways are so perfect. Never forget that we are born with unconditional love from God *but we learn FEAR while living here on earth.* You need to still remember that as a parent your responsibility is to protect them in the face of danger, when their decisions cannot be mature enough. *Every child must be protected to some degree from things that are dangerous*. God made it a pattern that babies would be given to adults to help them through the early stages of their lives. The same pattern is in the spiritual sense. *God knows that when we come to earth we need teachers to help us re-connect to the fact we are more than human beings.* God has put guides all along the way in life in many areas. Learning and understanding is critical in growing. God gave you your children to protect and to guide and in the early years of their lives allow them to make choices that won't threaten their safety. It's kinda like fishing; you let the fishing line out, then pull some in, let some more out and then pull in. Each time you let them make decisions, sometimes you might have to consult them for a moment and that is the "pulling in" and then when you see they understand, you let them go back out and try again. *This is a very beautiful way of teaching a child to gain confidence and prepare them for the decisions they will need to make in the future as adults.* So again I want to emphasize that *even though the children came thru you into life, they are individuals that came to become more of who they are.* You can guide them as much as you need to and care for them *the best you know how* at the time but you are only responsible for your own life and for your own choices. Not theirs. Never fall into the trap of attempting to make choices for them as they age, unless the choice puts their life in jeopardy or they can't make a decision. You can guide them, suggest to them, but ultimately *it is very critical to their growth that they choose on their own.* If all people would realize that 80 percent of the conflicts and problems we currently see on this planet could be resolved very quickly *because they truly spring from the belief we feel responsible for the choices of others, then this world could change so quickly.* The secret to who you are is very related to how you identify your responsibilities of others. *Stay away from feeling that you are responsibility for others and their happiness.*

When Buddha said that what we think we become, he simply was trying to convey that we have the power to connect to the God within us *but we first must see that in our mind.* What is important to understand is that you have the power in your own being to connect to all of what God has put "in you" from the beginning and the only way to connect is to see yourself as God sees you. We were created with God as a part of us. But why do we forget or loose sight of who we really are? We are uniquely different, and the exact reason that caused you to loose your connection to your source, namely God Himself, will be different from others. Let's look at a Family Tree as is often used in this world to obtain our genealogy. In the family tree that we as humans create for families, you are born into a certain position and you can never change that position. But in the Body of God, each self-conscious being, no matter where it originated, has the opportunity to rise through the different levels until it eventually reaches full God consciousness. Likewise, a self-conscious being can descend below the level of which it originated and be removed even further from the God consciousness. So you may ask what determines whether you rise higher or descend lower in the Body of God? The deciding factor is simply *"your sense of who you are"* or your sense of self, your self-awareness, or sense of identity. In this world we know that we are born into a certain family with a certain genealogy that can be traced back many generations. We know that our genes, and upbringing have affected who we are today or who we "see ourselves" as being. *But we must try to take into account that all of these ways of relating to who we think we are, don't really define us.* These factors have potentially no power over you unless you believe they do. For years I spent time searching my genealogy and had a great time finding some very influential people. One day I was sharing the names and stories with one of my children and he said, "Mom we are all related to everyone." "We are all God's children." I thought about that long and hard because he was right. What does it matter and how important are these findings if they only distract me from being the unique individual I am. If I believe that a certain relative and his life mission is my mission to, then I have taken away my free will to be who God has given me the potential to be. The plan of my life is going to be spinning around some long lost ancestor who also had a unique plan in his life.

> *~What I am saying is that we can't determine our life mission if we simply focus on someone else's life.~*

The words of wisdom came from my child and so never doubt who your children are as spiritual beings. *They have far more wisdom on the tip of their tongue than most of us have by the time we reach adulthood.* This is because *a child's spirit has a fresher memory of the spiritual being they are* and as we grow older, we loose more and more of our memory. At the same token, we can't find our life purpose and learn more of the spiritual being we are *if we focus on rescuing everyone around us or on feeling we are responsible for everyone's life.* And if we put so much emphasis on being related to this or that person then we need to make sure that *we are still willing to be the individual we have the potential to be.* We are individuals and we have the potential to take dominion over our individual self and change our sense of self *according to our "highest vision".* Keep in mind that our "highest vision" changes, as we grow to understand more and more thru the journey of self-discovery. That is why we always want to learn more because God is constantly striving to become more and we are a part of God and so we are also striving to become more. But "more" isn't according to earthly treasures to be obtained. "More" is more of spirituality and the ability to become one with The Father, as Jesus was. This is a part of the spiritual identity we all possess.

Recently I had a conversation with a man who is serving time in prison. He kept saying that everyone says he is just like his dad. His dad had a number of anger issues and drug problems and was in and out of prison much of his life. This young man even looks like his dad and his handwriting is like his dad's. So in a recent conversation I asked him to understand that no matter how similar his life seems to be like his dad's, ***he needs to break free of thinking*** he is just like him. I told him to see the similarities and then pass them off as just similarities. Take no more thought for what anyone says and keep telling yourself who you are and that you are a different and unique individual. I also explained to him that his life is on a journey that has the potential to bring him full circle to see his special mission in life. I wanted him to let go of the family tree and just be himself. ***Let go and let yourself be Y-O-U and no one else.*** Get out of your mind that you are a person that has a ***"predetermined destination"*** and you have no control over the outcome. Understand that the sense of self is changeable and it does depend on how you see yourself, how you imagine yourself to be and what you decide is real and is part of you. It all depends on the contents that you put into the container of self, or your mind. I am not saying to get an image of who you are and transform yourself into that image. What I am encouraging you to do is to find the real being inside of you, learn about who you are and become more of that person.

Let's look at an example of how we can loose our identity or our awareness of who we really are in the eyes of God. Take a white sheet of paper and imagine our Creator drawing a beautiful picture of your divine blueprint or purpose in this lifetime, on this white sheet of paper. This paper is what comes with you "internally" when you arrive on planet earth. As you come to earth you begin to experience life and as you begin to experience life you accept yourself as you see yourself on earth and many times it is a lower sense of your self. ***Lower in that it doesn't have the spiritual picture clearly reflecting.*** So as you begin the journey, you scribble on the paper with black ink, and ***those scribbles are experiences in your journey that distract you and begin taking you on a path farther from what the original picture God intended to go on.*** And if you keep doing this because you believe in yourself to a lesser degree than you really are, you will eventually reach a point where the scribbles cover not only your divine blueprint but also the white paper behind it. Eventually your awareness and the plan of your spiritual self has been covered over with a tangled web of black lines that no longer has a clearly defined picture. The blueprint you came with, as your spiritual mission *can never be lost* and so the black lines are not made with a permanent marker. For the truth is those black lines are drawn on a clear sheet of plastic that can simply be lifted off and reveal the untouched blueprint. I want you to understand that the fear we often have when making mistakes in our lives *is created in our minds* when we feel we have messed up so bad that we can't change the outcome of our future. As you understand that loosing who you are and the meaning behind the life you were meant to live, *is not permanent and can easily be recovered, then the fear of failure will no longer have power over your future.* Sometimes we must go down long and winding roads that seem so far from our destination. But these roads have the potential to teach you lessons you might never learn otherwise.

~Don't be hard on yourself if it takes awhile to get back on track.~

Simply understand that what you are going thru is important in your development of understanding who you are. Don't get frustrated and want to know everything right now. Be patient, love yourself, understand the journey can take some time and thank God for loving you enough to continually set you back on the right track. Life is a journey and in the journey *it is more than getting to the end. It is all about growing along the way* into the special individuals that God needs us to become. For our mission is not just about us but also about how we can raise God up and help the planet become one with God himself. With our love for ourselves and the understanding and patience we must have for ourselves we will set our feet on the right road to becoming one with God.

So, Who are you? In this world you are a human being with a physical body that is a product of the genes passed down in your family, and your upbringing is the product of the worldview and culture of your family and society. Yet you are still a unique individual and you can rise above your family background in many ways. The truth is you are a spiritual being having a human experience. You have complete freedom to rise above your current sense of identity and furthermore to rise above the sense of identity with which your individual being was born for. You can move past and rise even higher in your journey and this is why knowing that God is within you and God always wants to become more, also means you can become more. The very core of your spiritual being has a unique identity that sets you apart from others. But also God gave you imagination and free will so that *there is not a fixed plan* that cannot be changed as you experience life on earth. What I am trying to simply say is that God created you, a spiritual being, to come to this earth, to experience life and to improve life and become the force to help change our world for the good. You have the ability to evolve into more of what you were when you came. You have the freedom to become a son or daughter of God. This is where the power of your mind and who you think you are opens doors of possibility like never before. So if you see yourself as just a human being, who is suffering for no reason and who will live and die and be forgotten, with nothing to contribute to this earth, and that you have no power over your life, *then that is all you will be, at least in your mind.* If you see yourself as a mortal sinner, who is not worthy of God and His grace, and you deny you are a son or daughter of the living God then *your growth will be limited because you have shut off the source of life within your being.* That source is God within and knowing that God is within empowers you to take courage to use what is within to give God back what He has given you. Think of it this way. If your body becomes ill because your brain isn't functioning correctly, the body's lifespan will be shortened simply because the source of well being has been shut off. In the same token, if you choose to shut off the knowledge that there is a higher being within the human body of yours, namely the spiritual being that is housing God within, just shutting down the knowledge alone will shorten your life's ability to evolve and become all of what you have the potential to become. To reclaim the true identity with which you came into being, you can then build upon and become more than you were created to be, which is God's hope for you.

God created us to descend here so that we can use the Free Will He gave us to create a world that would live in peace and harmony. This was the plan from the beginning and has never changed. We are in the state we are in today because of our choices and *not as a punishment from God. Free Will doesn't mean we divide and conquer but what free will means is that we respect and understand our differences and come together to embrace the oneness of life.* Our differences are a result of free will and they will *help expand our understanding of life,* as well as helping us become one with God.

~When we understand others we open the door for them to understand us~.

As we deal with differences our first responsibility is to *"understand"* those we differ with. The power of understanding is revealed because in understanding another, we grow in wisdom knowing that our way of seeing things isn't the only way. *When we feel understood by another it is then we stop feeling the threat of our differences* and are open to love everyone for their differences and more important we are willing to change our way of seeing things because our hearts are open and love flows thru our being so that we want what's best for all. You see love is the power of healing the differences because when we feel understood, we feel a sense of oneness and the threats of our difference aren't threats. We begin to see that if we make wrong choices it not only affects others but ourselves as well. Our love for ourselves and for others becomes a power that helps us understand we are one people and we all need to look to what can help all of us. This opens our hearts. And when our hearts are open, God's love flows through us and to those we touch.

My message to you is not a new message but has been told many times by many people throughout the history of mankind. As you read try to reconnect to similar messages you have heard in music, in writings, in film, and even from other people you have encountered. Reconnecting is very important in your personal growth. When we reconnect it's almost like finding a missing piece of a puzzle. We find the piece that we once heard but kept in our memory. This memory stored information and you may not have thought much about it but your spiritual being, your soul, your I AM PRESENCE, retained that information because it unlocked a door for your own growth to manifest. Many have planted seeds along the way and as we gather them we learn that we are all on the same path and we all want a similar outcome. Reconnecting reveals the presence within you and in your own understanding that you are more than a human being, but a spiritual being. The keys that will be found in your self-discovery along the way will create in you a growth pattern *that will progress as fast as you are able to accept and understand the principles.* It's much like the simple growth pattern we all take on as we grow from a child to a man.

As I thought about understanding who we really are I found myself remember a story that I heard years ago. The story comes from the "Special Olympics" It reflects to me who we all really are in this world and the purpose of our lives. We are companions to one another, we are brothers and sisters, and when we see our oneness in humanity it is then we will embrace our purpose and enjoy life in a whole different manner. So often we get hung up on what we want and we loose sight of why we are even here in the first place. The story is about *"special needs"* children that compete in the same kinds of races that are found in the Olympics. In the story there is a race that takes place and the children are so excited about running together. They line up in the proper lanes and are wearing running shorts and tops along with numbers over the tops. Everything appears as if it were an Olympic race. *The excitement is beyond what one can imagine.* The parents and friends sit in the stands. The gun goes off and the race begins. A few minutes into the race one of them falls and can't get up. She cries because she is hurt. Those in the stand react. The children that are now diligently running the race all notice what happened and they turn around and go back, help her to her feet but she can't walk and so they use all their ability to help her finish the race. *"Together" they all cross the finish line. The emotion I felt when I saw them hand in hand walking with the girl across the finish line, was an emotion of deep love and respect for these incredible children, for they are more than children, they are spiritual beings that represent God and His unconditional love.* They may be mentally handicapped by what the world *"defines"* as handicapped, but *they have much to show us in how to truly love and what the real meaning of life on earth is.* The crowd was brought to their feet with cheering and you could feel the emotion unlike any you'd ever seen. That day those special children taught us how to truly live among each other. For in a race most run to win, and most long to be first but in this race these children forgot about the need to be the first one across the finish line. *Their joy was found in bringing the one who fell, across the finish line with them and together, in their eyes "they" won.* These children created a ONENESS among each other by their unconditional love, and *together they were all winners.* Their compassion for their friend was greater than their desire to be the winner. My favorite saying is by Jim Hendrix and it goes like this.

~*When the power of love is greater than the love of power only then will we find peace.*~

So often in life we get hung up in competitive avenues. We get focused on goals and live our lives around accomplishing those goals. There is nothing wrong with having goals but *what is wrong is when our goals become more important than our hearts.* When goals become the main focal point and nothing matters but fulfilling those goals, we loose sight of why God put us on earth in the first place. These Children knew the power that God put within them to love and *they were not afraid to show it.* In turn they taught those looking on that it's not about winning *but about working together.* The power within them is the power of Unconditional Love and all of us have the same ability to take a hold of our lives, open our hearts and BE THE CHANGE IN TROUBLED TIMES.

A similar story that has opened my understanding that *we are bound by chains of our own minds* when we define winning and coming in "first" is the most important goal for us, is the story entitled

"Everybody Won". Invisible walls of false ideas and false beliefs of what winning is all about imprison us. God designed our soul so that it can never be completely satisfied with this material world. Why did He do that, you may ask? *So that we will always seek beyond the material world and eventually we "can" re-connect with our Spiritual Being.* For the truth is that behind all of our outer desires and longings, *there is a longing for something more than what this world can offer.* We cover this longing with layers of desire for the things of this world. But the inner voice within continues to bring messages. I feel that this little story tells us that the joy is found *in how we "view" life's experiences.* When we are willing to look beyond our beliefs or ideas and allow God to show us how easy it is to embrace the simple things, then we grow and mature into the people that can bring us a better world and we become the change. This is the Story:

Everybody Won
(Author Unknown)
Last night was the last game for my eight-year-old son's soccer team. It was the final quarter. The score was two to one, my son's team in the lead. Parents shouted encouragement from the sidelines as the boys clashed on the field. With less than ten seconds remaining, the ball rolled in front of my son's teammate, one Mikey O'Donnell. With shouts of "Kick it!" echoing across the field, Mikey reared back and gave it everything he had.
All around me the crowd fell silent as the ball flew into the goal.
Mikey O'Donnell had scored!
Mikey had scored all right, but in the wrong goal, ending the game in a tie. For a moment there was total silence. You see Mikey has Down's syndrome and for him there is no such thing as a wrong goal. All goals were celebrated by a

215

joyous hug from Mikey. He had even been known to hug the opposing players when they scored.

The silence was finally broken when Mikey, his face filled with joy, grabbed my son, hugged him and yelled, "I scored! I scored. Everybody won! Everybody won!"

For a moment I held my breath, not sure how my son would react. I need not have worried. I watched, through tears, as my son threw up his hand in the classic high-five salute and started chanting, "Way to go Mikey! Way to go Mikey!" Within moments, both teams surrounded Mikey, joining in the chant and congratulating him on his goal. Later that night, when my daughter asked who had won, my son smiled and replied, "It was a tie. Everybody won!"

The truth is that when we simply embrace life as this young man was demonstrating, there is joy found in all of our experiences. The young man was so overjoyed with playing the game *that he forgot that certain outcomes would divide it into categories of how one "should" react.* In other words when we divide into categories of winning or loosing, *we train our responses to the outcome by what benefits our own desires or of what is acceptable by those around us.* So when we win, we give ourself the permission to be joyful but when we loose we create a loss and we feel a sense of failure and regret. *This young man didn't divide into the categories of winning or loosing because in his eyes everyone wins.* I am not saying we cannot have goals but *what I am saying is that our goals should "not" always be looking out for #1* but should be looking out for what can bring about a oneness with each other.

~If we loose, let us enjoy the victory of another in such a complete manner that we actually forget we are losers at all.~

When we focus on the victory of others we lose our own sense of loss because in all reality God created all of us to enjoy a sense of oneness. In loosing we are given the opportunity to share the joy of another. Do not divide and conquer and you won't feel like you lost.

Sometimes the only way to change a world is to simply "Be The Change" and soon enough others will be walking right beside you. The human spirit is so resilient and once we see how giving love and enjoying the victory of others, actually returns unto us more than we ever gave out, we will then understand the beauty of living together as one people on this planet.

As you begin the journey of self-discovery take into account how your life affects others. Being responsible for your actions as your journey awakens you is very critical because many times human nature, when learning new things, likes to convince everyone else around them that this is something they also should do. *Respect that each individual must come to the same conclusion that they also need to discover who they are within and allow yourself to become the example that silently begins to transform.* It is important that you specifically take this journey by yourself, going within and not dragging outside opinions or ideas with you or even other people with you. Stay silent to others, and expect that your journey of self-discovery will be uniquely what you need to experience. I thought about an Indian story and it goes like this:

SIOUX INDIAN STORY

My grandfather took me to the fishpond on the farm when I was about seven, and he told me to throw a stone into the water. He told me to watch the circles created by the stone. Then he asked me to think of myself as that stone person. "You may create lots of splashes in your life but the waves that come from those splashes will disturb the

peace of all your fellow creatures," he said. "Remember that you are responsible for what you put in your circle and that circle will also touch many other circles. You will need to live in a way that allows the good that comes from your circle to send the peace of that goodness to others. The splash that comes from anger or jealousy will send those feelings to other circles. You are responsible for both. That was the first time I realized each person creates the inner peace or discord that flows out into the world. We cannot create world peace if we are riddled with inner conflict, hatred, doubt, or anger. We radiate the feelings and thoughts that we hold inside, whether we speak them or not. Whatever is splashing around inside of us is spilling out into the world, creating beauty or discord with all other circles of life. Remember the eternal wisdom: WHATEVER YOU FOCUS ON EXPANDS...

--- Author Unknown ---

As you think about this little story keep in mind that in the journey of learning about ourselves we go thru stages of discovery. If we drag everyone down the road with us, we encounter different opinions, which can create inner conflict within ourselves and in turn stop our belief of our growth. We also encounter differences from what we need to understand about our unique individuality and what others need to understand about theirs. When we drag others into our drama we actually don't learn the specifics that we need to learn *because our journey becomes entangled with their opinions and judgments*. For example when I was younger, I tried to share my interpretation of difficulties in my life with some family members. I ran into very defensive accusations because as I learned how their family affected me, they became defensive and accusing. This experience caused me to not only go into myself but also doubt my new understanding. *Please note that opinions whether they are our own or others don't necessarily mean they are all together true.* The object of learning about our own individuality is in knowing that we have the freedom to choose, as we want to believe. We also have the freedom to change our mind and when we go back and forth in our understanding and often change sides of what we think is right or wrong, we are learning about how we see things. In this learning process we eventually begin to see things in a healthy way. We don't want to feel pity for ourselves because that will only stop our growth. *We want to lay things on the table and then see how our understanding can benefit our growth.* An important part of growth is found in seeing the value of having compassion and understanding for ourselves so that we don't live in regret. Each experience we go thru, each resolution we come to, and each time we forgive and encourage ourselves to learn the lesson and move forward, *we reach a new level on the ladder of growth.* So if we focus on the wrong things, and we dwell on mistakes of the past, then what we focus on becomes greater. The purpose of keeping the journey somewhat to our own inner being and consulting with what is within our being *is to help further your growth and at a faster pace.* I am not saying you cannot share and if you are going to a special doctor or in a support group *many experiences will help others in there growth* but if something you experience will offend another, it might be best to keep that in your heart, resolve it quickly, and move on so that your growth will reach the next level.

Some of us simply cannot work thru things easily on our own and really need to talk to others. If this is you, then feel free to do this *but what I am trying to say is that in doing this you might encounter your own sense of inadequacies because of the opinions of others.* The ultimate goal is to eventually be your own best friend and best confidant. That is your goal, to simply know that everything about you and what you need to do, is already within you. Namely God within your being from the day you were born.

THERE IS MORE TO YOUR LIFE

"A person needs a little madness, or else they never dare cut the rope and be free" ~Nikos Kazantzakis!

I have spoken of the foundational truths of God, Jesus, the Bible, religion and Who you are, and now I want to help you put these pieces in their proper place by helping you understand that they **serve as a foundation** in which you can see who you really are and why you are here, and build a better future.

~When you change your life, you change your future.~

Life on earth is really quite easy to understand. But it doesn't always seem easy because we loose these foundations when we get here. When you put together a jigsaw puzzle, it is always easier to begin the process by finding the edge pieces first and assembling them. I love jigsaw puzzles and recently I asked the question of how easy would it be if I **didn't** gather together the edges first and assemble them. **Now, here is a good example of how we as humans can miss "key points" in our journey in life.** Let me explain. I have been putting together puzzles most of my life and I am not young anymore. I have known that the edge pieces put together first are very important in starting to assemble the *entire picture*. But I have **never asked myself** if I could assemble it without assembling the edge pieces first. It never occurred to me that this question was a question because in my inner knowing, I knew the answer that would *"best serve me"*. I just assumed that this was the logical way to assemble the puzzle. But why ask the question now? I simply stepped out of the box, for some reason, and **challenged what I have always done**. I actually created a question in my experience that really wasn't important but I believe it was my Spiritual Being awakening me and in turn this thought made me really ponder over many things far and beyond the puzzle. It wasn't the puzzle that was in the lesson, for the puzzle was *the vehicle* that caused me to think more about life in general. This is where we don't' have to experience trauma in our lives to understand how to deal with it. Just thinking about something and walking thru it in our mind has the same potential to broaden our understanding, as going thru it. *You see you don't have to go thru hell and back to learn.* You actually can learn before disaster happens or when it happens you can handle it in a very helpful way for others to learn by. The Spiritual Being within you has all the information about you and what you need. So when thinking about the question of the puzzle I realized the question was to awaken me to understand *I had an inner knowing about something and had chosen to walk that path because deep inside I knew it was best*. Even though you might think that everybody knows that and this isn't really something great that I knew about how to assemble a puzzle, *I will tell you that you can push it aside or you can see it for what it is.* The truth is no matter how insignificant this natural knowledge seems, it is revealing that there is a Being within all of us that is working on helping us in this life and we are not alone. What is within us is our Spiritual I AM Being that is God within. So we are not alone and never have been. Next time when something very *insignificant* comes to your mind, you need to pay attention because it just might be something you have heard over and over again and you have become so used to it, you don't even recognize it. For me I knew that the Christ self within me was very much aware that life on earth is a journey in which we need to learn and come to a higher understanding and it begins with the simple things.

The Christ Self within all of us is our inner teacher and God assists us with other teachers such as the Law of Free Will and the Law of Cause and Effect (Karma). We have never been alone and never will be alone. The Ascended Host also guides us if we ask them.

For me, I am a person that is always challenging my own understanding. I feel that it is due to the fact that I am very close to my Spiritual Self and I am very aware of the need to journey and become more and so my human side is willing and ready to understand more. This is where growth accelerates. ***I believe that one should never think they know everything about anything.*** The reason I have never asked the question, about the edge pieces of the puzzled, is because ***it never occurred to me to be important.*** But it's never too late to be asked and maybe today is the day that such a simple question is ready to broaden my understanding.

"When the student is ready the teacher will come".

I have given you the ***edge pieces*** of the picture of life. I have assembled the pieces that reflect a deeper understanding of your life and a greater identity of your individuality by explaining the teachings that God gave man to help him. As the assembly of a puzzle, so is the assembly of our understanding of our lives. Think of the statement I wrote right under the title. ***"A person needs a little madness, or else they never dare cut the rope and be free".*** Without the edge pieces of a puzzle, ***there is madness in assembling the picture.*** Sometimes we simply allow ourselves to go thru madness in our lives but the hope is that one day that madness will have caused us to say, ***enough is enough*** and that is when we will dare to cut the rope and eventually we will be free from all that hinders our growth.

~Life is a journey and each step, no matter how hard it is, is very important~

When difficulties arise in your life the deeper understanding ***is*** that there is a picture of your "lack of understanding" ***that you still*** *need to see* in order to fulfill the spiritual plan you came with. There *is something* you need to overcome in your mind and *when you do it will change your way of seeing it and when it changes the way you see it, it will change your future.* Your future and fulfilling your spiritual plan is "dependent" on growing and learning *thru a process we call the journey.* It is also "dependent" on *your choices.* And to make better choices you need to understand things from a higher level of understanding. And to get to a higher level of understanding you need to be *on the journey*, making the choices you feel is best. The choices can give you a higher understanding *if you learn and grow from them.* This is why there really aren't wrong choices but they are choices that affect your growth or your lack of growth.

~You cannot get to the top of the mountain unless you are willing to climb it.~

Yes, a helicopter could take you there *but you will not appreciate the top of the mountain without the climb.* No matter what you see today that your life is about, you have the potential to **see so much more**. It is *in the journey* that joy is found, not just in the destination. So in order for you to enjoy the top of the mountain, you must experience the difficulties in getting there.

"When you have reached the top, you will experience a joy you never felt was possible and it will be because the journey helped you to "be ready" to enjoy the reward."

You see we understand this even in our human relationships. If someone always gives you something, you can only enjoy it so much, because the real joy is found *in attaining it*, in working hard for the reward.

So many people are "I" people because they want everything without working for it but the truth is *they are only hurting themselves*. Working for something not only gives you the reward you want, but you find that when the time comes and the reward is ready to be received **you have greater joy within because of the efforts you made in getting there.** *You find that the journey changed you and made you such a better person.* You find that the journey put muscles on you and in turn you can help others. You would never have this if someone just gave it to you. That is why God is *not* a Genie in a Bottle to grant your every wish. That would hurt you and God loves you. All of what you have gone through, good or bad, *was needed for you to get to this point.* But where will you go from this point forward? It is up to you but let me tell you that you can potentially rise to a height of the greatest abundance. *YOU* must first make the move; *YOU* must be willing to accept that *YOUR* choices create *YOUR* future. You also need to understand that if you make a wrong choice out of simply "not understanding" then by *getting out of the situation*, you grow and you can set out again on the journey only this time with greater understanding. This is why God doesn't interfere with your choices. Making a choice and having to get out of a bad choice *has enormous ability to empower you by taking away the fear you have when you make a mistake.* So if you can get out of situation, and it's not always easy, it helps you become the co-creator you are by giving you an experience that will help you eventually take hold of your destiny. When God created the worlds, He believed in everything to be possible and so for your creative abilities and for your imagination of your mind to all become empowered *you have to find the inner source* that helps you know who you are and what you can potentially do on this earth. **It all works together for your good and for the good of the WHOLE of mankind.** God gave you free will, and **He gave you His love** when YOU CHOSE to come to earth. You came on your own accord, with a plan that you felt would help you learn and grow and be closer to God. *God gave His blessing* when you asked to become embodied once again and He said He would help you as much as you wanted. But *this is "your" experience and so He will not interfere and do everything for you*. Doing everything for you will only keep you from learning and growing as you desire. He loves you enough to encourage you to grow on your own.

~*Your own ability to rise will be your power of knowing who you are.*~

Your struggles, and all you go through will teach you and you will grow to the higher level of the Spiritual Path **you have desired to reach.** He respects that sometimes we want to do things by ourselves because we are made in the image of Him and sometimes we want to be rescued, because the human part of who we are tries to hinder our growth. But because God loves us He also wants us to remember that it is to our own advantage we experience the results of our choices and find a way out of them. He knows you have the same ability to create as He does. He wants you to become independent of Him and *on the same team as Him.* He wants to watch His creative abilities that are in you to create on their own and in turn He experiences the joy thru His creation. He wants you to experience what you need to, so that you can grow wiser and more able to help all of creation. He knows that in coming to earth there are certain obstacles but He has not left us alone.

The edge pieces of the puzzle are representative of the things you need to understand *before you can put the whole picture together.* The edge pieces don't have to be there to put the puzzle together *but they make it much easier.* The foundational truths of God, and the purpose of life are not really going to make or break you *but they will make it easier for you to re-look at your life and see the masterpiece waiting to be assembled.* They also will help you get started by seeing who you really are. Do you know that you have the ability to begin an upward spiral of love and light in this world and at the same time cause others to do the same? Do you understand that if you can re-look at the troubles you have experienced, through different lenses, *you will see them as tools* to get you to a new place in which you can rise higher and begin to re-connect with the spiritual plan for which you came here to do? But you can also help others because they will see you as you rise and become more and this will inspire them. If finding the edge pieces of the puzzle of your life helps you begin to assemble everything else, *then they are worth it.* It is my belief that most of us, if we *really saw* the greater picture of our lives, we would *not* spend so much time *going in circles* over the details of the troubles. Let's begin to re-look at some of the things we, as humans, tend to get stuck on.

When I say, "get stuck on" I want you to look at a natural occurrence. Let's take an example. What happens when the flow of water in a river get's stuck going in circles at a given place in the river? It will spin in circles until something comes along and changes it's direction. I have watched the rapids of a fast moving river. Water has the natural ability to simply flow. It doesn't have a mind of it's own, so to speak. Water in a river is very much willing to go with the flow. Water in a river can be detoured by rocks, branches, cuts in the path, and many different things that come along. Water can also just drop off when the path drops off. Think about one of the greatest falls known to man, Niagara Falls. There are rivers that flow from long distances until they reach that incredible drop and then fall endlessly to the bottom. Did you ever notice that in this particular fall, some of the water turns to a mist? I remember watching the waterfall, and it amazed me to see that some of the water had so far to reach its destiny that it literally became a fine mist, and depending upon the atmospheric temperature it could turn to steam.

Then there are rivers in which we see sit still. Think of Mississippi River and how many times there are places where the river just sits, although we know it is on a progressive path. The truth is the river is symbolic of the River of Life. We are on a river and God would like you to know that He calls it the River of Life. Your life is constantly moving, constantly changing, and when you feel it has come to a standstill, you can be assured it hasn't stopped but has simply slowed down. Think of your life and the pattern since you have arrived. There have been days when the waters were moving so fast that you didn't know if you could handle it and then there were days when you felt life was sucking you deep into despair and you didn't know if you would live through it. Then there were days when you felt everything was going so good, that you questioned what might be coming down the road because deep inside you had focused on the bad times and when the good times came you didn't believe you deserved them. You didn't know why you were receiving such blessing because deep inside you felt a sinner and no good. This is because the edge pieces of your life were not in alignment with the picture. You know that if you put an edge piece of a puzzle in the wrong place, *you simply cannot put the picture together as it should be.*

The River of Life is constantly flow, always changing, always-becoming more. The reason for this is because God set in motion *that life would not stand still* so that you would have the opportunity to know there was need to be growing and to be changing from what you saw before, to what could be a better understanding. So when life throws a monkey wrench into the picture, we first ask *why*? Then we feel we are being punished for something we have done wrong. Then we feel ourselves going into a fight flight mode in order to survive. And lastly we get angry and lash out at others and God. Why? My belief is that if you really see the purpose of life on earth, these reactions will no longer be. When you see the importance of the "edge" pieces of your life, such as in a puzzle, you will see that God wants you to begin to assemble the picture of your life you came with. In other words, those edge pieces serve as a foundation but *without the foundation you will never be able to put the rest of the puzzle, the picture of your life together*.

You are in this lifetime right now and you are experiencing these circumstances right now. We don't come to each lifetime *with a memory* of the past lifetimes because we are to start again and in this life we will create new circumstances and when we overcome them, and learn from them, we grow more. If we brought with us the same memory of another lifetime, and we reacted the same way, and we found the same trials, we would not have the ability to expand our awareness and our understanding and therefore we couldn't move on any more than we did in the last lifetime. Keep in mind if you didn't successfully learn a lesson in another lifetime, you might learn it now in this one. But many times our greatest achievements manifest when we are presented with the same lesson, *only with a whole different scenario.* If you didn't move past something very critical in another lifetime, you probably chose to return again to achieve that goal because the truth is *it holds the key* to a higher level of attainment in the spiritual world. If you remembered the experience in another lifetime, you might just rely on how you tried to learn from it then and not be willing to see it from a different perspective, **which has the potential to teach you a higher understanding.** What I'm trying to help you understand is that you are a spiritual being who wants to successfully rise to a higher level in God's kingdom and because it can only be done by *your efforts*, you chose to return to earth for *your growth* and at the same time you can help others grow from whatever level they are on. You see when I say we are one WHOLE being of God, I mean that our lives affect the WHOLE and so when you struggle to learn a lesson and you find a way to understand it and then see the benefit of learning and moving on, *you actually inspire others to do the same.* Another important part of your own journey and how it affects others is in understanding that when you intuitively know there is something in your plan that needs to be done and you do it, *you then affect your future* and the potential for greater abundance in your life and the lives you are connected with in the body of God.

So, lets get back to the River of Life for a moment. Think of your life as the water flowing down the river. The water is moving in the direction of life but all the sudden it comes to a rock. The water then takes a detour around the rock and then it sees another rock and has to detour again moving far to the right. Your life sometimes changes direction. When everything seems to be steady and predictable you are sitting back just taking in everyday life but all the sudden something changes and it sends you into another direction. You ask yourself what happened, and you wonder if you did something to cause it. Because you don't really understand the deeper meaning of your life you have a tendency to *allow your mind to wonder* what you did to cause this. You will tend to blame yourself for creating this mess. When your mind wanders, it creates *incredibly false pictures* but it isn't entirely bad, because any picture you imagine has the potential to get your attention. However it also has the potential to send you into an *emotional rollercoaster* in which you really don't get the answer to why things changed and you get all stirred up with false emotions. Now, you could be a person that doesn't blame yourself but everyone else, and this also has another potential to get you on another path in which you can go in circles. Then there is another scenario in which you don't blame anyone but God or bad luck. And finally you could simply just know that there is something from this you need to learn and so you look for what it is and you move into the direction of growth. You can see that life is a river and there will be obstacles but ***how you respond to them determines how fast you grow and move on.*** I have known many wonderful people that have so much love in their hearts for their family and friends yet when trouble comes they take upon themselves all the blame. They feel they should bear the burdens of others and they do this in an effort to save those around them. But doing it this way may appear to help others but ***it doesn't allow others to learn what they need to*** and move on in their lives. We cannot save anyone but ourselves. Jesus said for us to pull the beam out of our own eye first and only then can we help others. The other important part is that when you take the blame for ***everything you also put yourself in danger*** of loosing ***your own ability*** to grow. It just might be that you are in this place, trying to save others, to learn that in your efforts you are hurting them instead. They must learn from their experiences. You can be there when they are going thru them and help them see beyond them but you can never save them. Also, if you choose to take the route of helping them thru their experiences you first have to pull the beam from your own eye to do this. This is a ***foundational necessity*** that you need to fully understand in order to create your own healing. You need to heal yourself, you need to understand your life, and you need to grow with new knowledge and all of this can only take place when you first pull the beam out of your own eye.

To pull the beam out of your own eye, you need to see what life is really about and why things happen to people. We know about karma to some degree. We know that karma is a universal law God put in place so that we would not self-destruct.

⁓*Karma is essentially a teacher set in motion.*⁓

So when you create results by choices you make according to your understanding, ***you will receive back unto you what you send out.*** So if you make a choice to take matters into your own hands and punish someone for their actions, you have first forgotten that they have created actions according to ***their own understanding*** and because they are also ***on their own journey*** you are hindering their journey, and secondly ***you have inflicted new challenges on yourself*** by taking matters into your own hands. I am not saying we should put ourselves in danger from a person that is so far down the level of human understanding that they endanger everyone. But what I am trying to get you to understand is that Karma or what Jesus explained as reaping what you sow is a natural teacher to help us when we have a lower understanding of life and the purpose of it. God is not an angry judgmental God that will send you to hell if you make a mistake but ***God wants you to learn from your choices and move on.*** God put in motion a safety mechanism so that we would not totally loose our opportunity to manifest what we came to do in the plan we came with. Let's say you are a very highly evolved spiritual being and you have a very important mission on this planet at this time in the earths history. Let's say life has hardened you and you have chosen certain paths that have caused you to forget the spiritual being you are. Let's say your job and the many important people your work with are just a job to you, you just go through the motions and have lost touch with your heart and soul. ***Your job has been given to you as an opportunity to experience the very life changing challenges that potentially can help you rise to a higher understanding.*** However, other challenges of your job have caused you to loose family and friends not related to your job. You essentially feel alone and angry because your job seems to have alienated you not only from those you worked to provide for, namely family, but also from the deeper part of your needs that define what you long for in life, and from your spiritual self. ***Your life has become empty***.

Let's look at what happened for a moment. Your life purpose is incredibly important today as it was when you were born. You came into this world thru a specific family that would bring you the highest growth and help you rise by the challenges presented. Somewhere along the line you became ***so attached to the journey in life*** that you literally lost your memory of the spiritual plan. Just so you know this is normal for most of us. What you are experiencing right now in life has the **potential to awaken you** but the only way you can be awakened is to begin to see **who** you are. You begin by first knowing that all you are going thru in life are to serve as only tools to help you grow. You begin with faith that you will soon understand, if you keep walking with the desire to know more. The **faith will get you going in the right direction** but because you have been so alienated from your spiritual self, you will need to make an effort on your own to set up a pattern of beginning to learn and grow with spiritual teachings. What happens to many very important spiritual people is that they simply have lost their memory. The river of life is constantly flowing and the directions we take when the river gets disturbed **create a new scenario in which we journey in a different direction**. It is in our own spiritual desires to become MORE, that we put those obstacles in the plan that we made before we came. We didn't do this to sabotage our journey but we knew that **if we could overcome them, we would rise higher, in a shorter time**. We knew that if we could achieve overcoming this obstacle we could potentially rise much higher at a faster pace. Now isn't that normal when someone is trying to climb the ladder of success in life or if someone is trying to excel in sports. Think about it. If someone wants to attain a faster speed in running, they will push themselves way beyond their current ability. So when you decide you want to take on a greater obstacle in life and you know if you can learn and grow from it you will catapult yourself so far that you will achieve a greater victory, then you will put it in the plan. Human achievement is very similar to how our spiritual achievement is designed by us when we are in the spiritual realm. We wanted to become more but in order for us to truly understand and achieve this, we knew we would need to experience a monkey wrench in the path we took. We allowed it to be so, because when we made this plan we saw **as a spiritual being** and not as the ego or carnal mind saw. In other words we saw from a higher mind when we choose certain details of our plan. We have the ability to do whatever we want **in response to the obstacles we encounter** and the universal law of cause and effect, or karma as we also call it, **is to help us stay on the path of evolving and becoming more**. So even when we make decisions that only hurt us, we are given the results of our actions by what returns to us, to get us to re-think our path and see that our decisions didn't really serve us in the greater picture of our lives. And in turn we can make better decisions. It's never too late to live the life of abundance.

When we hit the place in the River of Life where we seem to be going in circles, we find that we dig a deeper hole. These times are the most *critical times* for they can actually *make or break us for a long period of time*. In the River, this spiraling affect can actually create a vacuum where everything is sucked down into it. So whatever gets sucked down into the whirlpool of the waters spinning faster and faster is virtually out of the picture or out of visible reach. We don't know where it is and we feel we will never see it again. The same goes for us when we attach to an experience where we are going in circles in our emotions. We can get lost in this downward pull for an indefinite amount of time. Let's consider the example of someone we love, who has died. The experience is emotionally very hard but then as the experience should become a memory, we don't let go of it. When we don't let go of it we live it everyday as if it just happened. We not only subject our own selves to the same emotional loss but we also subject everyone around us to the same loss. We not only affect ourselves but we also affect the WHOLE of mankind. When enough times passes we find that we cannot live our lives anymore. We begin to feed upon the negative emotions *as if they sustain us*. Like a food that isn't good for our overall health, so it is with the emotions we feed on. An experience in life, such as this, is not intended to be the end of our story, but actually can help us grow because of what it presents to us. Sometimes we are reminded when something happens of how we reacted in the past over similar experiences and so life presents a *new picture of a similar one we already went thru*, to challenge us to try again to move into a higher understanding. This is why many times, people who feel there lives are going smoothly, all of the sudden hit a bump in the road and it reflects to them in their mind the thought, "Here we go again: this is the story of my life, every time something good comes along something comes along to destroy it." But is this the truth. *NO!!!!* The reason it is happening again is because this time you need to believe you do deserve something good and the only reason you find yourself spinning in circles over an emotion that has told you this always happens to you, is because it is critical you take on a ***new belief not only of your life as a whole, but you also resolve what you can do to take matters into your own hands and stop the negative emotions.*** People that are spinning in circles and experience one trauma after another need to realize that someone is trying to wake them up. ***That someone is your higher self.*** God is not to blame. The fact is it is your higher self that wants you to be successful in the plan you created. I have known many people that have experienced these things. I know of some who experience the loss of family over and over that are dear to them and each time this happens they ***hang on to the loss***. It gets worse and worse with each one. They eventually make themselves emotionally sick. The truth is it keeps affecting them in such a detrimental way to basically get them to wake up and learn that death isn't the end of life. What you are experiencing is an effort to help you move on and become more aware of what your life and the plan of your life is all about. **We create our own demise** by our own choices or ***by our reactions to things that happen in life*** and these are based ***on the level of understanding we currently have of why things happen to us.*** Things happen to us to help us and ***not*** to destroy us.

The important part of what I want you to understand as you think of your life in connection to others around you is that ***you can look at their lives but you can't change them***. The only thing you can really do to help them is to begin to help yourself first. See their lives as ***their journey*** and love them and support them in understanding but ***don't take on their journey*** because when you do you ***hinder your own ability to keep growing***. You can listen to them, you can try to help them but keep in mind that the only way their situation will change ***is if they choose to make different choices for their lives.*** You are first responsible for yourself and ***not in a selfish way but in a loving way.*** If you can really understand that when you take hold of your life and make the strides to improve it to the best ability you have to understand right now, you also affect or help those looking on.

There is so much more to your life than the struggles you have on earth. Remember how I have already explained that God created you to help Him create more. Remember that you are not just a being that has no purpose but you are the most important plan God ever planned.

"God created human beings to be a part of Him."

He wanted us to create also. He wanted to experience life thru us and in turn He would become more. We are all becoming more of who we are by being in the River of Life together. Do you understand what this means?

"The madness you often feel in life is only there to awaken you to see that this isn't what life is about but simply a tool to awaken you."

Yes you may have to exert effort to get out of some of the circumstances you find your life going thru but that's ok. If you step back and think about the value that God has in your life that He cared enough to even awaken you, then you will count the troubles as tools to help you look beyond everything that seems so overwhelming.

"When you get a clear vision of why things happen and how God sees you, you won't question the importance of your life anymore."

Yes, you will find the difficulties still hard but if you can step away from them and look at how they have brought you to a new understanding, then this alone will give you courage to work through them quicker and one day soon you can spend your time doing things that will show even greater abundance.

"The troubles seem overwhelming today but they are only steps on a ladder and soon they will be a distant memory."

To help you see there is more to your life, I want to try to illustrate *"your journey"* and how it can potentially become the ***most powerful tool you have in your toolbox***. When you start out in life and come to earth as a human, you loose your identity of the spiritual self you are, this we already have talked about. ***Your journey is the fuel that takes you to your destination*** but if you choose to disembark and no longer be conscious of your own decisions you will begin to slowly separate from your higher self, which is like a death.

"Keep in mind you cannot loose your higher self, but you can become separated from it and this creates the alone feeling, which triggers anger and fear."

Many people choose this and their death is slow and agonizing because the whole time they are dying inside, their spiritual self is trying to awaken them.

"It's like there is a battle going on between your lower self and your higher self and you are suffering the whole time."

Their spiritual self wants to finish the plan but the part of them that has become mortal, human, has taken on the ego and that part wants to destroy their spiritual plan or never let it manifest in this life. The ego doesn't want to die but the path it takes you on leaves no other alternative. So how does your spiritual self wake you up? Well, the law of cause and effect will be one avenue that will naturally try to save you. In getting your attention, even if it means bad things keep coming your way, there is still a potential to ***shake you up enough so that you will want to change things in your life.*** You see God wants you to ***come to the end of your troubles and get tired enough to choose you have had enough of all of this.*** This will be a decision that you can make and it will bring you change by your own choice. However, if you have resigned yourself to life on earth as always being this way, in some ways you are saying I give up. This could go on for a long time, especially, if the power of your spiritual plan is very significant in our world today. *So those that suffer the greatest actually have the greatest plan to change their world.* But they can never begin to change the world until they change themselves first. *God is never willing to give up on us and so His laws, along with the Ascended Host, will continue to try and wake us up.* Now let's say you are now AWAKE and you decide you want to begin the process of re-connecting to whom you really are. Let's say you have begun to see through the maze of obstacles in your life and you have come to a place where a difficult decision must be made in order to go forward in the right direction. I want to tell you something very important. When you get to a *turning point on your journey that is critical*, you may see intuitively the importance of a decision that must be made in order to fulfill the spiritual plan but you might be lingering on whether or not you are ready for it. As time goes on, there might very well be something that tells you of the urgency of making a decision. Keep in mind that *making no decision is really making a decision.* Intuitively you also might see that in your making a decision for your necessary change in direction of your path, you see how it will save those you love. It takes time on the journey to see *the depth of this kind of scenario* but when you do see it, it would be wise to respond as quickly as possible. Now here's another catch in the journey. Let's say you make the necessary decision and it opens wonderful opportunities and brings you to a future you have longed for but you find that *something is holding back the abundance.* This is because your spiritual plan may be directly linked to helping others or directly linked to something you came to do in this lifetime. You will then see a new part of the journey that you need to work thru. This part will help you grow and when you grow you will help others grow. You may have been called to not only fulfill your own plan but also to help others to fulfill theirs. This would explain why when you awaken, and respond and journey in the path that leads you to your ascension to a higher spiritual place in the kingdom, others will follow by responding to the opportunity they are given. If you were told that the journey you were on up the mountain entailed helping others up the mountain, it might overwhelm you. Sometimes what we don't know is ok. It's possible that the pattern of your life up to this point has been in helping everyone else and so you have now come to a point where your personal needs in life long to be fulfilled. However, it is evident that the timing *isn't in your favor and you are now required to walk further without your needs fulfilled. This is where the journey becomes very hard and often long.* Many loose heart at this point in their lives because they long for deliverance from all the heartache they have endured. Although they want to be strength and help to those that trust them and need them, they long for a little strength for themselves. However, the pattern of the journey they are now on *requires they go further and there is no other option*. They choose to go on or give up. I will tell you with all my heart, I understand this very well. It has been my journey and yet when I came to a place where I had made a choice to switch directions and begin a new journey, something deep inside of me told me to just begin and when I get to the next step I will have gained more strength in the journey. It is when we are willing, a step at a time, even when we don't know the way, that we put our hand in God's and in those who are there to help us, that we begin to see the pattern of the journey. I knew deep inside, my hearts pain and longing, and yet I knew that I would never see the abundance I longed for unless I was willing to walk a little further and take the next step. It would require faith and assistance from those in the Spiritual realm, whom I call the Ascended Beings. There were some humans that tried to help me but they couldn't give me the assurance I so longed to have. They loved me but their words gave me no promise of anything, just empty "maybes". It was probably the most trying times I ever had. But that is all they had to give me because they didn't know either. You see although we are all connected and although when one rise's others can rise, as humans we often cannot help one another because we really don't have a *higher understanding of what is really happening*. I was given a vision of the future, a higher understanding and so without telling them; I simply walked on with courage on my own. I would reveal as I went, some of what I learned but most I kept deep in my heart. WHY? Because if I said anything and they responded with any doubt, I would have questioned what I knew. I was **still so human** and with the ego and the way it sees things, I couldn't take a chance that their reaction to my words or my understanding would cause doubt in my heart. **I needed every bit of strength to keep going.** As I began to see the pattern that was happening I would have an inner knowing that my vision was truth. I would continue to be faithful in what I knew I needed to focus on, I would give my heart of love and light to all who cared for me and I would receive back from them what they **could** give me. We began a journey together, and they didn't really understand it, but I now knew that their future depended upon my willingness to pursue **in spite of my heartache.** In some ways I began to see the future in a beautiful way and in other ways I felt the length of the journey and it was my greatest challenge. The journey is about growing and becoming who we really are and in doing that sometimes we must **go with faith.** I knew that everything depended on me doing certain things and **only then would others be empowered.** As I reached new levels of understanding, I had wondered before I got there if I would have the strength to keep going. But the beautiful part of the journey is that the strength we used to get from one point to another, **added more strength to us and when we finally reached the point we longed for, we would be healed already from the journey.** You see we all have longings and needs to experience in life and when we begin the journey sometimes we are **so weak from the longing** that could be from a lifetime, that **we don't feel we have the strength to finish our lives.** But the truth is I can tell you from my own journey that when I didn't know how I was going to get to the end, let alone one more step, **somewhere I found strength. Each step took me to the next and each time I got to the next step I was a little stronger.** I didn't look at it that way because I simply focused on the day-to-day living and enjoying each moment as it came. **By the way that was my secret in enduring.** I couldn't look too far because I felt my knees weaken. So I looked **just for the day and I enjoyed the moment.** I felt that God would bring me the joy right now and I would be thankful for what He has given me up to this point.

What I want **you to understand** is that it is important that you know that when you finally arrive at the place that you have longed to heal you all your life, *you will see that there is little healing left to do and what needs healing will come so quickly that you will begin to live your life with such joy that you never thought possible.*

~You will see that the whole time you were on the journey, and you were struggling to keep going and to help others, that you were growing stronger and healing all along the way.~

You will see the beauty of what you send out and *how it has returned* unto you by your love for others. You will see that God has created laws in the universe *that can ultimately save you* and *has the potential to create the most abundant life you ever dreamed possible*. God loves you more than anything. When you start on the journey of your life, you don't see the troubles ahead and you don't know if you can finish but when you get closer to the finish line *you all of the sudden see the heavens open up and the joy you feel changes you in such a beautiful way that you never desire the things of this world again.* It is a joy that I cannot explain to you because it is beyond words. But today I want you to know that I know and have seen what is waiting ahead for you on the journey.

~No matter what you understand right now, I ask you to use the strength you have and begin~.

It may seem long, the journey, at times, but it will pass quickly and the more you walk and stay focused on learning and growing, the more strength you will gain and you will begin to see the beauty more than struggle. It does seem hard to fathom but I ask you to believe me and continue to walk. This is the greatest joy you can imagine. Just think how you may feel when you do return to your spiritual home, you will have such fulfillment in knowing you finished with victory and you will be able to raise the level in your spiritual home. The victory waiting will be the greatest feeling you have ever had. I want you to experience this and I want you to know that you can, *by just continuing*.

As you continue to understand the spiritual side of you keep in mind that when you are going thru trying times God is experiencing your pain and your sorrow at the same time you are. God wants you to have victory and to enjoy the life He has given you. God wants you to rise above the past and all that hinders your happiness in the future but the only way to rise above is to forgive and go on. The way we forgive becomes much easier when we look at life as I have already explained. God never wanted you to experience this life and then to allow it to overcome your potential for happiness. You are like the flower. God brought the rains to water, and the sun to encourage growth and God saw that it was good. But God also saw the things on earth that could hinder your growth, like disease, floods, and all manner of pestilence. God knew they were here on earth but hoped in His loving heart that you would press onward, stay focused on the life ahead and eventually produce the most beautiful, fragrant flowers known to mankind. It was God's hope that your life wouldn't succumb to the pressures of living on earth. And as those pressures came, you would see who you are and look beyond this life and continue to grow and learn and become the co-creator or spiritual being that you are. You are a god and It is written, Ye Are Gods, you are a part of God's being. God is in you and lives always there waiting to help you press onward. My hope is that you will look at the experiences in life as lessons in a classroom. They are teachers to help you become more of who you are. If you can see your troubles in a *different light*, you will be able to overcome all the darkness that you have allowed to be part of this journey you are on. It is your choice. I ask you to consider stepping away from what you know is your life right now, and take my hand and lets see what God has to show us. Step away from all your beliefs, all your emotional attachments, and your heartache. Take a journey with me to another planet and view life from a different perspective. When you return to this planet and you return to your reality, I hope that you will want to see things differently. This is your salvation from your so-called "heartache" on earth. Instead of seeing the troubles and the scars and the prison walls around you, *as all*

there is, see them as a springboard in which you can **go beyond** what you currently see as all there is.

I begin with our minds, because it is ***in our minds that our world becomes our own reality.*** What we see is what we get. How we see things formulates our path in which we begin to walk. We've talked about the power of your mind and how you see things determines how you respond to circumstances. ***It is the mind; the things you tell yourself, that become your reality***. When you take on these beliefs it is then that you create the path you walk.

~Your mind literally has the power to transform you into what you think you are.~

There are layers in your mind. On the surface your mind has a list of positive affirmations that you are telling yourself in an effort to empower change in your life but in a deeper layer you may find that when change doesn't happen, you empower the deeper thoughts that you carry that you will never be successful, never be happy, and don't deserve this or that. ***These are the parts of your mind that have the ability to change you.*** No matter how many band-aids, so to speak, you put over them; it won't change things because this is something critical that is ***blocking your progress*** on your spiritual path. The truth is that you must truly believe that you do deserve happiness, you are worthy, etc. You must heal the deeper levels of your mind and only then can you begin to really appreciate the special person you are. Keep in mind that the negative thoughts you carry with you, are not the truth, and are not your reality. In God's eyes there is love and appreciation for you. You must begin to understand that the reason you do not have the abundant life that God promised is because ***you don't understand the value of the experiences life has put in your path*** and in turn you have told yourself lies, that you will never have what others have or that you have failed or whatever. So if you follow a process of just telling yourself positive things, it can only create a false feeling inside. No positive affirmation that isn't truly connected to how you see yourself can do anything more than create a false sense of security. This is the pattern of self-help in our world. There is nothing wrong **with beginning** to tell yourself you deserve happiness but if you don't **internalize it** by changing the way you "see" things, self help can **only go so far** and then you are back at square one. I honestly believe that self-help is defined by helping yourself and so **you must be the one to change**. But it's not just that simple. If you choose to change a behavior by learning a laid out plan, or rules that someone says to follow, it will only work for a while. The key is to see yourself differently and that can only happen if you take on a different way of seeing things in your life. This will create the change you need to help you so that your behavior becomes natural and the changes **become a part of who you are and not whom someone thinks you should be.** No doctor, no book, and no theory can work unless you truly see the change necessary and this is where **you become the one in charge of your own destiny**. You make the decisions on your own as to what will benefit you in your progressive growth.

I learned through my own struggles that many things, many people, and many prayers help you begin the process. To truly grow spiritually and learn the lessons in life it takes time. It takes effort to take a step at a time and to keep in mind that nothing happens quickly. Be willing to look ahead but **don't go too far and too fast, just a step at a time**. You see, when you are crossing a creek, you see the stones ahead that you need to place your feet on in order to get to the other side but if you go too fast you loose your footing and slip into the waters. Life is this way. A journey of a thousand miles begins with one step. Don't focus on the destination but focus on the journey. **For it is in the journey that the richest rewards are found.** I think it would be good for you to realize that as you are walking and taking each new step in life, you can be experiencing things you've never seen. **There is joy along the way and if you don't pay attention you will miss the best parts.** You see even the fact that you are in a place in your life right now, and you are suffering with the circumstances of life, there is a lesson, and a joy waiting from the very moment you decide to take a new journey. A journey in which you ultimately want to experience the abundant life that God has waiting. But in the steps you take to heal, to rise above, and to understand, there is waiting for you *treasures* in every step. These treasures are gifts that God wants to give you as you experience the healing from each and every part of the journey. You may ask why life is so painful but I want you to know that in getting thru the pain, and beginning to rise above it, *there is an incredible amount of wisdom and joy as you begin to walk out of the troubles you have encountered.* In walking out and in understanding, you will find new strength and a great sense of self worth *will be yours for the taking.* You deserve to reap abundant joy from the experiences you have overcome.

Sometimes the hardest part of changing our lives is just *in making the decision* that this is what we need to do and then it is in committing to finishing. We can start on a journey and then get weary and feel this is too hard and give up. It is very important that even though there will be times when you want to give up and when you no longer feel you made the right choice to take the path you are on, *you must keep going,* and not give up hope. When the road seems hard, that is when you can know you have reached a place where the bump in the road is too hard to climb, but it is most likely presenting itself because *it is a critical turning point in your life.* Many people have walked entire lives without reaching their goals because there came a time when something became too difficult and they gave up. *Don't get so close to your victory and give up right when everything could have changed for the best, in your life.* It is only too hard if you see it that way. Keep going, stay focused and believe that the strength will come and when you rise over the bump in the road, you will see a beautiful new path waiting for you to take on. Also know that each bump is a victory and there will be more along the way. Just keep going and one day you will see that the clouds have lifted and all that once was your world, all that you focused on in talking about, is no longer important. You will experience *a knowing* that the problems were only vehicles to help you see who you really are and why you are here on planet earth at this given time in history. Yes the tears of yesterday are now understood and you have come to realize that there is pain in living on earth but the pain is only to be understood and you can turn the tears into tools to help others get past the same.

I wonder if you realize that when someone comes to earth and has so many troubles to walk thru, part of overcoming and rising above is so that you can help others. You may have been asked to walk the walk you experienced and then to formulate with love and compassion a way in which **you can help someone else have the courage to move past their struggles**. The people you help may very well be the people who can go on and help in a great way to bring change to this planet. You never know who will be capable of the greatest influence and you just might touch their lives. But if you had never walked the path you walked and if you had never suffered as much as you have suffered you might not be able to show others the way **out of the suffering**.

There are many beliefs that you have of yourself that get you nowhere. They keep you going in a closed circle. These beliefs have attached to them fear, guilt, no love for self, anger, vengeance, failure, hate, control and unforgiveness. With the beliefs you tell yourself and the emotions that are attached to them you have literally created your own divisions in your being and without knowing, **you have taken away a good part of your ability to take hold of your life**. In other words you have taken away the connectedness you can have with God. Jesus said the kingdom of God is within you, and he truly wanted all of us to know that God is within us. As you find yourself on the journey of growing from who you think you are to who you really are, you also find beliefs that you have allowed in your mind to become the so-called "truth". In other words what **you think** is your reality doesn't necessarily mean it is. These beliefs we carry can help us, by revealing **something more** than our limited view of our experience. The way beliefs help us is **by challenging us thru their power over us**. When we see their power we have to question **why** and that is when **we see them as a wake up call**. They may very well be wrong and keeping us from becoming whole. But they **must be faced in order for us to understand** their power.

~To face them, means to look at them for what they are and to see how they help us or cripple us. ~

245

They can be good but many times they are not. The greatest lies we tell ourselves must be thrown out but in order to throw them out, *we must first recognize them*. When we recognize them, we are taken down a challenging road in which we are asked to re-look at what put those lies into our heads in the first place. Why did we believe something that has no truth and not only hinders our growth but actually paralyzes us in many ways from ever believing the truth about our life? These kinds of beliefs are many times taken on in an effort *to survive what we are going thru at the time*. But as time goes on we find that we have said them so many times in order *to survive that we literally have taken them as truth.* As we are trying to survive we are also loosing our "spiritual" identity and we no longer believe that there is more to our life here on earth. In the survival mode, we focus on what can keep us going and many times what keeps us going, takes us further away from our "spiritual" identity. Others that look on can see what we are doing to our own destiny but we cannot see and we are digging a deeper hole as time goes on.

So if you are ever going to see who you are as a spiritual person and what you came to this earth to accomplish, you must first align your beliefs with God's truths of "you" as a spiritual being. *How you feel about the journey is in direct relationship with your emotional beliefs of yourself.* If you feel like your life is depressing, and always going against you, then in order to get on the right track of healing, you need to see all the struggles you have experienced as tools to help you become stronger and more able to not only experience real abundant life for yourself but also to help others believe there lives are much more. If depression has been much of your life then there is probably fear and anger attached. You also feel unworthy or worthless and life seems so difficult from day to day. In order to get out of depression you need to begin to believe your life is good, and there is a special plan waiting for you to embrace. Do you realize that you are a loving, unselfish being who is in the image of God and your life is to experience life, good or bad, and then allow yourself to become MORE from the experience? If you could see you are not separate from God or from all who walk the earth, then would you not reach out to help anyone in need? When you help others, you help yourself and together you both rise to help God. We are ONE and we must come to this understanding in order to become the Change in this World. Everything in your life is given to you to help you learn and become more. Nothing is to be lost. Like the fishes and the loaves that Jesus used to feed the multitude. He gave what He had and when he went to pick up what was left, he gathered more than he gave. Why???? *Because what he gave multiplied and as others were blessed the blessing returned in the form of abundance* and that abundance had the ability to be given out to more and more until all would be fed. Don't you understand? *We have the tools to bring enormous blessing not only to our own lives but also to all who live on this planet.* Jesus wanted us to know that when we give, we receive more abundantly. But to give sometimes requires us to first pull the beam out of our own eyes and when we do, we are able to help others. Giving isn't always monetary and many times the best giving is of our skills and ourselves. I have watched more so recently with admiration, the rich and famous reach out to the very poor of this world. I believe they will receive the greatest of this blessing for themselves. For when we reach out to another it appears we are doing the goodwill and we are, *but the greatest gift is what we give ourselves when we give of our hearts.* When we give of our hearts the blessing we receive is so abundant that we realize the key to abundant life is right here within our own hearts.

God gave us the universal laws that would keep us and feed us. The power of Free Will is to serve us and when we realize our free choices teach us and help us to grow it is then we want to make better choices. The power of Karma or you reap what you sow, is to serve us.

"When we realize what we give out, we receive; we realize we are in control of our own abundant life."

I think if people that are hurting in life, suffering beyond what they ever dreamed, if they would simply walk into a Children's Hospital, and take under their wings a child dying of cancer, they would not only heal the child's lonely, long days, but they would see for themselves their own ability to heal the world by taking in their hearts love and compassion for one so young and without hope. When we look beyond our own heartache and then reach into the lives of others, **we forget why we hurt and we begin to see our own courage by embracing the courage of others.** We are all connected and when we begin to see how we each help one another, that is when we become ONE, **that is when we see God in us** and that is when we learn that God is with us and not against us.

Let's go back to what I have already said about "before coming to earth" you laid out a spiritual plan with the help of a spiritual teacher. Now, we don't know the plan so what we are going to do is look at what you might be going thru in your life. Let's say you were abused as a child and then when you married you married someone that also abused you and your children. Now, when you come to this world you are faced with the reality that there will be tempting forces on this earth. We can call them dark forces **because they refuse to bring light** and help to those on this earth. I have known numerous stories of horrible circumstances in which people are so distraught over and yet these people are such loving people by nature. I have tried to figure out what is happening when people find their lives turn into chaos and stay that way many times for a lifetime. When we talk of dark forces we need to keep in mind that their goal is to stop the growth of personal Christhood or anyone who wants to have the mind of Christ. Dark forces are simply forces that have no light in them. They can exist anywhere and in any living being. They work on total confusion and destroy any goodness a person might have, but they can only do this if you don't recognize them and therefore you need to bring in more light to counteract them. You **can't** go around accusing everything to be dark forces and so this is not what I am trying to suggest. I want to try and give you a way to look at your life and **intuitively think about it**. Until you can get past some of the trials you have been facing, you must try your best to look at them differently so that you can **begin** to not let them take over your mind. **I am trying to help you find a space in your mind where you can begin to breath again.** Your mind may be full of thoughts that relive your trauma and so you become consumed and when that happens anything that comes along will attach to the already impossible circumstances and you can't breath. You can't find a way *in which a seed can be planted* to make your world slowly transform. Again I say to you, look for the *open door* in which you can begin to transform your life as you currently see it as. Don't worry about how long it might take and don't look too far ahead or you will become discouraged. Just take today and look for a way *in which you can plant a seed* in which new life can spring forth.

I believe that many times the dark forces go after the souls that have the greatest ability to make a difference in this world. If you feel your world has been shattered over and over, again I say that you may be a very special soul that has come to this planet at this time to help the world. You cannot possibly help the world until you help yourself. Do you know that you have within you the ability to not only put aside the endless record that is played over and over about everything you truthfully have gone thru, but you can actually pull yourself out of all that has plagued you all your life, and start on a new road of self-discovery. People that come to earth with a very important spiritual mission or plan are the ones that the dark forces will strongly attach to. They will disrupt your life in such a profound way, *that you literally will have absolutely no idea of any plan*. You have actually been so traumatized that you have amnesia. It is my loving goal to help you reconnect to who you are and why you came but we first must recognize the problem and take the beginning steps to get you in the right direction for change. Anyone can get out of what they are currently suffering, and so you are the one that must decide if you are ready for this adventure.

With all that you have suffered all these years you will naturally take on the belief that you are cursed or you are being punished for all you have had to endure or whatever. And you will in no way believe that you are a special spiritual soul, that has a higher understanding of the world as a whole and that your mission was to do something very important to help the world.

One of the plots of the dark forces is to create the ***greatest possible amount of chaos in your lifetime so that your life's mission is so distorted*** that you never manifest the purpose. In their attempts to do this, dark forces will seek out others around you who are weak in mind and who have a lower understanding of the spiritual realm and use them to expose you to severe abuse. This is not to put anyone down or to categorize anyone. But what I would like for you to see is that ***your trauma may be an all out attempt to destroy the special spiritual mission*** you came to do. The people around us are from all walks of life and many are also having tough times. Keep in mind that their lives may also have a very special mission and so the dark forces would ***like for all of our lives to be so confused that none of us can help God*** bring greater meaning and abundant life to this earth. When you see those around you this way, I hope you will not begin to point fingers or accuse anyone of keeping you from your purpose. If you go that route you will have to be responsible for hindering their growth. The best route to take is to find an understanding ***that you can grasp of your life***, and to begin to weed out any negative influence that hinders you. You cannot change anyone but yourself. Don't go accusing anyone, just walk away, or silently go inside and have a knowing that you must take hold of your life before you can help anyone else. It won't always be easy and many times you will be confronted with the same trauma you have dealt with much of your life. Try your best to simply walk away without infliction of words or actions. If violence is part of what you struggle with then you need to find a place where you can stay away from the violence. You must take ***an active approach to your own growth*** and sometimes that means going to authorities or getting help. Live as peaceably as you can ***but be firm in taking a stand for your life.*** This is about change and ***change comes with courage*** and sometimes you have to put your foot down. Sometimes you cannot walk away with peace. ***I would say that it would help you if your actions in response to violence don't lead you down another difficult road.*** Whatever happens you must take a stand for what is right and leave vengeance, no matter how angry you feel, to God. For the truth is "vengeance" is discouraged by God because He wants you to heal on your own because what you are going thru *is about your journey. If you take vengeance then you have another road to deal with.* God is trying to help you out of how "you see" your life, the easiest way possible and *He doesn't want you to complicate the situation by creating more problems. It is in your best interest.*

The interesting thing about Karma is that our *"intent"* that creates our actions are the very teachers that help us grow. So if you are to hurt another by accident that is different than by intention. However, *the truth can never be avoided.* This is why *the heart must be changed* in order to change the actions. Karma is to teach you and when someone hurts another, they will learn in one way or another by how it affects their lives. Another thought on the matter is that maybe in this life you haven't been abused but you were in another life and part of your experience in this life *is to receive the healing from the other life.* As I explain different scenarios, please don't cause yourself to create a picture of your life and then never waver or be willing to see it differently at a later date. These thoughts I am trying to get you to think about are *only guidelines in which you can begin to look at your life* differently and not take it so personal. Yes, it is personal but if you are a spiritual being on a mission and you have been distracted for most of your life with abuse and heartache, *when will you be able to put that aside and look from a fresh perspective?* When can you step away from the trauma and see that all you have gone thru is definitely terrible *but is a distraction to keep you so occupied that you never accomplish the real reason you came to earth?* I feel in my heart that if people knew better they would do better and now is the time to know better. If you will make this decision and if you will follow through by taking advantage of all of the avenues of healing, you will find that there will be an extraordinary amount of help and support given unto you in this world and from Above. This kind of decision opens up a door in which God and the Ascended Beings, if asked, will help you out of your struggles. Sometimes the best road to healing is found in just understanding what you have been going through. In understanding that your struggles were put upon you to distort the picture of your life and to distract you long enough so that you would just give up, you can find enormous strength in rising above them. In understanding that your struggles are tools to help you, you will then re-look at your life and take courage to begin again. You are not alone in obtaining the help you need. You first have the Christ self within you and you have angels and ascended beings that have been assigned to help you overcome all the obstacles and manifest your Christhood. All you have to do is call to them with an open mind and you will receive the help and guidance you need in order to take the next step toward healing.

The next step is in understanding that when you are exposed to severe trauma and abuse, especially in childhood, it is most likely that *your soul will become somewhat fragmented*. There is also a possibility that your soul might have chosen to embody in a situation where there was a high probability of abuse. You might ask why would I choose this? Well, it's possible you wanted to learn a specific lesson that would help you resolve something in your psychology or you might simply have wanted to learn a lesson in which you fully understand that you can only rely on your Christ self by going within and establishing a connection. This is very important because to establish this connection is how you will find your original spiritual plan. Now there is another reason why you might have purposely chosen a difficult childhood and that is that you are a very mature soul who wants to help others. You chose to do this by experiencing a very difficult situation yourself so that you will know what it feels like and can therefore be more effective in helping others overcome the negative effects they are going thru. This is where pulling the beam out of your own eye is the only way you can see your plan. In order to fulfill your mission to help others, *you must first heal yourself*. There is also another possibility of why you are experiencing abuses in this world and that is to bring judgment upon the soul or souls, who abused you and all the dark forces working through them. This was one of the reasons Jesus allowed himself to be crucified. In committing this abuse against a person with full Christhood, these souls, and dark forces working through them, brought about their own judgment. As I have said before, we are all God's children and we are all working to manifest our Christhood but many are working for themselves. The only way to help them is to bring upon them the judgment that they create against others and that is really their only hope. You can only change yourself but in changing yourself you cause others to ultimately change.

Another very critical part in your own healing is when you realize; you will need to manifest a flame of a forgiving spirit. It is **only forgiveness that can set you free** from the imperfections found in your life. Let me help you understand the importance of forgiveness. To truly understand you need to realize the truth that the basic law of this universe is the Law of Free Will and the very purpose of life is to grow, to move on, and to ultimately self-transcend. If this is the purpose of life and yet you are not fulfilling it then what is preventing you from growing and from moving on. **I believe the underlying problem is your sense of identity.** You have the identity of yourself according to what your life has been up until now. But if you were to lay aside all the details and go back to the beginning when you first arrived, you would see your identity in a very clear picture and it would be very different from what you see right now. This alone would help you to move past everything that is stopping you. But because you can't see your identity this way, right now, we need to continue to walk in the direction where you can reconnect eventually. So the part that is keeping you from growing, and from moving on and transcending your current state of consciousness, your current sense of identity, **is non-forgiveness.** You see, when there is something you have not forgiven, there is something you are holding on to, and there is something you cannot let go of. Recently I heard two children talking. They both experienced how their dad had hurt them emotionally. Both of them said they forgave their dad but only one would not talk about it anymore. The one that let it go actually forgave but the one that held on to it had not fully forgiven and so was always talking about it and making comments. I thought about this in view of my own perception of forgiveness and I realized that as long as I kept something in mind and held onto it, I had not forgiven. So when we remain emotionally attached to the things of this world and the things we have dealt with in this life, we are actually holding ourselves back from moving on. We hold ourselves tied to a limited and imperfect sense of identity and we are essentially worshiping an idol of our own making.

~By not forgiving, we are taking away our own freedom to move on.~

For a long time I believe I forgave but just didn't forget. However, in forgiving we loose a memory of what happened because we don't bring it up anymore.

So when you don't forgive, you don't move on and you become still or stagnant in your growth. And if you stay too long in one place, you will become subject *to the second law of thermodynamics, which means that a downward spiral, a negative vortex, of energy will begin forming around you.* When that vortex becomes too strong, it will begin to overpower your feelings and your thoughts, until you begin to believe either that there is nothing outside the vortex or that you cannot escape the downward pull of the vortex. *This is what causes people to believe there is no other way to live than in opposition to what you cannot let go of.* This is also why people believe that there is no way to escape the cycle of violence or revenge. They feel they simply must continue the cycle because they must have revenge, or they must set things right by committing another act of violence to supposedly neutralize or make up for previous act or even to stand their ground. *The intense energies that accumulate from this negative vortex prevent people from asking a very logical question, When Will This Come To an End?* Think about this in terms of your personal life and of countries at war for centuries. How are we going to stop the violence? *Is there an ultimate act of revenge that will settle the score permanently and bring about an end to the violence?* Only those *who are not trapped* in the downward negative spiral can see the solution. There is NO PEACE through revenge! It is not even possible to attain peace in this manner. *Vengeance creates vengeance from your opponent. It's a vicious cycle.* Just like in physics, for every action there is a reaction. It is simply a law of the material universe. And when you take revenge, you are reacting to what was done to you but your reaction becomes a new action and it creates a reaction from your opponent or even on a broader scale from the universe itself. ***Unless we learn to forgive and move on and that means to totally forget and start again, this cycle will never go away.*** I want you to understand that the people on this planet ***that do not want peace are few compared to those who do want peace.*** Many of those ***who want peace*** are caught in a spiraling vortex of revenge that was created by those ***that don't want peace.*** Whether we are talking on a planetary scale or on a personal level, you need to apply this thought to your situation or how you are applying what I am trying to tell you. Many say they want peace but they are not willing to stop the cycle of revenge. I hope you can use this principle and step away from the problem, or outside the box, and look at a new understanding of how energy vortexes of anger and revenge keep you from seeing the truth. They ***keep you from logically and rationally seeing the reality*** because they are so empowered ***by your emotional energies*** that they do not even stop to think. This is where we can be the change in a troubled world. If you can see the need to break free from the thinking and the actions that create a magnetic pull on people's emotions and overpowers them, ***you can actually begin an upward movement to break the spell.*** I think that many times the ***pattern of problems*** in this world continues because those that take on the power, are those that are working against God. ***This is where we, who see what is right and what needs to be done, must be the action and the change. We must have the courage.*** So in order to be free from our traumas in life, we must forgive and give those that have hurt us no more power over us. In forgiving we free ourselves from their evil.

So as we experience abuse, we also take on a limited self image and we feel unworthy or no good by how we are treated. The experience causes us to feel so violated by the abuse that we feel we could never again be worthy to face God. ***This is the ultimate lie and it is extremely important to see thru this lie and accept it as a lie and then dismiss it.*** You need to know your Father in Heaven and His unconditional love for you ***that cannot, nor will not ever go away from you.*** And there is nothing that could have possibly happened to you in this world that you cannot overcome and leave behind. When a soul has been deeply wounded it can be very painful to think about the entire situation surrounding the abuse. What I want you to know is that although someone abused you, what caused your soul to be hurt was **not the outer act of abuse but your reaction to it.** This might be difficult for you to accept right now but when your soul is somewhat healed; **you will begin to see it differently.** The important thing is to realize that I am not saying horrible things shouldn't affect you but I am trying to get you to understand why some people can have the same trauma, almost identical, and **have a totally different reaction to it.** Let me explain something further about what happens when your soul has been abused. When this happens **your soul will have fractured and some of the fragments have become separated from your soul.** This will leave empty spaces within the structure of your soul and **it is those empty spaces that can be filled with impure energies or even dark spirits that seek to control your soul and your ultimate purpose you want to accomplish.** Because there is not enough soul substance left after the abuse and because of outside forces trying to manipulate your soul it can feel like "your own will" has been taken away from your power. One reason for this could be that the soul substance that is left might not be strong enough to take dominion over the rest of your soul. As you begin to heal your soul, you will magnetize some of the lost soul fragments back to you and you will also begin to expel the foreign energies and beings that I have called dark forces. This will be a way in which you can begin the journey of reaching a greater understanding and wholeness of your being and you will begin to take dominion of your life and your will, back. Just like salvation, it is not an automatic process. The reason that there is no automatic way to salvation, which by the way is what you are working on right here in saving yourself from destruction, is because God wants us to take dominion over our life and **if you don't do the action, you are not using your free will to actively come back to God.** In doing something, you gain strength and wisdom and you begin to exercise your own abilities and this gives you confidence and sets you on the right track. **It's in the journey that you gain back your identity** and when you arrive at the destination you will find that there is more joy to come. Focus on the "doing", the active part you take, the journey and you will be amazed at the joy you will find along the way.

Each day you will find confidence. This is what Jesus came to tell you salvation was. It's not about a certain church but it's about becoming one with the Father and the only way to become one is to reconnect with your spiritual self and take on the mind of Christ. "Let this Mind also be in you", isn't that what Jesus really wanted to help us find. The truth is that **no force in this world can TAKE away your will.** When the forces of this world expose you to severe trauma and abuse, your soul is in such turmoil that it can **voluntarily GIVE away** its will. The soul can feel it has made such a terrible mistake, that it has been so wounded and the situation you are dealing with is so chaotic that it could not possibly do anything on its own, to resolve the situation. Have you ever experienced this? I have and it's not a good feeling. When I went thru this at different times in my life, I once succumbed to believing this was my life and I need to just make the best of it. But often when we are in this situation we know how hard life has become and when we resign to just living it the way it is, it gets worse. *The reason it gets worse is because we must change and God wants us to change.* It gets worse before it's gets better because God set up the universe so that we create our own circumstances by our choices. *This might seem unkind but it actually is a fail-proof design or at least a warning that we are in imminent danger.* If what we are doing, we have resigned to continuing because of how we believe we are not worthy, continues on the path of destruction, we will continue to get a wakeup call. If we put the **wake-up call** on hold or just hang up, we will get another one down the road. The **wake-up calls** are brought by "what is within you, your spiritual self or I AM Presence" and when receiving more of the same abuse or trauma, **what is within you is trying to tell you something.** WAKE UP AND LISTEN. Until we take hold of our lives, even in our weakest moment, **nothing is going to change but in fact will only get worse.** But it gets worse because God wants us to move beyond it and **not because He is punishing you.** The physical abuse might change if we get away from it but mentally we will be tortured by the same feelings and so God wants us to overcome and to **not only overcome** but also re-connect and truly fulfill our spiritual plan. It's not just about helping the world although that is what we ultimately **can do.**

Love yourself enough to focus on pulling the beam out of your eyes first and then you will be able to be the kind of help for others, they need. You see God loves you more than you realize and God is not an angry, hardhearted person. He is not capable of anger. He is full of love. For me it was years of resigning myself and years of believing I was unworthy and *"I"* had created this by believing this was the truth. I knew that if I was going to live, I had to re-look at my beliefs and in order to do that I had to remove the beam from my eyes. But before I came to this full realization I prayed God would save me and this I requested based on beliefs I had thought were true because religion taught these things and I had believed them to be all there was to life. What did I believe? I believed I could do nothing for myself *but that was a lie*. If we reap what we sow, and Jesus said pull the beam from our own eyes, *then it was ME that had to take hold of my life.* One day I realized that I was going to die *trying to live thru it* and I asked myself, if this was really what God wanted me to do. Did He want me to totally hand my life to Him and just die in His arms? That is what religion teaches *but this just can't be.* The teachings were still implanted in my mind but when I *intuitively* saw something that was what caused me to re-think. *This is where it takes time.*

~Hear what is within you, your intuitive voice, and your spiritual self and know it is trying to awaken you.~

Did God create me to live thru hell and then just crawl up in His arms and He would take me to heaven? If that were the case then people would want to die all the time. But *God's message was to LIVE* and not to just curl up and die. The "pieces didn't fit". God made me in His Image and so what did that mean? If God used His *own power* to create and he told us to take dominion and multiply what He did, *that doesn't add up to resigning myself to all this heartache and believing there is nothing more I can do.* So I just give my free will away and do nothing with my life? *NO this is not the truth!!!!!* I began to realize that my *intuitive "knowing"* all these years, that there was more to the message of Jesus and to what God really wants of His creation, *was*

God within me, crying out to wake up. I decided to take my "will" back, to jump into the river of life and to have faith that God has not brought me this far, only to send me to a so-called hell. This was what caused me to step out of the box of the so-called reality I thought was all there was and take a chance ***that I simply needed to have a different take on the same words.*** I needed to see differently but in order to do that I would need some help and that is when I began to pray to the Ascended Beings which by the way includes Jesus. This gave me an open door to begin to see the greater picture of life on earth and the reason for all we go thru. Your life is very, very important and you are a chosen vessel that has come to earth at this time to help the world in your specific plan.

So taking back your life is a conscious decision and ***can only become your reality by an act of your own will, FREE WILL. You gave it away through an act of will, and you must take it back the same way.***

In certain methods that are given thru self-help avenues these methods present ways in which you can convince yourself, your outer mind, to do something and there is a result that happens by this action. Take for instance positive thinking. It is good and ***it can get you on the right track*** but positive thinking can only go so far. What happens is you are given an outer security ***that you can be healed*** and for a time you will feel the healing because positive thoughts are what helps us. However, in the end, you must consciously take back your will by making the decision to go deeper and accept full accountability for your own situation. So if you just use an outer ritual to make yourself feel better but you don't change the inner beliefs that have created this lack in your life, it will only be a Band-Aid and ***ultimately what you struggle with will return, often in a greater force.*** Another reality of severe abuse is that it is hard to accept personal responsibility for the situation that others have inflicted on you. I am not asking you to feel accountable for what others have done to you. And I am not asking you to feel that you must be a bad person to have such things happen to you. What I want to ask you to do is to ***accept accountability for your "reaction" to your situation so that you accept the fact that*** *what hurt your soul was the decisions you made, the false self-image you accepted, while the abuse was happening or even afterward.* I also want you to give love to yourself and know that the decision you made was the best possible decision at that time for you, considering your state of consciousness or your understanding of your life, which is also based on your soul maturity. This is very important when you find yourself re-living an abuse in your adult years that happened when you were a child. A child perceives things at their level of consciousness at the time and so if you carry the same reaction with you into your adult life, you are actually bringing along with you the interpretation that you felt from a lower understanding because you were a child at the time and that was the best you could see things.

Now you are an adult and you have a higher level of your souls maturity. So if you could go back with this "level of soul maturity" to the time when the abuse was inflicted, then you could make a better interpretation. It might not be easier to take the abuse but you might not be as traumatized, *because the trauma is linked to your interpretation*. So if your soul maturity is at a higher level, then your reaction will be different. When you come to this understanding, you can allow yourself to re-experience the situation and *replace the original decision with a better decision*. The damage that was done to your soul *was done through decisions you made according to your understanding at the time of the trauma.* In other words, the only way the damage can be permanently *undone* is by you making better decisions that replace the old ones and many times this requires you to find a new interpretation of what happened. The help of a therapist is very good if you can afford one. And yet for others they seem to be able to get thru a lot on their own. This is where you need to see what would help you. You may choose to get professional guidance for a time and try things on your own once you get strong enough. This is your life and if you are trying to really find joy and a new way to live, then you need to exercise free will choices. Don't be afraid of the decisions and don't be afraid to get help. Look at what you ultimately want to achieve and know within that you are quite capable of making your own decisions and what you decide is good. As things change in your life, then you may adjust previous decisions and this is good too. I do want to tell you honestly that when trauma for you has been very hard, you definitely need someone to talk to.

~God wants you to know that change is always a part of the journey in life. ~

So if you walk a certain way at a certain time in your life, **then you needed to.** And when you decide to walk another way, **then you need to.** Change is part of growing and the ultimate meaning in life is to eventually become one with God and to be able to exercise your ability to co-create with God. That is why you must rise above your current limitations.

Keep in mind that it takes time to heal, especially from childhood abuse. Be patient with yourself, and **remember to love yourself unconditionally thru it all.** If you are feeling pain so deep, then allow yourself to cry and to bring up the pain but remember to not allow that pain to be your entire story. The pain, the tears, and the anger is to help you release it and move beyond it, not to hang onto it and let it be what you live every day. Once you are free from the trauma, you will feel spiritually reborn, and you then will begin to express your Christhood and fulfill your divine plan.

Like I mentioned before your spiritual plan just might be to help other victims of abuse and be able to show them how to be healed. As you find your way to heal yourself, you will have one avenue to help them do the same. Look at your struggles with a different perspective. Yes, you can go on reliving the pain everyday for the rest of your life and **you will have created your own hell on earth,** or you can take the courage to see beyond them, heal your hurt and **then use the tools and the understanding you gained in rising out of it, and help others.** It's your choice and no one else's. Another possibility of why you have gone thru what you have is that your spiritual plan might have been **to raise awareness about abuse and help society put an end to it.** Whatever the reason, believe there is a way to heal and believe that your life can ultimately have the greatest abundance ever.

Develop a new attitude when facing abuse or anything else that troubles you that ***everything happens to you as an opportunity for growth***. Abuse doesn't have to be physical and very evident to others. It can be mental abuse, and a slow agonizing way of taking away your power of your own free will. It can also come from just everyday stress of life when you don't feel understood. ***Life's difficult situations are really an opportunity to learn something about life and about your own psychology.*** Any situation you encounter is simply an opportunity ***to let go of some element or attachment that has a hold on you*** from this world. This attachment is embedded in a lower understanding of what life is about. In other words before we have a higher understanding of life, ***we have the best understanding possible at that time in life.*** I don't want you to think of yourself as lower but when you come to earth and reason as we often do about life, on earth, your understanding is not what you understood as the spiritual or higher understanding you had before you came to earth. We take on ***the best understanding we can*** according to the circumstances we are brought into when we come to this world. Some more mature spiritual beings will actually retain alot of their higher understanding and therefore, many of life's circumstances don't attach to them and they simply react differently. They are often seen as teachers for us. But no matter what, we all are of great importance to God and all of life. If your life has taken you down a deep road of struggle, then you may have been chosen to go that way and then rise out of it and you will in turn be able to have a greater understanding at how to help so many people that need to desperately rise above even the greatest of troubles. What I'm saying is that even though it appears you have been very unfortunate because you will have to exercise a greater effort to rise out of it, you are actually a very special, chosen being. ***With great difficulty you can acquire greater strength. With great adversity you have the potential to become one of the greatest teachers ever.*** You see true greatness isn't what the world sees as acquired wealth and status ***but true greatest comes when you become one with God.*** This will ultimately help you rise in God's kingdom and ***your heart will lead you to the greatest joy you ever imagined.*** When you help others achieve joy, ***your joy is multiplied.***

When you give back life to another, *your life is increased*. It's not about wealth and status, which is how the worlds lower consciousness, sees the meaning of life. But that isn't joy. It' might make life easier while here on earth but it only goes so far and when life is over, those joys are over.

I want to clarify this about everything being an opportunity. I am not saying that everything that happens to you is acceptable according to some ultimate standard that fits into the great scheme of things. Abuse, violence and all sorts of horrific atrocities *are not in any way part of God's plan or vision for this universe.* But *when* they happen, we need to approach those things with an attitude *that can help us move quickly beyond them.* If we are to face these things then let us not allow them to take us under. If we are to face these things then we need to be able to move past them quicker so that we can continue on the road of life. They may create mountains *that seem immovable* but if you have the right attitude and not let them be immovable, then you will learn what you can given the situation and become a better person in spite of them appearing. *Have the attitude of perseverance and not surrender.* Remember on another level of the Law of Cause and Effect that no one can escape the consequences of their actions. IF someone abuses you, that person will make personal karma and that person can never escape having to balance that karma. When you understand this Law that God has put into affect from the beginning, you can overcome one of the major blocks on the spiritual path. Just look at history on a broad scale for a moment. Have you not seen millions of people thru the ages, which have allowed themselves to be dragged into conflicts with other people that have gone on for many years? If you just look at this fact in accordance to how far removed we've become from why something happened in the first place, *you would see that your own trauma from childhood to now has become distorted in facts.* So if people are still feuding today over something that happen hundreds of years ago, it probably all started because one person did something to another person. Then one decided to punish the other for the action. *When people use that state of consciousness in which they feel it necessary to punish someone for doing them wrong, they actually are punishing themselves.* When you seek revenge over another, you will inevitably misqualify God's energy and produce negative karma for yourself. You punish yourself because you can never go on, never get past something and you remain in a constant conflict that literally destroys your life. If you understand it this way, you will see that *it really has no significance what the other person has done to you.* By the other persons actions against you *they have already created their own karma* and because the law states you reap what you sow, they will have to reap anyways. But if you choose to inflict the same action in revenge on the person, *now you have to answer for your own actions.*

In all reality, if you can understand this, you might understand *how you action of revenge only delays your own joy* that you can potentially have if you are working on bettering your life. Your action against someone because they did something against you is only hurting yourself. Many people have allowed themselves to be trapped in a *negative karmic spiral in which both sides seek revenge.* This creates an ongoing spiral, which can develop into family arguments or even wars between nations or religious groups. The Middle East is a great example but even more look at the wars between races of people. Then when you realize the reality of reincarnation, you will see that many people bind themselves to re-embody with the same people over and over again. Let me ask you something from another perspective. If someone abuses you and you pay them back, *you connect yourself to that person and so why would you want to create a karmic spiral with that person and have the potential to reincarnate with that person over many lifetimes.* Do you realize *you are only hurting yourself* and making each embodiment harder to get thru? If you forgive and move on *you release yourself from the ties that bind you* to that person. So it is in your best advantage to forgive and to not act in such a way that only creates more karma, more work for you to work thru. If someone is abusive to you, why not simply leave that person behind and move on to better things?

You might ask, how can I leave that abusive person behind? The best way I have seen to work is to simply look the other way and become non-attached to their actions. Forgiveness is very important. Many times when people hurt me, I found the emotional pain was the hardest to get beyond but I knew if I inflicted pain back then I would be pulled into their conflict with me.

~*If we refuse to be pulled in then we will not create a karmic tie.*~

When you do turn the other cheek, you will have the victory on your own personal path of transformation. So even though it isn't right what happens in life, you can still use the circumstance to help you grow and in turn you will be much further ahead. When you take steps like this, it is then that you begin to see the rewards and often the rewards are even greater because ***they create a new perspective*** in your mind. The victory within ***starts with an inner decision*** that you are going to begin to grow and no matter who steps in your path, you will keep the focus that the situation is an opportunity for growth.

Sometimes it is hard to understand why taking this approach is going to have a greater victory in the long run for you. Let me try to give you an overall view so that you can decide for yourself if this is something you want to do. Many people feel like they are victims beyond their control. Many times we will ask ourselves "Why does this always happen to me?" Often we feel that we could not have chosen the difficult challenges we are facing in this life, right now, but the truth is might have very well chosen this path. Let me explain. See yourself again as a spiritual person who has embodied numerous times. Thru lifetimes you have made certain imperfect choices and have created personal karma.

~*Karma acts like a magnet that draws your soul back to the material universe to resolve it.*~

When you are in embodiment in a lifetime, it is hard to see that a situation is a result of your choices because you are so overpowered by the emotions and the circumstances. However, when you die and return to the spirit world, you are now considered out of embodiment and you also escape the involvement of what you had gone thru in this lifetime. This is very important. Many times you will hear that people communicate with those that have gone on. Many times healings of past struggles with those people come as a result. So when you leave this lifetime and are no longer in embodiment you can look at the situation from a higher and less emotional perspective. Now let's go back one step further to a time before you came into this life stream. You met with your spiritual teachers and created a plan that is designed at helping you rise to a higher level on your personal path. ***When you are not embodied you can see things from a less emotional perspective and you are not empowered by outer circumstances.*** So when you choose your next embodiment, you often will choose to embody in circumstances that offer maximum opportunity for spiritual growth. I am not saying that you will choose the easy road. ***Believe it or not every soul has enormous courage*** because in all reality planet earth's current conditions are very difficult and it takes courageous souls who are determined to learn their lessons and move on with life, to choose to come here. ***Many souls deliberately choose circumstances that present major challenge*** which gives them an opportunity to balance the karma that has hindered their growth for lifetimes.

The essence of growth is that you are willing to leave behind your attachments to the limited image of yourself and the world. Let's say you are trying to break free from an identity obstacle. In past lives you have been unable to fulfill your spiritual plan because you have attached to a crippling part of who you are in this lifetime, namely your name or namesake. So a choice to come to this earth and be able to break free might include very difficult circumstances that force the soul to deal with this. The reason the soul makes a decision that is difficult to get past unless they face it, is because that once you become embodied in a physical body, it is very tempting to seek ***to avoid challenges and difficulties.*** You will find that many people spend a lifetime trying to avoid challenges they face in their life. This is the fight that goes on when in embodiment and it often prevents the soul from learning its lessons and therefore progressing on the path. When the soul is still out of embodiment and is still with it's spiritual teachers, they will create a plan that is so difficult *that it will be hard to ignore or to get out of. The reason is because this soul is very strong and wants the maximum opportunity for spiritual growth. But if they achieve victory, they will experience a joy beyond their expectations.*

We have talked about not taking revenge and so one might wonder where we draw the line in allowing people to have their way. Jesus came out of compassion to the entire world and their struggles but he didn't come to say it was ok to remain in the situations they were in. *He knew that if they understood things with a higher understanding they would see the difference between human suffering, that seeks to make people feel good about remaining in a bad situation, and true empathy which seeks to help people rise above their limitations.* Jesus was a true spiritual teacher who wanted his students, those who wished for a more abundant life, to be empowered by coming to a higher state of consciousness. Jesus wanted us to *use tragedy as a stepping-stone on our path to a life with more abundance.*

Let's look at emotions and how they consume us. If you have lost a loved one, you are overwhelmed by emotional energy. But if you step back from your situation and see the planet as a whole, you will see that you are literally swimming in an ocean of toxic emotional energy and your personal energy field is only a drop in that ocean. If you do not take measure to protect your personal energy field, you will easily be consumed by the energy that surrounds you and this is why so many people become overwhelmed by sorrow over a loss of a loved one and literally sink into depression in which there seems to be no escape. This is how some people, when experiencing personal tragedy, become overwhelmed by sorrow and actually sink into a permanent state of depression where there seems to be no way out. *The truth is they become immersed in not only there own emotional state but have actually jumped into the ocean that contains the mass consciousness of the world-accumulated emotions.* In some cases, dark forces that are seeking to derail your own personal spiritual progress can direct such emotional energy at you. *Emotions are the inroad for controlling people.* Emotions by nature are fluid and easy to manipulate. You need to be on guard as to how your emotions, your thoughts, and your sense of identity are all connected. Once you internalize and begin to change your sense of identity by accepting that whoever you are called by is insignificant in the spiritual world and you are first and foremost a spiritual being. Your given identity on earth in this lifetime is for a reason and is to serve you in your higher understanding of your life.

I haven't covered every detail of every kind of scenario because I want you to learn the **principles** of how to take any scenario and find a higher understanding on your own. Today is a new day and no matter what part of your journey you find yourself on, **it is the best part to begin**. Begin to take hold of your life and have faith that God will be with you always. Nothing is too hard for you too handle. You are a courageous soul and you can do anything you put your mind to. **Believe and you will achieve the power to take back your life.**

CHANGE BEGINS WITH YOURSELF

It's not what we do that is as important as why we do what we do. As I begin this chapter I ask myself how many people in this world *really are completely happy and content with their lives.* Does your life lead from one crisis to another and you would like to get off the merry-go-round and begin to understand the greater purpose? Do you have an inner longing that there is more to life than what you are experiencing right now? Change begins with your "self", first.

Many times we understand change is necessary and we want to change. But what happens when we suddenly revert back to our old ways? What takes us only so far and then halts all progress? Do we simply loose sight of the goal or has something else caused us to retreat? In understanding the deeper reasons of what keeps you from changing, you will then be able to have the power to really change yourself. There is value in every aspect of life, from the past, to the present; *power in knowledge frees us to believe that abundant life is possible.* Maybe we simply don't understand the value of the past and the potential of the future.

In order for your life to change and become a *source of strength* to you and to others, you *must* ask yourself how you can produce the necessary change in your own life. Necessary change becomes evident, as you understand things more fully. *Knowledge is power* and will help you make a better decision of how you want your life to be. There are many things that hinder our ability to change and so I will try to cover some of the very basics. It is important for you to understand that *my words will not give you everything there is to know* but they have the potential for you to open your own mind and begin to hear God speaking to you.

I begin with love because unless you love yourself, you won't be willing to look at the truth that can change your life.

~Love is one of the most misunderstood emotions on this planet.~

We all desire love and yet most of us have a definition that is derived from our experiences and emotions attached to them, in our lives on earth. It's earthbound because it his how *the ego sees love*. Much of the time it is attached to conditions, and it can change in the blink of an eye. In the religious world they speak of God's Unconditional love but *they don't know how to give it to others*. My experience is that many want to, but in religion they are *boxed in by their beliefs* and are always encouraged to get others to come to there religion and so *unconditional anything* is simply only spoken about. It's ok if you don't agree with me, but think about it next time something comes in opposition to your church. Do they encourage you to encourage others *to feel good about their opposing journey from the one you are on* or do they encourage you *to pray for them that they will see their wrong?* This way of right and wrong, good or bad, and so many opposing opinions is the ego's way of reasoning. *It is very hard for the ego to see the value of unconditional love because they are always trying to convince themselves and others they are right.* Unconditional love is about seeing someone's need to be on a different path than yours and *loving them all the way. It's about giving them the courage to grow on the path that they are one because they need to be on that path so they can grow independently on their journey in life.* It isn't about dividing and conquering and trying to sway someone in your direction. *It's about a constant flowing of love that goes on and on based on*

absolutely no conditions. Love is desired more than anything else in this world. *Yes, even more than riches and power.* People that seek for riches and power, still have a deep inner longing for love. They may hide it but they desire love above all things. Riches and power feed the ego *but when they have had their fill, they are still unhappy and they search for love.* Why is it that we as humans seem to search our whole lives for love and yet it can't be found? The truth is that love is found deep inside your own being but you cannot connect to it because of how you feel about yourself. *Love is easy and a joy* but most of us see it as difficult and forever getting in the way.

~Love is a part of the energy that created you.~

Love is what God's being and light consists of. So why do we search for love from outside our being. Part of it is the experience in the material realm. We have this belief that *if we don't feel we have it then we need to get it* and so when we don't feel we have love then we look for it in someone else. We need to love ourselves first and then we want to give our love to others. Love is a force that flows constantly through us and unknowingly while in the material world. Our spiritual being knows it desires to give love out to others, but we have forgotten we already have it inside. The love we have for ourselves creates an abundance of love that can be given out. So if you feel unloving towards the people of the world, family, friends and even your spouse *it's because you do not have the love you need to have for yourself.* You have lost touch with the love you already have within and so when you don't *think* you have it, *you create an avenue of great loss and sadness, an empty feeling.* Don't get me wrong. There are many people that have great confidence that they are very loving people and even manifest love for others but their love is not stable and becomes fragmented when things go wrong. For instance if you are in a loving relationship and you break up, they say the first thing to go is your self-esteem but I believe the first thing to go is your sense of love for yourself. *If you don't have something, you can't give it away and so it is, with love.* The power of love is underestimated and when we talk about change and how it begins with *yourself*, it's important to understand how fundamental love is. ***Love is what created everything in the universe. Love is the foundation, the central force behind everything ever created.*** When you understand the importance of love in ***all of life***, then you realize how you have "in the palm of your hand" ***a key to your transformation.*** We all know about love and we have seen its power in how it can transform our human lives. But the power of love is so great in the Spiritual Realm that it becomes the driving force behind all life and all potential for everything to become more. I want you to know that you can facilitate your healing a little at a time by ***one very important key to opening many doors*** of greater understanding through ***simply loving yourself.*** This will take some work but loving yourself ***will open up so many doors*** in which you can heal and rise above.

Jesus spoke of loving your enemies, of Loving God with all your heart and soul, of loving your neighbor as yourself, and throughout his life he showed us by giving love in the most difficult situations. Think of him when he was dying on the cross. Do you realize the pain he was suffering and the anguish deep in his heart? ***It wasn't just the nails but it was the thought of how he had given so much and this was the heart that did these atrocities.*** Yet he cried to the Father to forgive them for they knew not what they were doing. Keep in mind this cry was while they were driving nails into his hands and his feet and they had stripped him of his clothes and were throwing dice as to who would get them. Do you see this kind of love in our world very often? I don't, ***but I know it has been here*** through countless spiritual men and women who have chosen to live here long enough to show us how God's love is. And I know it is here always. I know I see this kind of love often in children. So today I think the first thing that we need to look at when considering changing ourselves ***is what love has to do with it.***

God has made it clear that loving Him is connected to loving yourself. God is one with you, He is in you, and ***so loving yourself is critical in loving God. If you don't love yourself, then you must not love God, because God is a part of your being.*** Jesus came to show us that love is the key to everything in life. Think of love as an energy vibration. *Love brings a higher vibration, which is in direction correlation to light.* Jesus lived to show us that whatever life throws your way; *you need to respond with love.* And the reason for this is to show you that if you respond to everything in love, *you raise the energy around the whole situation and within yourself.* This was a way to help you understand that you can actually apply this simple truth and it would help you *keep a higher vibration of love in your presence* which would in turn make change much more accessible. *The higher vibration of love is likened unto a beam of light and if you keep that light around your being on a more constant basis then you will be able to see more clearly the reality of your life and it will help you grow quicker.* You see, just in our visual world we know that *operating in the dark is very long and tedious* but if we really want change to begin on a more stable foundation you can just apply the simple message of Jesus so long ago. *Turn on the light or the love.* Light and love are in the same vibration of energy. *So if you want to see more clearly then apply the love, the unconditional love Jesus encourages you to posses.* This is one of the *major blocks* in religion and because of the nature of religions philosophy that theirs is the only way; it will remain as it is. *When you love others unconditionally then you find that all the reasons you didn't love yourself, disappear.* When you give to others, you give to yourself. So when you accept others and *their journey* with a heart of unconditional love, *you also accept yourself.* When you condemn others *you simply sit in the dark.* And when you stop condemning and start loving, based on NO conditions you see that what you send out returns to you and often double-fold. When you send mercy you receive mercy, when you send love you receive love, when you send compassion you receive compassion, when you send tolerance you receive tolerance, *it's simply God's laws set in motion. You can argue about it but it won't change God's truth* because God has made it so. *God knows the best teacher is thyself and so if you reap what you sow,* you will feel the effect and *you will decide* if you want to change. The only thing that can change is Y-O-U. So if you want to sit in the dark because you don't believe you can make the change or you don't believe that you reap what you sow, *then sit in the dark. You have free*

will and that is your choice. No one should interfere with your choice. And when we see you make that choice ***we love you no matter what because our love is unconditional.*** Giving every individual the right to live, as they want, although sometimes they have to face consequences when it affects others, is important. If someone is a murderer I am not saying you should unconditionally love the fact they murdered someone. I am saying, separate the action from the person they are and love them no matter what. ***To love others especially when they have gone down wrong roads is so helpful not only in their healing but in yours.*** To forgive and love means you understand not only them but also yourself. You see loving and forgiving heals you the most. To grow we need to give ourselves the best scenario to begin and these are the things that will help you begin. We are what we think we are. When we change, the whole world changes because ***we see it differently.*** The power of change begins with you. I recently watched a program where someone in prison was dying and had been there all their lives because of a horrible crime they committed. This person wanted to die outside of prison and asked for parole. A family member of someone killed wouldn't give her that last request. That is her choice but as I heard why, I realized that her choice was blocking love in her being. She said it was because she didn't "feel" the person's remorse. When something so horrible happens we can empathize with the victims family so much and I feel a great sense of love for this family member. I understand that the loss of their loved one ***cannot ever be remedied.*** But sometimes we can be healed when we give understanding and love to someone who will not be here much longer. When we understand nothing will bring back those we love, maybe something like this has ***come to us to help us heal.*** Maybe the family member's higher self is trying to help her heal before the prisoner dies. And maybe giving mercy to the prisoner will help the prisoner heal. Whatever the case, opportunities like this often challenge us because our first reaction is that we want them to suffer as our family member did and we have, but sometimes these opportunities ***are in our best interest.*** Opportunities do come and sometimes we just pass them by because they are too painful. It's ***understandable*** but for some reason I believe there is a deeper reason that it would be in the best interest for this family member to use this situation to grow from. Forgiveness is not just for others but also for ourselves and it can heal us in ways you never thought possible. *There is something that her higher self wants her to overcome because she has the potential to do other things in life.* The woman prisoner is not going to live and so would it help to help another even when our human nature wants us to make them pay. *If we could see that in giving love and forgiveness we heal ourselves* and if our lives will go on, we have a greater potential to become what we still can become.

Another thought I want to share is if your life is bringing trouble to you, you may have created this by your actions in the past. You may have not always responded with love in situations. I know that it isn't always easy to respond with love when the situation is difficult. In responding with love in difficult situations, you don't have to agree with the anger or drama but you can try to understand the person that is very difficult and not *react* to it or simply just voice you can see their side. There are exceptions, but in general we reap what we sow. *It's not time to panic when I tell you this, but it is time to have a higher understanding of how love can, bring you abundance.*

If everything in life is from energy, then light is also energy and love is energy. If you are experiencing negative feelings of fear and anger then you are receiving a lower level of energy. *It actually is energy of less light.* When we experience troubles, we are receiving a lower vibration of God's light and *this creates a void in us.* We feel alone, and we feel that life is unfair. Think about any experience you have gone through and try seeing what I'm saying. Many times when this happens either once or on a constant we feel God is punishing us, or we feel angry with Him. *The truth is He would have never done this to you. You created this all by yourself.* What you send out you receive and so if you want to receive a higher vibration, a higher level of God's light then you *must give that out.* This is where you need to see that karma is to help you grow but *growing can only come from your ability to understand and put it in action.* If you don't understand, or you don't *want* to understand then you will continue what you are doing until you have had enough and you want a better life. ***Change becomes something that you are in control of.***

If you want to get to, let's say California, you get in the car and you start driving. If you have trouble with the car, then you fix it and keep going. But ***everything is your choice when you want to go somewhere.*** Yes, problems arise, like money, or time but essentially that ***is also in your control.*** What I am trying to say is that ***no one is to blame for your life, but you.*** The important part of any scenario is that we need to take responsibility for the things ***we can do differently*** and ***with the things that are not in our control, we need to take action in the best we can.***

Let's get back to "love". We know how our intentions and our hearts have a direct influence on the amount of love we can receive. We also need to understand how being ***honest with ourselves*** and seeing our lives as they really are will help us understand anything that hinders our ability to receive love. ***Honesty is the only way to see your situation as it is.*** Let's say you have been walking down a certain street to catch a bus but lately you have found yourself dealing with construction, holes and barriers. This has caused you to fall and hurt yourself, be late, and experience frustration at levels that have created bad days at work. ***Do you have control over what you are going through? Yes, you really do.*** But if you choose to continue to walk down that street, you will experience the troubles ***until the conditions on that street change.*** Now, you might find this particular street is the fastest way to catch the bus and so you choose to continue to use that street. There are other streets that are safer but ***it is your own choice*** in the matter. This situation is an illustration of knowing the facts and yet choosing how we will live our lives. We can complain, as many times we do but the truth is ***we make the choice*** and we really shouldn't spend time complaining about it. Sometimes it is very evident to others that we should make different choices in certain matters but we still choose to walk the same path no matter what anyone says. Honesty in seeing life as it is can save you a lot of frustration and help you begin to grow sooner. When you are around someone that keeps making the choices that make their lives more difficult than need be, keep loving them and if they want to hear advice then do it with kindness. I have noticed throughout my life that many people keep doing the same thing over and over, **not because it is the best way**, but because they either see it a certain way or are just set in their ways and don't want to change. If that is you, **that is your choice**. Only you have the power to change yourself but I can try to help you **see something differently** and then you need to decide if it's **in your best interest** to change. As for the circumstances you are experiencing in life I would ask you to stop blaming anyone else, including God, for your life. And take hold of the fact that **you do have control over your life**; therefore **what you are experiencing has a direct relationship to you as being responsible for creating it.** I am not saying that everything in your life is your fault. But everything in the pattern **of what your life reaps as a result of your direct actions, is of your doing by your choices. This is not a blame game but if I can get you to take responsibility, then we can begin to change the outcome.** Your choices you made were based on what you saw **as the best for you at the time**. HOW CAN THAT BE WRONG? This is where the "journey" begins to enlighten us. What you thought to be the right way for you to walk, lets' say five years ago, you may see it differently today. **That is the beauty of the journey**. Don't start the blame game **on yourself**. Just understand that you saw it one way at one time and now you see it another way today. **Shouldn't that be something you should be rejoicing over?** If you take the **attitude of gratitude of the growth of your journey**, you won't have time to put yourself down for making mistakes, because you will be seeing the beauty of the path and **you will actually be captivated at the power you do have over your life**. There may be some blatant errors you know were obviously wrong in choices you have made in the past, but look at it in an impersonal way so that you can learn the lesson and grow. When I say impersonal I mean, see it for a lesson to grow by and **don't attach the emotions of guilt and regret.** Just learn and "move on" because that is **why it came into** your journey. Do you think for one minute all the lessons of life are there to trap us and disable our ability to move forward? **No**, they are there because you wanted to experience certain situations so that you could move past them. If you didn't move past them before, then **NOW is** *your opportunity for your victory* in rising above them. **Don't pass it up; it's a chance of a lifetime!!!!** This will also reap a sense of gratitude for the experience. *How you see everything has the ability to help you or hinder you.* See things with a higher understanding and then you won't have to walk down a road in which you have to cover the same territory over and over again. *Let's see it for what it was, and move on.* There is a lot more for you to experience in your life but *if you remain on the same spot* for the majority of your life you will essentially not move ahead.

In taking responsibility for your life think about a basketball game. In the game each player has a responsibility to play the position they are given and to work for the good of the team as a whole, winning the game. You are responsible and if you make a mistake and it costs you to loose the ball then it was your choice in certain moves you chose to take in the game, that created this. What I am trying to help you see is that *it is to your advantage to take responsibility for your life and your choices*. If no one takes responsibility then there is **nowhere to begin**. On the other hand if you feel everyone is to blame, and it isn't your responsibility then no change can happen. So in a nutshell, if you want to really change your life, you must begin with yourself and *that means putting the power back in your hands so that you can make your own choices.*

If you are experiencing anger and fear, you are probably feeling the affects of what you have sent out into the universe. When we misinterpret our journey and we don't see that it's not to destroy us, we tend to use anger and fear instead of thankfulness for the journey. *We send out anger and fear and we receive more. But if we want to receive love and acceptance and feel growth, they we must send that out.* The only way to do this is to see the experience differently and that is *when change occurs*. If you want more abundance in life and you want to avoid unpleasant circumstances, then *you need to begin to change* how you feel about yourself and others. You need to change your attitude of life and your approach *by changing what you understand*. What you understand is in direct relationship to your state of consciousness.

~So if you respond to a situation with love, then you send an energy impulse of love into the universe and the universe will reflect that love back to you in the form of a positive energy.~

If you enter into a relationship where blame and confusion, and backstabbing are present it is to your best advantage to get out of that situation. But let's say you can't, let's say you have to live with it. Maybe you are a child and your parents have created this world around you. Maybe you can't just leave and so how can you not only survive but also grow. With every situation, good or bad, there is an opportunity to grow and become more. ***How you respond*** to the troubles you experience has the potential to not only help you but so many others watching you. Many times our greatest obstacle is how we see things. Even those that inflict pain and suffering are individuals that are also suffering. If you could see them as people that are so hurt they hurt others, you might feel the pain in their heart. It's hard when they are lashing out at you but look into their eyes and see them as wounded individuals. They are in more pain than you realize.

~To see a person separate from their actions helps you to love them in spite of what they do.~

You are given the choice to make your decisions in all matters and so do the best you can and stay with it. ***Remember that your purpose in life is to grow and become more aware of what your life is about.*** So in order to not get hung up on things that are happening you need to detach from the hurt and pain and realize it is going on but it's not about you even if they blame you. Go within, and find your reality of how you feel and the deeper part of you. ***Yes, things happening around you seem like your reality but they the results of others struggling with their journey.*** What's important is to know that what you are going through is not to destroy you and even though you are trying to live through it there is an opportunity waiting to grow from it. Find

279

the best avenue for you at your current level of understanding and keep the confidence that it is the way *for you now*. Don't beat yourself up if your choices go against the grain. There are no real solid right and wrong ways in many of life's situations but always consider the best way possible.

Love is everywhere and is available from all spiritual beings. All you need to do is ask for it. However, *to feel it inside, you must want to receive it*. If you send out hate, anger, and fear, *then you are creating a habit of responding to situations in a negative way* and you have created a *downward spiral of the same*. The interesting part of receiving love is that if someone has created this downward spiral *they probably can't receive love, because they don't love themselves enough to say they deserve love*. Here again, the abundant life that desires love unconditional *cannot be received until you change what you feel you deserve*. What is within you must heal. You see many times God sends love to the most unlovable but they don't see it because *their mindset doesn't recognize it and therefore doesn't have the capacity to embrace it*. God could send out all His love unto just you, but you wouldn't feel it, as you should. So the inner key is to take hold of your life, to send out the same as you want, because doing these things, taking this action, prepares you for what you desire. If you do it with the wrong intention you still won't receive it because your heart is not open to accept it.

So, when you have created this downward spiral from what you send out, you have also created more negativity, which can only be reflected back. Think of a mirror. You look into the mirror and *what you are is what you see*. If you want the image in the mirror to change, then you need to change the image, which is you. You *can't blame the mirror* for reflecting a wrong image back, because the mirror *only reflects what stands before it*. You stand before the mirror and all of what you are is simply being sent back to you. The same goes with negativity or any feeling you send out.

~If you send love with wrong intention then the same kind of love with wrong intention will be returned to you.~

Life is about learning and becoming more. Karma is a law that God instilled in the Universe to help us continually grow *even if we aren't purposely setting out to do so.*

Let's look at the many people that were involved in the death of Jesus. Each of them were on their own journey. *How they each were involved is about their own experience.* So no matter how awful an experience is, you need to see that all humans are each on their own journey and each have the potential to reach a higher understanding. We are not separate from each other and we can all help one another thru the experiences we go through. So with all of this in mind, *we can start by understanding there are many lives that can benefit in every experience.* When we look at our lives and the situations we are in and we look at what we are experiencing we need to look with an open heart, and honestly. We need to not be quick to condemn or judge but ready to understand each situation.

~If you have an honest heart with love, then you will look through loving eyes.~

You will stand for truth, and you will not be quick to judge. You will look at how your attitude can help others.

Difficult times are opportunities to bring so much healing and this healing comes from love. So the only way to change your life *is to change your approach to life* and to find a way in every situation to bring love, forgiveness and understanding. This will change what is within you and *what is within you can potentially heal your heart.* When you send out love, you will have the ability to receive the unconditional love that is returned unto you. Those that have not understood this must understand it before they are ready to receive it. I have often talked to people that will argue with me about this. They say, I gave them love but all I got was more of the same hate and anger. The truth is if you give mechanical love, that is not true love, but is a form to look like love, then you will receive the same back and that is why you feel it doesn't work or it doesn't' change. However, you may give true unconditional love to someone and they don't send it back. ***Understand that Karma doesn't always return right away and there are situations where it doesn't return in this lifetime.*** But it will be saved and returned like a savings account in another lifetime. But in general most of the time what you send out will be returned to you in this lifetime. ***This is where the attitude of what you send out enters. If you send love and expect a return, like a reward then you are sending it out with the wrong motive.*** Unconditional love is based on nothing ever returning to you. So if you give so that you can receive then you will receive the same kind of giving. Loving and giving with a pure heart is what will bring the growth of your life to fruition. What I want you to see is that ***certain attitudes you carry in your heart*** can be very helpful in your ability accelerate the necessary growth. Being honest and having the right intention is critical because if you don't send out ***true unconditional love***, then you will not receive it and you can't receive it until your heart wants to be honest and open. Your heart must want true love. ***It all works together and there is no fooling anyone. You cannot deceive this law, for it is true to itself.***

So let's talk a moment about how someone can go to heaven. We have somewhat covered the basics about love and our need for it but love ***is a flowing presence that permeates a soul when in heaven.*** In order to get entrance to heaven you have to have within you the higher level of consciousness. And to have this, ***a transformation of what is within you has to take place.*** Jesus illustrated this presence you have to have through his example of the "wedding garment" in Matthew 22:1-14. To explain what he meant to people that had a lower understanding of the spiritual life; he used the illustration with that of clothing, or garment. ***But the higher understanding was of a changed consciousness to fit the vibration of heaven, which would allow entrance.*** The garment was to help them relate to what they understood at the level of consciousness they were currently at and give them a picture of how they could enter the kingdom. Many churches believe that the wedding garments symbolize the **good deeds necessary** for Christian life and also the fruits of the kingdom of God. This is typical because most of the times a lot of teachings talk about the outer appearance. Even in today's interpretation by churches, they are taking scripture as it was written for the people of those days who didn't have the ability to understand as we have today. They are using the **same level of consciousness to explain these verses** when in fact there **is a higher understanding** and it has **nothing to do with outer appearance.** If you focus on the outer appearance you will also be left out of the kingdom. In order to permanently enter Heaven, you need to go through an **inner transformation of consciousness**, which comes when you have a higher understanding of what Jesus really was saying. You may not understand everything but you **can understand the "language of how to love unconditionally"** and that is why Jesus spoke to them much about what real love is. They may not have the higher understanding in the lifetime they lived in the Bible days, but they could reach heaven with understanding that in order to have **the frame of mind that created unconditional love they could attain the transformation they needed.** And in order to have this frame of mind they would need to change what is within, their consciousness, by changing their attitude and intentions in life **because that would change how they respond to people naturally.** To put on the wedding garment you must make a conscious choice and that is reflective of how your mind sees things and feels about life. **This is why you cannot fool anyone but yourself.** God knows if you can enter by what **you have allowed** your mind to contain. You simply cannot enter, **not because God keeps the door locked, but because you haven't taken the time to choose to change how you see life and in turn you do not have the ability to enter the kingdom. Your level of Consciousness raises the energy vibration to a higher level and in turn allows entrance.** That is why a "mechanical way" simply won't allow you in. You have to raise your level of awareness.

This is why this chapter is critical. **Change must be with you. You cannot fool anyone but yourself and you are the only one to blame.** The blame game simply won't do you any good but if you choose to walk it, then you need to walk it. To put on the wedding garment means you have the Christ consciousness and have left the carnal mind. When the carnal mind is left behind, you no longer are offended in situations.

Many people find it hard to love in difficult and hurtful situations. But through the years, because I love so easy, *I have had a hard time not loving someone* when they do terrible things to me. I learned at a very young age that when someone does something to hurt me, I find my mind separating the action from the person. Onlookers have often accused me that I deserve to be hurt because I allow people that are very hurtful into my life. I am not a person that is not aware of people' intentions but *I see the good in them*, as if it is worn on the sleeve. I know the bad they inflict and I know they continue but I see the possibilities of how much love they have to send out and that is what keeps them in my life. *For me I cannot turn off the flow of love* that course through my entire being but for many when terrible things happen *they just turn it off like a faucet.* They still have the ability to love *but by their judgment* and their hearts attitude they justify that love is not deserved for that person.

Let me explain to you the truth of love and the force of its power. Love is also explained in creation as light. Love is a pure energy that completes us as humans. It is a very well accepted fact that *energy cannot be created or destroyed*. Energy can be harnessed or hindered *but not gotten rid of.* The truth is that God created the worlds with His love or light and His love exists *whether you feel it or not.* The only way you do not have his love is because *something in you* has hindered it from entering. Your mind, your conscious awareness or what is within, is what allows love to flow or hinders it. Again *you become the force* of whether or not you have abundant life that is full of love. You see when you understand that *it is you and your choices* that give you what you need in life, that is when you realize you also have power to take control of your destiny.

~God created you to be an open door where His pure light could flow into this world.~

This is the natural ability **you have and always have had**. The reason you do not experience this light is because you have shut the light **off by how you feel about things, and your current level of understanding, which has lowered your vibration below the higher frequency in which light resides.** To have a life of love and abundance it is ready and available **when you set up the conditions you need to receive it.** Those conditions are in raising your vibration or level of consciousness.

In our world we learn what we **think** love is, by our life experiences. We all grow up in different families and some in different countries. God's love is unconditional and what that means is that **there are no conditions that you have to fulfill to receive His Love.** It's free and it's always available in the fullest form. God's love is what completes us and so if you are missing His love, then you **are "feeling" alone.** His love is there for you whether you receive it or not. Now human love is a different story. They say love comes in all sizes and I guess that is a good way of looking at human love. As I have already talked about human love is often based on conditions. Many marry for various reasons. Many times parents put a lot of emphasis on obedience and **relate it to love** when it comes to dealing with their children. Sometimes when people who have grown up in a very dysfunctional family search for what they never had in family, in a relationship. However, the unfortunate possibility when you grow up in a dysfunctional family is you will be drawn to saving someone and **you will recreate the same scenario in your own life.** The truth is that the same scenario happens because it is something you need to resolve and move past and it is drawn back to you so you can do that. That is another reason why people will say, "this always happens to me." The reason something continues to happen on a similar situation is because **you are required to resolve** your emotional ties to it and move on, in order to reach the next step in the ladder of your growth. So instead of thinking of yourself with bad luck, think of this in an impersonal way for growth. Again our growth is based on how we see things because how we see things reflects our readiness for the next step waiting for us to take.

There are many reasons people marry and some are from true unconditional love. Not all human love is bad but what happens is that many times people confuse love with need or just settle for something that is not good for them. Whatever the reason for love in marriage, or love in family you need to understand how important it is to *have God's love first*. Without fulfilling the love you long for from God, your fears will remain within. *God's love is what heals and secures your inner being.* When you feel comforted with His love, you are more able to know love in this world when you see it. So love is based on our understanding of it and if we simply have never experienced being loved unconditionally then we will have a hard time understanding what that really means. However I do know of some very loving people that had terrible childhoods and yet they know how to love unconditionally. Miracles happen and we can never know who knows about the real kind of love from God. So when we have difficulties in loving, we need to have an understanding that somewhere in our psychology we haven't fully comprehended the kind of love we long for. That kind is God's love but if you feel you don't have God's love, then we need to first realize that the only reason we don't have it is *because we don't open our hearts to receive it.*

Let's talk for a moment about Psychology. Our minds are very powerful and literally *they are what can make or break us.* I have thought many times of the old saying that boys don't cry because it seems that society labels people according to gender and age. This is unfair. To begin with, do you understand that in heaven we are neither male nor female? This is a biblical statement. It is critical to overcome psychological blocks that would hinder us from achieving our spiritual plan in this lifetime. In our world change is hard but change happens every day. Many people believe that people can't help the way they are. However, I feel that in this particular time in man's history there may be more than I realize who are willing to relook at this statement. We are not a product of hereditary and environmental factors and once we grow up there is nothing that can be done to change us. If everything in everyday life is always changing *then why do we get in our mind that we are un-changeable because of these factors*? You have every ability to be in command of your own destiny. Nothing can stand in the way of you achieving peace of mind, growth within, and happiness. The only person that can stop you by unbelief is yourself. Something I noticed in the past several years was that if you look back over a course of time, you find more and more of the feminine part of humanity, making large strides for change. I feel that this is what is supposed to happen. I am not talking about extremes but I am talking about changes that benefit humanity as a whole. There is a feminine and a masculine side of God. We are made in God's image and likeness and this alone should prove to you that God is both male and female.

So what creates block in our psychology? We again look at energy. Everything is energy and energy is at different levels. ***Growth or lack of growth is due to the flow of energy.*** Spiritual growth is necessary because it has the ability to transform toxic energy that we store up in our energy field. God's energy is flowing all the time to us and the level of vibration of the energy that we receive is in direct correlation with our level of consciousness. So if we want to receive more light or higher vibrational energy then we must raise our level to receive it. Toxic energy can exist within us from the energy we receive and is miss-qualified with negative energy from our mind. So in other words we might not be receiving the pure energy of love and light from God but we are still receiving energy, but just at a lower vibration. This energy flows thru us and if we hold psychological blockages we misqualify the energy and it becomes toxic. Let's take the example of going to a Psychologist for help. Lets say that you have certain issues you need to resolve so that you can live a happier life. Why is it that many times you cannot make headway no matter how long you have been going?

> ***"First of all I want you to know that your progress is totally dependent on your willingness to change and your understanding of your role in the matter."***

The doctor can only help you ***help yourself***. If you are truly committed to growth then you need to first stop miss-qualifying God's energy, and the only way to do this is to resolve the blocks in your psychology that are the culprits creating toxic energy and wrong karma returning. I have always believed in "balance" and so in helping you resolve this problem, you need to first understand that you can begin by sending out more positive energy than the toxic energy you are transforming. The toxic energy exists from ***an ongoing crisis in your mind*** over things that you have experienced either in this lifetime or another. They are blockages in your psychology and they block your ability to love and be loved. You generate toxic energy from how you see life, namely yours, and your interpretation of what has happened in your life. Keep in mind that two people can experience the very exact trauma and yet each has a different reaction to it. ***The reaction is determined by their state of mind or mindset or level of consciousness or understanding.*** All of this springs for how you really understand what life on earth is all about. The acceptance you have in your mind of false beliefs whether in this lifetime or another is a memory you might carry from lifetime to lifetime, in your mind. If it has to do with another lifetime and you don't know anything about it that is not going to matter. The way to healing all of these blockages and resolving all false beliefs is in understanding the truth. You either make a choice to rewind over and over the filmstrip of what goes thru your mind and creates havoc, or ***you can have a higher understanding and move past it.*** You can make the choice to leave the past in the past and see the story from an advantage in which everything can help you become a better person. Anyone that isn't getting help with a professional, is because they are not taking charge of what they need to do ***to help themselves.*** The doctor can walk with you because he or she is well trained to assist you but they cannot do anything for you. This is where your interpretation of the kind of help you are seeking can lead you down another road. If go to a doctor and believe they will heal you, you have a distorted picture. They have studied and become experts in the field of the mind but only you can create the change. It is their place to guide you and help you when you need help but they can never be your savior. This is critical in creating a trusting relationship with the doctor. No one can save you but yourself. Like in accounting with a balance sheet, if your income is lower than your expenses, your progress is negative. The same goes with what is in your mind, the amount of toxic energy you possess must be lower than the amount of new, positive energy you generate if you are going to find new strength in your psychology. This can only be done by taking upon yourself to resolve the major blocks in your mind and the only way to do that is to understand the truth about life and your journey. *If you understand the spiritual truths of life, life will become a source of strength.*

To resolve psychological problems you need a greater awareness of life and how everything is in your control in many ways. When you understand fully that you are the result of your choices then you want to make better choices. Studying and reading for deeper understanding is very helpful. Sometimes going to group sessions can be helpful in seeing you are not alone but the greatest help is *in knowing that you are not helpless and you are not alone.* God is within you and it is by your choices that your life can change. Just in choosing to see circumstances differently and choosing to love someone in spite of what they have done to you will empower within you the ability to love yourself. *Remembering to separate the action from the person will help you to see they, too, are struggling to live their lives and enjoy the abundance God has for them.* There is no quick fix but it takes time. Keep in mind if you go to a group session, you may hear much of the same and therefore this can hurt you if you interpret it as everyone has these problems. When you understand you are not alone and others experience the same it can be reassuring but if you still don't understand that your circumstances can change when you make the effort, then a group session can only be a place where all of you cover the same ground without solutions. However I have known of wonderful groups that walk with you, care and empathize with you and in turn help you to see new ways in which you can take charge of your life. The truth is that in order to get past anything in your life, you first have to see your responsibility to take hold of your life. You may be lucky to have people there to help you but they cannot do it for you. If you are lucky and someone is helping you then use that time to really work on the problem. Don't find yourself using their help to just sit back and do nothing. ***Help has come to take off some of the load and this is the best time to gather strength to change what you couldn't change when the burdens were greatest.*** Have you ever thought of the doctors that sit and listen to you in an effort to help you? Do you know that their greatest reward is to see you heal and move on? They know their business, they have studied the mind, but they also know you are the only one that can make the changes. When you heal you help them in their lives. Like I said before we are all connected and when we help another we help ourselves.

I want to address something deeper that can only help those who are ready. When we talk about "Who you are" it is a subject in which it is hard to really understand and ***even harder to explain*** because when you come to the material world you become attached very quickly upon entering, to a certain level of energy. That energy is in direct relationship with your embodiment and your embodiment is given a name and relationships that attach you on the outside and even more on the inside. This is a problem when we talk about the human identity vs. the spiritual identity. But the greatest problem is not what is on the outside but what is on the inside. It is the greatest because it is often not so visible and therefore you quickly think it isn't a problem. When I say energy I want you to remember that EVERYTHING is energy. I do not speak about "some" things, but EVERYTHING. This is one mental block that you must try to overcome when trying to understand at a higher level. There was a book written many years back about "The Impersonal Life" and I have often thought of it's importance in understanding the reality of Who You Are and your true ability to take hold of the real reason you are here in the material world at this time. The impersonal life is so real to the way you need to see yourself. Try to see yourself as ***impersonal energy*** but when life throws you a curve ball and you react with emotions, you are reacting to the energy in a very personal way. We are all God's energy. But when you live in the material world you take your energy to different levels by how you react and feel about things. It's hard to explain but I am going to keep trying. Let's say two people in the same family experience the same trauma but one has very little scarring or problems from the experience while the other cannot get past it. Why? Well, you can try to facilitate your own reasoning in this matter by thinking of possibilities. This is a great opportunity for you to learn from an experience. Why do you think these two people had such a different view and reaction to the same experience? Your explanation may be very different and this is where I want you to know differences aren't necessarily wrong. We understand by what level of energy flows thru our bodies. We can define energy as light, consciousness, understanding or awareness. But we are all on a journey and at different places. The differences in our understanding are not wrong but *are necessary for us* in our personal journey. Wherever you are on the path, you need to be, and so embrace how you feel, and your interpretation of the question I just gave you. I will tell you my interpretation and it's *not because it is the only interpretation* but it's how I see it at my level of understanding. It's possible in my eyes that the reason for the major difference in the two people's interpretation is from the energy they currently have in their bodies. It could be from the level of understanding or even from a past life experience in which their energy when experiencing something similar, was shattered. It's important to understand that past lives are very real but we don't need to try to figure out who we were in another life. It's just not necessary. What is occurring in this lifetime and the experiences and our interpretation of them, is what we need to look at and not past lives. We carry with us the struggles from lifetime to lifetime but we don't carry the details of the circumstances when the struggles happened. It's simply because it's not the issue. *The issue is the emotions we attach to and how they hinder the light from flowing through our body.* We need to see the struggle we carry, take an observer point of view, not make it a personal problem, and then work towards healing. Healing comes when you observe that what happened has no personal attachment but is only something presented so you can *remove the emotional blocks in your being that is keeping the energy broken up or the light from flowing through your body.* Your being is directly linked to your higher self and the emotions often block the flow of your pure light. To allow your true identity as the spiritual being you are, flow unhindered through your lower body and be able to manifest your divine plan, you must get rid of the blockages. So this kind of experience is actually brought about to help you remove the blocks that your higher self knows you must get past. The impersonal view of your life helps you to not take on more in the process. For instance the Buddha talked about the middle way and to understand a little of what he was saying is to basically see the **middle way as a way to Balance.** As humans we take things from one extreme to another and the **middle way is a resting between those extremes.** In resting we create balance and balance will give you the ability to re-group and see things as they are. Anytime we go from one extreme to another we loose a part of our ability to grow.

~Balance allows breathing room and time to meditate and get a better picture of life and your purpose in life.~

So in this situation where you are the one who is traumatized it would be advantageous to simply take the middle road and not go one way or another, but begin to understand and "impersonalize" it so that you can see a higher understanding of the purpose of the experience. In order to understand the power of your embodiment on earth, you need to see how certain things affect you. There is a little exercise that you might try to do and it will take some effort. Whenever you talk about yourself to anyone or even as self-talk which by the way is many times far more than to others, replace the word I, myself, and anything that refers to you referring to yourself, with "it". So if you were to say to yourself, "I don't know why they hurt me so much" replace it with this "It doesn't know why they hurt it so much." This will help you see that the identity you have on earth **is not the real you, but the life you are living through your body which is your vehicle.** If this exercise is hard at first it will tell you **how attached your are to your identity.** When you are very attached that is when you are always trying to convince yourself and others of your actions. It is your way of protecting everything you think you are in your identity. I am not telling that you cannot be who you came to be in this lifetime but what I would like to help you achieve is healing. Sometimes in order to heal we simply have to see ourselves and our situation as if we are the observer and replacing your talk about yourself with the word "it" will help you be able to see your life and the experiences for what they are. They are vehicles to help you get a grip on your identity that is your spiritual, higher self. When you can achieve this process many problems with the emotions you have about your identity and the things that happen to you will disappear.

Many people loose their sense of identity during trauma. Your sense of identity includes how you see the world and whether you define it as good or bad. Many people that are constantly driven in thought that the world is evil, by religion, they keep within them this fear of the world and anger that God brought them into the world. This can hurt their ability to reconnect with who they are and this sense of identity is lost by trauma. *Their thoughts are energy and when their thoughts connect with their emotions the energy passes through colored lenses and how they see their memory of life is influenced by attitude and opinion or reaction to something they are struggling with.* Their feelings that are generated from their emotions are also influenced by the colored lenses in which these thoughts pass through. If they feel guilty or responsible for bad things, if they believe they are no good sinners, or God will punish them, all of this contributes to their own demise.

The power of our minds has the ability to take us on detours. It can be our stubbornness or just simply how we see things. I guess we could say that it is sad in so many ways *that our minds have so much control over us but the truth is if you can see that what you feel and have understood in your limited awareness is not the truth, then your mind, when it sees the truth will be so liberated that you can literally move mountains and this power of the mind is the most amazing power in all the world.*

"Once you understand how energy and the correct flow of the right energy can change you from feeling helpless to becoming the change in a powerful way for yourself and others, you will find that life on earth is full of abundance."

This is when you will uncover your true spiritual identity and the purpose for which you came to earth at this time and this alone will bring you to sit on the highest pinnacle and see the Kingdom of God on earth. *It's what you can see thru the right consciousness that can be able to bring you from a life of dependence to a life of independence.* The moment your sense of identity begins to change, your thoughts will also begin to change and your emotions that once you carried with heaviness of heart, no longer have any ability to weigh you down. True freedom comes when you are free to see life and the beauty of God's abundance is just waiting for you to allow it to flow through your body and soul.

When something emotional comes, lets say someone dies, think about his or her life, and think about what they brought in the time they were here. *Life is about what we can bring and leave to help others with.* When you focus on their life, you begin to have a greater appreciation for their willingness to share when living. Yes you miss them but they are not gone, in fact they are standing right beside you. *They cannot be seen with the human eye but they are still among us.* The difference between heaven and earth is a difference in vibration. Remember that your thoughts can become your emotional blockages and so sending out love is the key to keeping your heart with the highest vibration. Many times we fight against anger, which is from a fear deep inside. Anger often is based on a sense of injustice or a need to blame, which in turn creates a need within us to make them pay for what they have done. When I say make them pay, it might not be with physical force but might just be in the form of alienating or humiliating by avoidance. What ever you do to pay back may cause you satisfaction for a time but in the long run you have created karma to return unto you for your intentions. But lets say you were abused as a child, you can actually create anger against yourself for allowing the abuse to happen to you. The only way out of the anger you have put upon yourself is to forgive yourself by understanding that it wasn't in your ability to stop the abuse. Love yourself unconditionally, understand you did the best you could, and forgive and move on.

~The only way to totally overcome anger is to rise above the feeling of a separateness from your creator or from other people.~

The truth is you are one with life and with your creator. God is in all of us and we are all a part of the whole and so when you take on the sense of being separate and you become angry, you actually become angry at the whole, which is also yourself. The same goes for love. When you don't love others, you are actually not loving God who is in all people, along with not loving yourself.

To change yourself you need to see life differently so that you don't take everything as an extreme. Understand that God never intended the negative conditions on this planet and ***evil was never part of God's plan.*** Evil exists ***only in the absence of light*** but is not the opposite of God. However Evil is a part of life on earth in the here and now. It is allowed because it can enhance spiritual growth by opening challenges to be driven to desire the life we came to live. The Buddha and Jesus both believed that when dealing with dark forces, the most important thing to keep in mind is to remain non-attached and turn the other cheek. Many people don't want to believe in evil spirits and maybe this has to do with the fact that when confronted with them it is easier to believe they don't exist because they don't have a way of escaping it. This is also used in trying to understand different theories. When something can't be measured they would rather believe it doesn't exist. If something can't be understood they would rather believe it doesn't exist. Evil spirits ranks high among one of the things that can't be measured or proven and so most tend to ignore the topic. But evil spirits do exist and ***they are simply a concentration of imperfect psychic energy.*** There are techniques that are very helpful in invoking protection from evil spirits. When you invoke a high frequency of spiritual energy, it becomes far more difficult for evil spirits to enter your energy field or put thoughts into your mind.

Changing your perception of your world means you must first be willing to ***change your understanding***, and that will ***change your***

beliefs and ultimately reveal to you the perfect plan of your individual life. Have you ever been enlightened by someone who really does seem to help you understand that the root of your problem isn't in the outer circumstances of your life but is found in your inner beliefs. The part of you that is within is what really is the source that stops your growth or accelerates your growth. And your perception of the past is what is the root of your belief system. *In other words if you could see any experience, good or bad, as a tool for your growth process then would you fear the past?* Would the past loose it's grip over your destiny? I would like for you to try and understand the importance of changing your beliefs and leaving behind the past. And in leaving the past behind you must first come to terms with its "value". The strength within you is very powerful and yet because you are divided within, by beliefs that have attached to you thru experiences in life, you are not "one" and are not unified in strength. This division within you will cause you to sit with a very prominent doctor that is trying to help you heal in your life's experiences, hear him, believe that what he says is true and then walk out of his office week after week never changing your pattern. Think about it. You are a good person and you want to rise above your current limitations in life that seem to be like a ball and chain holding you back. So what is it that has to change first in order for your future to change? Many wonderful people, such as yourself, would love to live in peace and to enjoy life to it's fullest. I believe that the heart of all people is like God and when I say that, I want you to know that I believe in you and that you long to love and to be loved. The problems we have are simple. *We, time and time again, spin our wheels trying to find happiness in life and yet we seem to go off into directions that only bring more struggles.* I like this one story that I heard many years ago and it goes like this.

Chapter One
I walk down the street.
There is a deep hole in the sidewalk.
I fall in.
I am lost....I am helpless.
It isn't my fault.
It takes forever to find a way out.

Chapter Two
I walk down the same street.
There is a deep hole in the sidewalk.
I pretend I don't see it.
I fall in again.
I can't believe I am in the same place.
But, it isn't my fault.
It still takes a long time to get out.

Chapter Three
I walk down the same street.
There is a deep hole in the sidewalk.
I see it is there.
I still fall in...It's a habit.
My eyes are open.
I know where I am.
It is my fault.
I get out immediately.

Chapter Four
I walk down the same street.
There is a deep hole in the sidewalk.
I WALK AROUND IT.

Chapter Five
I WALK DOWN ANOTHER STREET.
~Sancheeta~

The key to healing our "broken vision" of who we think we are and why we do what we do is found in becoming "one" with our present "self" in this lifetime and our spiritual self that resides in the spiritual realm. This is how we will reconnect to the real purpose of our lives in this lifetime. Unity in our own thinking helps our thoughts no longer battle one another. In finding a "oneness" within, we first must be willing to defeat the enemies within. The enemies within are simply your own trained thoughts and emotions you believe to the "your truth". They could actually be the beliefs of family, friends or even your minister if you go to a church. The first step to healing comes when we understand **we have control over our lives.** When we begin to see that **IT IS BY OUR OWN CHOICES** that we continue on a path that leads to more of what we are dealing with, that is when we take back our life. God wants us to take control of our lives and Jesus lived to show us that we must be in control of our lives. Ask yourself a few questions. Have you ever considered how often you force yourself to do, say, feel, or think things in order to fit into society, in order to accommodate some kind of standard put upon you from outside yourself? Have you ever considered that as you grow up, you are conditioned or maybe programmed, even brainwashed - to accept many things that are "norms" in your society, without ever questioning them? Have you ever considered that some people live their entire lives by following the norms of their society, in anything from religion to fashion, and they never actually have an original thought or make their own decisions? In other words many choices we make while still struggling in our mind about our life, can often lead to more struggling, simply because of **"why" we make certain decisions.** This is why it's important to begin today a journey of self-discovery.

~Why we do what we do is more important than what we do, because it unlocks the door to our healing.~

When we understand why we do something, we also reveal **if the choice is ours or someone else's.** If we make a choice simply because everyone in the family does it this way, or our friends are persuading us or whatever, and it is against what we want to do, then we only walk down ***their*** path. We still might learn from the choices of others but really the power comes **when we have chosen something from our own perspective.** The healing comes when we see how valuable it is to make our own decisions and have freedom to grow. Whether you fully understand a lot of what I am saying, or not, it's important to try and take "baby" steps. ***Take the steps you do agree with and begin the change.*** When you begin and experience some of the results it is then that your level of consciousness rises and you see the worth or the value of the experience. ***This will help you decide if you want to take more steps. When we experience for ourselves that is when we awaken.*** God allows us to experience life by our own choices because we are individuals who have come to earth with a unique plan and the only way we can fulfill it is ***if we begin*** our own journey. ***Making choices and experiencing the results of our choices helps us to grow and to see the next step we need to take.*** Don't allow fear to keep you from taking the first step. When you learn to ride your bicycle as a child, you cannot give this learning experience to someone else. ***You have to learn for yourself and in learning this you are open to learning something beyond this.*** Experience by our own choices opens the truth that ***what we think we are, we become*** and the only way to change our life is to change the way we see things or the way we choose things. But you can never move forward if you don't make your own choices. Many times our choices in life are made to fit in society or family, or whatever. The power of making good decisions, I believe comes when you make decisions based on your heart and intuition, and ***when it is your decision.*** However, every decision has the potential to not work in your best interest due to circumstances. Like for instance, lets say you have a son who wants to walk to a friend's house after dark. You want him to learn to be on his own and so your heart tells him that it's ok. However, your heart is kind but it isn't in his best interest and he gets lost. ***What I am saying is that there needs to be an understanding and a love for yourself that sometimes the decisions we make, although driven by the heart, don't always turn out good.*** The important part of what I want to express to you is that you need to understand that life is a journey and nothing you do or say or choose *is perfect.* To grow beyond any decision that might have been wrong you must learn from the experience and become wiser as a result. ***This is your journey*** and through out your lifetime you can continue to grow and evolve and this will re-connect you to your spiritual self that holds the reason why you came in this lifetime. Many times we want our families approval or our husband or wife's approval. All of this is good when keeping the peace but God made us to be independent thinkers. God wants you to be able to work through your choices on your own and if you make mistakes, ***which we all do,*** then learn by them and understand the value of the lesson. When we understand the value of the lesson, and see for ourselves how we can grow from the experience, that is when we change what is within ourselves therefore changing our belief of why we want to do something differently next time. Become empowered within and use your own intuitive power to see what you need to do.

Many good men and women, who are doctors, spend their lives trying to help you sort out the problems that plague you. They have great understanding of many techniques that can help you rise above your troubles and begin to live the life that will bring joy to you and your family. Oftentimes when a person goes to these doctors and they don't get help or there lives seem to only get worse, they blame the doctor. Whose fault is it? God created us with something that forces us to take hold of our own destiny. Free Will is what I speak of. Free Will to live by your choices is the choice you can make everyday. What is within you and all of us is God within. The guiding hand of God lives in all of us. If you have read the Bible you will remember that we are made in the image and likeness of God. The reason we loose sight of this "permanent" part of our being is because we base our "free will" decisions on a ***"limited understanding"*** of who we really think we are AND WHAT SEEMS IMPORTANT IN THIS LIFE. Therefore the true self within us, the very real presence of the Living God becomes a permanent fixture that has no power in helping us make the right choices, simply because "WE HAVE TAKEN THE POWER AWAY". We took the power away when we felt we knew better ***by simply fitting in with what others think we should do.*** I'm not saying that everything you do when you base decisions on experience from life on earth is wrong.

But what I am saying is that you need to talk it over within, you need to trust the inner wisdom that God gave you, and look at how your choices can help you or hurt you. You can hear the voices of people around you, as tools of understanding and if you choose to follow their advice *then make sure it is "your choice" and NOT theirs.* You have to answer for your choices and so let it be your choice. As you choose in life, remember to do things with a clean conscious and a good heart. Anything with quick gratification for the sole purpose of pleasures on earth *needs to be seriously pondered over.* Anything done in a selfish manner will reap a selfish result because what you do to others you do to yourself. When you think of others and think of how you can be closer in heart with your creator, you add unto yourself blessings that will reward you "within" and bring peace and joy to your heart. Sometimes this means you might have to work harder and you might have go without but God will NEVER leave you alone and will reward you with His love and more of His understanding. This and this alone will give you more peace than anything you could possibly attain in this life. *You might blame God for your troubles in life but they are not His doing but actually a result of your choices.* God allows His presence to remain alive and well, *but silent so that as you walk and make choices in life and begin to realize the power of your choices and how they affect your future.* You also can understand that most choices, even if bad for you, *in the long run, bring healing and opportunity to make better choices in the future.* Life on earth is a growing experience that has the potential to help you become one with the Living God and this is a happiness that is beyond your human understanding. For it is the God within you that quietly lets you misuse your freedom of choice and suffer because of your own choices *so that by these errors you are given an awareness into the fact that there is MORE to your life.* Our mistakes are NOT to destroy us but are *WARNING SIGNS along the way to help us choose differently next time.* They are like road signs when you are driving on a highway and they guide you on a safe trip. And sometimes we all know that road signs take us on a detour and that detour adds more time to the trip but in the long run the detour has the potential to take us safely to our destination. The detour also has the potential to teach us something we needed to learn in order to get to the next stage of our journey. Sit back and learn about yourself. Observe why you get into certain situations in life by your choices and grow in wisdom so that you will eventually make different choices.

You may ask yourself why is this so complicated. It is not complicated at all. **WHAT YOU FOCUS ON, IF IMPERFECT IMAGES WILL REAP MORE IMPERFECT CONDITIONS.** Focus on God and you'll experience God's perfection. **LIFE IS REALLY THAT SIMPLE.** The truth is that when you came to earth you brought a part of God in you. You are not separate from God and God is never on the outside somewhere where you have to reach Him. God is within you and you are never alone. *The alone, lost feelings we have when life seems so hard and so challenging is only because we have forgotten that God is always with us.* This aloneness is a result of the division or the wall you have created in your being. The division or wall within you has separated you from God and *you alone can tear down that wall.* You have within you the ability to NOT feel alone when you know you are not alone, and to become one with God. God allows you to create your experience in life to help you become MORE of the spiritual being you are capable of becoming. In reality, you are who you think you are. And in the here and Now, you are who you think you are. As I said before, *the key to oneness is understanding that there is currently a gap between who you really are and who you think you are and THE ESSENCE OF LIFE IS TO CLOSE THAT GAP.* A house divided against itself cannot stand. Your house is your mind and therefore it is vital to bring it together and keep it together as "ONE" flowing presence within.

In life we find that there are many people who like to control others and situations and believe they are helping others by forcing them to do something. Oftentimes parents who feel so responsible for their children try this approach. But whatever age the person is at, the truth is that forcing anyone to do what others think is right, only stops their own growth. The greatest gift in helping others see the need to change *is helping them find within themselves the reason to make different choices* and the beauty they will experience when they see how important their lives are. Doing it this way allows them the privilege of utilizing their God given "Free Will" and seeing that their choices can really make a difference in the their lives. When someone sees by experience how they do have control over there destiny *then they not only change their lives but they change their beliefs of life*. This is how the power of God's laws, Free Will and Karma, has the ability to change the entire planet earth. Like that saying *"Give a man a fish and you feed him for a day. Teach a man to fish and you feed him for a lifetime."* When we help others to believe that their lives have incredible power to change not only themselves but also those around them this is when they no longer fear to live and they begin the journey of finding out who they are and what their purpose in life is.

In teaching other people methods of healing we often try to encourage them to walk a certain path so they can get the "idea" of how it can benefit them. There is nothing wrong with this teaching. The problem with "a teaching" that "sets up a path" for wholeness that is rigid and supposedly should work for everyone, is that sometimes people *only adhere to that path* and never venture to try other approaches that could further help them excel in their healing. Don't attach to only one teaching but be willing to see the value in many ways to achieve the same goal. Too many times we attach to "a belief" that there is only one way to heal or one method that will work for all people but God wants all of us to know that He *knows each learns differently and therefore different ways to achieve the same goal is a gift from God.* It also gives us the understanding of how important free choices are and how, when we make free choices we also take control over *our own* healing. No one can heal anyone without them wanting it for themselves. Free Will is critical because when a person is allowed to explore other approaches to healing, *they begin to see that the power of their healing is found in their ability to choose freely*. Take an example when a child is learning to ride a bike and the parent is so attached to the fact that they are the only good teacher of this skill, they never allow the child to explore different ways in which they can create that sense of balance so that they can successfully ride the bike. The parent actually will do harm to the child if they force the child to do it there way and ***only*** their way. Many times it's good to help someone by showing them how you are successful in doing something but then letting them learn by experimentation. If you show a child how you learned to ride a bike and then let them explore new ways they can learn, not being strict in them doing it your way, then you will find that they will not only learn to ride the bike, ***but they will learn to believe they have an ability within them to learn from an inner voice***. The key to becoming whole within is found in learning ***to believe in our own inner abilities*** and to believe that all we need of God and of our spiritual understanding of who we really are is found within our inner being. So the truth is that when we allow "free will" to be a guiding light in teaching us new things that are necessary in growing, we gain confidence in the skill but also in knowing we have the ability within, to grow and become successful. ***We stop looking for answers on the outside or in outer circumstances and we begin to look within*** and find that God provided us with all the answers to everything we need to know in order to grow beyond our limited belief.

The first very important step is found in that little story about walking down the road. You'll notice that in the beginning chapters there is a "belief" that nothing is in their control. They are lost, helpless and "don't take responsibility" for there own actions. They believe it's not their fault. **This denial and this feeling of helplessness, that you don't have control over your life or are a victim of circumstances is one of the first obstacles you must overcome.** You ***are*** in control of your life and ***you are not supposed to be victimized by circumstances***. You choose to be a victim when you don't take control over your own life. Take responsibility and look at the options you have in making changes in your life. You cannot change things unless you look at things in a healthy manner. The definition of insanity is ***not for those who feel insane*** but for all of us. ***"DOING the SAME thing Over and Over but EXPECTING A DIFFERENT RESULT."*** How can we expect things to change unless we are willing to take courage and slowly bring about new change on our own? When fear becomes an obstacle within that is when we will not be able to move past the struggles. When we are willing *to let go* of our beliefs that keep us in a "fear of never being anymore than what we are", then that is when *courage takes flight*. For the truth is that courage doesn't always roar, but sometimes courage is the quiet voice within your being, at the end of a difficult day that says, "I will try again tomorrow". You'll notice that in the next chapter of that story he pretends to not see the hole, and falls in it again, wondering why it happened again. *Isn't this how we often approach problems in our lives that seem so evident to others but yet we have not come to our own conclusion that we can do anything about it?* **We continue to deny it's our fault and therefore we continue on the path we are on.** Until we admit that we are the only one that can control our destiny, we will keep finding the same circumstances happening in our lives and we will continue to have the same results *FROM OUR OWN CHOOSING*. The primary key to healing and to allowing ourselves to receive the help from others, who want to help us, is in realizing it *IS in our control and it IS our choice to change our belief within*. When we change our belief about ourselves and what we deserve and what we can control, *it is then that the past no longer has control over us.* You'll notice in the next chapter that the person walks down the same street, SEES there is a deep hole in the sidewalk, REALIZES THAT, *BUT BY HABIT he falls in the hole again*, **but this time the fall opens his eyes.** He now sees why he keeps falling in the same hole, and he takes responsibility and sees *IT IS HIS FAULT.* **He is awakened to the fact that his choices keep him doing the same things.** The same things keep happening *not* because someone is out to get him, *not* because God is punishing him, *but because HE CHOOSES TO NOT SEE THINGS AS THEY ARE.* **When his eyes are open, it is then he chooses to go on a different road.** This is a valuable truth for all of us. Sometimes we have to go through the same experiences time and time again *but the value of all those times is found when those times eventually awaken us.* Without the troubles we would never learn. Troubles are not to destroy us, but are to help us progress on the spiritual path to understanding who we are and why we are here in this lifetime.

When you learn the lesson of a difficulty it is then you are ready for the next step to your spiritual path. A step at a time we progress and a step at a time we learn and can share with others our own journey. Nothing is lost or wasted. Just because you have suffered greatly in this life, doesn't mean your life is no good. Actually those that suffer much have a great plan that if embraced can literally change the world.

When you open your eyes and realize that the roads of life and the circumstances that keep happening to you are for your growth and for you to take hold of your life, ***you stop blaming everyone else for your life and start to take hold of your own destiny***. When you see how important it is to learn and grow in every experience, you no longer fear or regret, but you move on and find greater compassion and understanding for yourself and others.

I would like to help you understand how powerful the wounds of the past can have in our lives and how they alone can stop us from ever believing we deserve a better life. Many times we are unaware that our parents or people in the past that have been a major contributor to our lives, have any power over us. If you are strong-minded and have overwhelming confidence you might feel that no one is telling you how to live your life. However, many times when we fall into despair or when troubles arise in our lives, we find a part of us that we thought didn't exist because in our strong, confident lifestyle we got thru so many things that others couldn't begin to overcome. We considered ourselves as victors and not victims. However, ***when life throws us lemons we don't seem to be able to make the lemonade we always encouraged others to make when they struggled.*** What is it about the human psyche that can appear to be altogether when times are good and then crash and burn into a deep pit where we cannot get out. ***The wounds of the past have a quiet hold on us and they chain us to a belief of ourselves that was long ago forgotten, or so we thought.*** I believe with all my heart that troubles come into our lives to help us overcome old beliefs we once attached to. You see, although we were so strong most of our lives for those around us, we all will fall into a pit of despair once again. Those times are not to destroy us but to help us become the people we have the potential to become. *Those times reappear so that we can once and for all rise above their hold.*

For all of us, wounds of the past exist. When trouble comes into our lives and our world seems to be falling apart, we begin to see how our past still has a hold on us. Many times you will hear people who are not willing to take hold of their lives, blame the reason why, on something or someone that hurt them long ago. They will make excuse that this is why they are the way they are. They base their choices to continue living in denial that they have no control over what is happening to them, because of how they are suffering from what someone did to them years ago. It might be their health or it might be a relationship in which they feel an obligation to someone and they won't stand up for themselves. They justify that it's getting better and yet soon enough it not only reveals that it's not getting better but it's getting worse. They won't take hold of their lives, not because they haven't done this in the past but because they have reached a new level of their own inner being in which they have exposed wounds of the past and in that they can't see how they must take new steps to get past these wounds. *This is where taking dominion or responsibility is critical in moving past certain circumstances.* In order to rise above, you must first confront the fear or problem, and then be done with it. Being done with it, means forgiving and moving on. *If you don't do this, then you will always meet the problem again.* Your growth depends on your willingness to rise and be done with something that only keeps you from achieving a more abundant life.

Maybe you are one who had an abusive father that made you feel guilty for having fun, or maybe he abused you physically, sexually or mentally. Maybe you had a mother that left you feeling obligated to her and therefore you couldn't really explore your growing up years. Maybe you were a caretaker and couldn't be a child, and grow socially with others. Whatever the case, wounds are all wounds and they all *can* have a major affect on your own ability to take hold of your life. But remember that wounds are not the means of an end to your growth. They are only *presented to you* so that you can heal and move past them and see how you have the ability to be what God needs you to be.

> **~The power, wounds have over you is found in the emotions attached to them.~**

If we keep repeating how this or that has hurt us and that is why we are the way we are, **then that will be our story**. But if we face the facts that these things happened and begin to see we are not to allow this to be the end of our story, we then open our eyes and realize that we can't make any more excuses as to why we remain on this same crippled path. Don't keep reliving the past abuses. **If you do then you are allowing those that abused you to continue to have control over you.** Choose life. Jump into the River of Life and out of the boat that has entrapped you in your limited belief. Let Go Of The Past!!! The only reason you keep playing the same song over and over in your head is because Y-O-U keeps choosing to play it. No one else wants' to hear the same song. If this is the reason you are stuck in the past then **you are** the only one that can choose to let it go.

Sometimes we ignore the need to confront our reality. If we are financially strapped and we allow our family to believe nothing is wrong, then how will we face our reality? Many times our children can grow into more mature human beings by understanding that their parents are human too and need help also. Many times when we face the truth of our lives, we actually give them the courage to be honest in their lives. Pride is what keeps us from admitting things but maybe if we could look at the truth of our lives and stop pretending, maybe God can help our children by our own life's experiences. Sometimes parents feel that they have to be the constant strength, the ongoing Rock of Gibraltar in order to help their kids be successful. When we feel this heavy load of responsibility **we take on the need to put on a front and in turn we not only can't resolve our struggles but we also can't show how others can resolve their struggles.** Sometimes we feel we have to hold the weight of the world on our shoulders to help our kids be strong. But sometimes it's our own struggles that help them see we are human, too and we also show them how to deal with life when and if this happens to them. We teach them not always in the best circumstances when everything is going well for us but *we teach them when things fall apart in our lives by how we handle things.* True courage means facing the reality and finding a plan to take our lives back. By our honesty and our courage we help them to face life's experiences and not be afraid. We give them tools that they can use when life becomes a challenge. Life is never perfect and so why not simply live the truth and become an example as God sees the need for you to show the way. Honesty, truth, vulnerability, and a willingness to lay the cards on the table and find the best solution will not only help you reconnect to who you really are in God's eyes but will also help those who look on to become united within.

The wounds of the past come thru physical and emotional abuse of some kind. I think both are very traumatic but over the years I have come to realize how powerfully deceiving emotional abuse is. Many times we don't even recognize the signs of this kind of abuse. Verbal attacks, constant criticism such as intimidation, manipulation and refusal to ever be pleased, are ways in which the victims self-confidence and sense of self-worth are beaten so far down that they simply loose trust in their own interpretations of life and in their own ability to take hold of their life. This kind of emotional abuse can create deeper scars than physical abuse and yet oftentimes the subtleness in which it takes place isn't identified until the person goes thru many personal struggles. When the person begins to experience personal struggles, they feel like they don't understand themselves and they don't realize that abuse has been inflicted upon them subtly for years. The truth is that if you are physically abused much of the damage caused is emotional. In emotional abuse the greatest scar is their loss of belief of themselves. Whether they blame themselves for the abuse or are so convinced they are worthless and believe no one else could possibly want them, there ultimate fear is being alone. I have known many women who have lived in relationships where they have constantly blamed themselves for everything that goes wrong. They continue to doubt their self-worth and often give the abuser the benefit of the doubt, and make excuse for them.

Emotional blackmail is also very powerful in manipulating a person into doing what he wants by playing on that person's fear, guilt, or compassion. Women in particular tend to place other's wishes and feelings ahead of their own. ***They can be made to feel guilty simply for thinking of their own needs.*** I think a true sign of emotional blackmail is when someone makes a statement they never loved you and then tells you, you will never find anyone to love you. You are betrayed on every angle because you trusted in a love that now is denied ever being there and they finish you off by telling you will never be worthy of anyone loving you. How cruel!! So how does one overcome this kind of hurt? For one thing we can't make anyone love us and we can't live anyone's life for them. We are only responsible and in control of our own. To overcome this kind of hurt and any other kind of hurt, we first must love ourselves enough to say we are not to blame. This isn't our fault. We did everything we could to love and to desire love in return. The only one to blame is the one that has abused you and your trust. But do we spend our time blaming that person? This is very important to understand. We could blame those who hurt us and we could spend the rest of our lives voicing our hurt and in turn ***we would be choosing to remain a "victim".*** I, for one, have never wanted to be a "victim". People that have abused me have accused me of being a victim but the truth about myself, whether they believe it or not, is that I never have played that role. It's a waste of time, to be honest. Yes, I have passed thru corners of the emotions of feeling victimized but I quickly pulled out of it. I realized a long time ago that those that hurt us really are hurting inside of themselves. I saw their pain and when I saw that, I understood why they do what they do. We overcome the hurt that others inflict on us by standing up for who we are and ***not taking their opinions as truth.*** We also overcome the hurt ***by forgiving them and moving on.*** Some forgive, but don't forget. The truth is, ***if you forgive and don't forget then you are always thinking about it and so forgiveness becomes useless.*** The key is to move on. Moving on after forgiving frees you and ***those that inflicted pain no longer have control over your destiny.*** Your destiny can never be achieved ***if you are going in circles.*** Mental abuse is often done by someone who is critical and always finding fault.

They can never be pleased with anything you desire to do. Keep in mind deep down they struggle with ever being pleased with themselves and that is why they put you through what they do. They don't understand how each person has a right to dream and to contribute to the world and even if nothing ever becomes of your work, *you at least found your voice*. The power of overcoming is not found in what *others think, say, or do as they judge us*. The power of overcoming is found *when you walk right through the opposition and believe you are worthy* and you can do what others don't believe you can do.

Many situations create challenges in life that seem harder in your walk. Whatever you have suffered in your life, you will rise above it *if you make the determination to make it happen.* It's not what has happened in life that is as powerful as *how you feel about what has happened.* So if what has happened has crippled you, then how you feel about it is *emotionally charged* and until you get past it, you will remain somewhat at a stand still. But if what has happened to you has helped you to see beyond it and become stronger, *then you will be empowered* and you will be able to take the next step in the ladder that will help your spiritual self grow. These things happen and they give us *opportunity* to grow but if we choose another road, then we are allowed to *follow our choices.* God wants you to take the roads *you need* in your life, if you feel that is what will help you. If they eventually don't help you, then *He hopes* you will take another road. He wants each of us to take our own Free Will and use the freedom to accelerate our own growth, by our own choices. *Only when we use our free choices will we grow as empowered individuals.* We do carry scars from childhood and some of those scars are hard to overcome but the important thing is to realize that what happens to us doesn't define anything about us. Anyone can use and abuse anyone without good cause. *What happens to us in this lifetime was necessary to gain a skill of rising above it and moving on.* It's not fair that some people experience their own hell on earth. We can take the pieces of our lives and become better people not only for our own selves but eventually to help others. The people that can reach out to help another are those that really understand what they are going through. Whether you are experiencing poverty, abuse or disease, you have been given an opportunity to view the troubles differently and to begin to rise above how your mind sees things. Become a voice of change and reach out to help others.

~When you reach out you will heal your own heart. This is the circle of life.~

God created us as co-creators of this planet and we are one with God. When we heal, God heals and others heal. When we inflict pain on others we hurt ourselves as well as God. Our Oneness affects the whole. Your life is an opportunity to move past what hurts, and to begin to love your life. When you see that the past is a tool in which you can grow, then you no longer fear it.

~To know thyself is the greatest power you can possess.~

I want to try and help you see who you are by first explaining the powers you hold in your mind of who you "think" you are. A little story that really helps us understand the power of our own beliefs is found in this story of "The Golden Eagle". Here is a magnificent bird, which often causes us to stop and stare when he flies high above us and yet this eagle *doesn't know who he is* and doesn't have a clue as to what his purpose in life is. He looks like and Eagle with the awesome wings and stature. He has the bold keen eyes and the coloring of him is beyond magnificence. But because he is raised with chickens, he believes he also is a chicken. The funny thing is that he doesn't look like one and when he sees another of his kind flying, *he* is taken back in awe. Even he sees the magnificence of his own identity but he doesn't relate himself to being the same. He has lost who he is. Doesn't he see a resemblance or is there such a *large beam in his eye that he sees only thru the eyes of those he lives with.* Many times we get lost in our lives on earth and we only see ourselves through those around us. We not only have a beam in our eyes, *but we have been blinded by our lack of worth.* Is that how our vision gets clouded and we don't see who we are because our family or any other influence has such a powerful presence? Has our identity been lost because the beam in our eye deceives us? A message is given to awaken him but ***he is so convinced*** he is a chicken, he remains in ***his trapped illusion*** and one day he dies without ever claiming his identity. Is this how our story will end? Will we have clues along the way that we are more than our current understanding of what we think we are, but never enough courage to believe? When the eagle saw another eagle fly overhead, did he see any resemblance or was he so convinced he was a chicken that it never crossed his mind? There are levels of our loss in our identity. Some loose it slowly, like a slow death, while others loose it quickly in trauma. Some have a remembrance or see a resemblance while others can't see anything. Either way it's sad! This is often our story. We live and die, identifying ourselves with others around us and ***never realize the great importance of our lives***. Our minds contain our identity in a self-made box in which we see ourselves a certain way and cannot see who we really are. God gave us a magnificent task to accomplish in this life but because life and the circumstances become so overwhelming we simply loose sight of who we really are. ***We can't see thru the obstacles, thru the struggles, and thru the lies we alone have told ourselves.*** What is within us is put to sleep and we use our mind to define who we are. Here is the story:

THE GOLDEN EAGLE
A man found an eagle's egg and put it in the nest of a backyard hen. The eaglet hatched with the brood of chicks and grew up with them.
All his life the eagle did what the backyard chickens did, thinking he was a backyard chicken. He scratched the earth for worms and insects. He clucked and cackled. And he would thrash his wings and fly a few feet into the air.
Years passed and the eagle grew very old. One day he saw a magnificent bird far above him in the cloudless sky. It glided

in graceful majesty among the powerful wind currents, with scarcely a beat of its strong golden wings.
The old eagle looked up in awe. "Who's that?" he asked.
"That's the eagle, the king of the birds," said his neighbor.
"He belongs to the sky. We belong to the earth--we 're chickens."
So the eagle lived and died a chicken, for that's what he thought he was!

I bring to your attention this very profound but simple illustration. **WE ARE WHO WE THINK WE ARE.** Many different people have said this many times, many different ways. The truth is that *it holds the key* to motivating us in believing that there is MORE to who we really are and what we have the ability to become in this lifetime.

To know yourself means freedom to grow beyond what you currently see your life as. You are an extension of your Creator and your identity body relates specifically to what you came to do in the material universe in this lifetime. Think of your spiritual Being sending down an individualization of itself. Visualize your spiritual Being taking a part of itself and sending it to earth at this time. The reason you would do this is to become More of the Spiritual Being you are. In the Spiritual realm there are many mansions, many levels of attainment and every spiritual being has the opportunity, if they so desire, to become More and raise higher in the kingdom. Coming to earth isn't easy and takes great courage. The denser energies that inhabit this planet are unlike the spiritual realm and so coming to earth is for a specific reason. Before a spiritual Being chooses to descend to planet earth, he is helped by a spiritual teacher *to plan a life that would be most beneficial for his growth* and sometimes that can entail overcoming emotional scars of past lives. *In the plan, it is for the greatest ability to overcome and achieve a higher understanding of life.* It might mean you are born in a certain country or certain conditions or even with a particular family. All of which may create a challenge but gives the opportunity to move past and heal certain things that have held you back from a higher level of consciousness. As I have already explained, Jesus came to help us know that we can take control of our own lives and the main purpose of life is to attain the Christ consciousness or the Christ Mind. So when we sit down with our spiritual teachers *we plan the life we feel will benefit our growth the most.* But when the spiritual Being, we are, sends an extension of itself into the material realm in the form of the human body, it forgets everything. When we arrive on this planet we have an inner knowing but often we shut out that voice, within and go about living our lives *without an awareness of who we really are and why we are here.*

Let me explain something very important before I go further. On earth we have been led to believe that God's will is outside of, separate from and is even in opposition to our own will. *This lie is so profoundly crippling* that it keeps us feeling separated from God when in fact God is within us. Of course, the will of God is always in opposition to the will of your mortal self or ego and the prince of this world. Your mortal self and the prince of this world is completely trapped in the duality consciousness, which is the consciousness that springs from a "sense" of separation from God. It is by their very nature that they "see" themselves outside of God's will or in opposition to God's will. The will of your ego and your mortal self will always feel that it is being *restricted* by the will of God. Furthermore your mortal self will try to get you to believe in the illusion that in order to follow the will of God you have to give up your own will. That you have to surrender your own will to the will of God and submit yourself to this higher authority that wants to control you. This belief cripples your ability to see who you are as a spiritual being. *It cripples you because you give away your identity and individual power to take hold of your life on earth.* Let's look at Adam and Eve for a moment. There is a common belief in the story that when they rebelled against God in the Garden of Eden, they gained their own will and when that happened they went against God's will. When in fact they empowered their mortal self and ego to run their lives. Before that they were actually helped by their spiritual teachers who helped them in the plan of this lifetime. They lost connection to there higher will they came with. They were created in the image of God, with their own free will from the very beginning and in rebelling against God's will *they simply lost that freedom of free will by giving it to the mortal self and the prince of this world.* When you understand it this way, you understand that your greatest possession in coming to this world is your individuality. *Your greatest desire is to express that individuality.* If the mortal self and the prince of this world can make you believe *that expressing your individuality is incompatible with following the will of God, you will be a house divided against itself. The truth is that you have a longing for wholeness, which can only be attained by following the will of God and at the same time expressing your individuality.* So if you believe your individuality and the will of God are incompatible, you will never feel whole or fulfilled in this lifetime. This is where you need to realize how important it is for you to get rid of this dualistic illusion. *If you are going to re-connect to who you are then you need to understand that the will of God is not separate from your will.* God is not an angry God in the sky as I have already expressed in earlier chapters. He is not waiting to punish you for your every wrong move or mistake in life. God's will is *not* in opposition to your will, meaning the will of your spiritual self. So many people that believe that He is in opposition and see how they have different desires than what religion teaches often *are resentful against God for the very fact that they are alive.* They also feel God is responsible for bringing them to this earth and putting upon them many limitations and difficulties. *This is how people begin to believe they have no control over their destiny.* Their reasoning is simple and justifiable but it is *born out of a dualistic interpretation* in which they have separated their own will from God's will. *They feel God created them, and gave them free will but because they used it and made mistakes in the past, God has abandoned them.* In many ways even your mortal self doesn't believe these lies but *simply uses them as a tool to drive a wedge* between you and your higher spiritual self. It's important to see that "imperfect beliefs" keep you from seeing beyond your identity on earth today. The key to reconnecting is to *first come into full acceptance that God's will is your will and your will is God's will.*

Let me give you a little picture of your spiritual beings desire so that you can understand how important your life is on this earth. I hope that this will help you see the amazing being you are. Sometimes when life has been difficult and you have experienced great heartache and struggles you tend to feel your life is worthless. In the spiritual realm you are an immortal Being. God created the earth and also created co-creators out of His own being and *that is who you are.* Think of yourself and understanding that God wanted the earth or the material universe to be filled with His light and *so His co-creators volunteered to bring God's light to the world of form.* Spiritual Beings decided they wanted to serve the Creator and so they sent a part of themselves to the earth *to bring God's light.* Bringing God's light will raise the material universe to a higher vibration. So you are a spiritual being who came to help God and at the same time help yourself attain a higher level in the spiritual realm. *To know thyself you need to understand that as a spiritual Being you could only send a part of yourself to the earth.* Also keep in mind that *you are not separated from your spiritual parent* which is your spiritual being. This is where you can understand that the original will of your spiritual being is not in opposition to God's will. You are not created by some external or remote God who then forcefully sent you into this world without any choice of your own. *You chose to come here to bring God's light and you had a choice whether you would seek further growth in the spiritual realm through the experiences in this life.* In all truth you chose to come here to bring God's light to this world and you chose this *out of love.*

Many things you struggle with in your life are a result of the influence of life on this planet. These illusions or beliefs *that are not reality have taken you down roads that are not in alignment with your original purpose for wanting to come here.* When you truly know thyself and reconnect to who you are, your life will attain the greatest sense of joy and purpose. You will then realize that you are an extension of a greater spiritual Being that embodies a particular quality of God. You will then *appreciate the reason for your individuality* and how important your life is in bringing into manifestation God's kingdom on earth. *You are a part of a great number of Beings who came to this earth for a higher purpose.* This alone can give you a sense of meaning and divine direction that will give you the ultimate fulfillment for which all spiritual people have a deep inner longing for.

Your life on earth is not about misery and lack but about abundance. To see the abundance waiting for you to embrace, you must be willing to see any and all illusions of what you are currently experiencing for what they are, simply illusions from the real you. Abundant life is not about material things but *it's all about knowing thyself.* Knowing who you are and why you are on earth at this time. *It's about feeling God's light flow through you and coming into alignment with your original plan.* Every aspect of your life is an expression of that original plan and serves to fulfill it and bring to you the ultimate state of abundance which will *raise your level of understanding and in turn raise the vibration of the entire planet.* You see your life is more than just about you but *it is about your loving desire to become more of God's consciousness.* You might ask what do you mean? Remember you are a part of God and God is a part of you and you can never be separate. You are here to not only become More for your own level of consciousness but you are also here *to help others and to bring the light of God so that more light is in this world.*

To know thyself you also must keep in mind that *the power of the identity you hold in this lifetime is connected to your power of will, determination, direction and purpose.* You made a decision to come here and so the entire purpose of this life stream is born *out of your own act of free will.* I have already explained to you that you are a co-creator but you need to further understand that your act of free will to come here is *an extension of the original decision made by your Creator which is "I will create".* In order to bring yourself in alignment with your higher will you will have *to begin to think beyond the "self" that is focused around the physical body and the mortal self.* When we focus completely on ourselves and what we can gain in this world, we leave no time or room to think of long-term goals or spiritual growth. To focus on the reality of who you are, means you will see that you are one with all life and you came from the same source as God and are an expression of God's Being.

~Your spiritual self that sent you did not have any selfish desires.~

This Being is in perfect alignment with the will and the vision of God and has a greater purpose for sending you to the earth. *That greater purpose is also in perfect alignment with God's vision of all of creation.* What I am saying is that to know thyself you must look beyond *the narrow sense of identity you hold in your mind* of yourself in this life and reconnect to the greater sense of Self that you truly are. This is how you will ultimately find happiness, fulfillment, purpose, and self-worth in this life. Reach beyond your physical body and *give of your own true Being.* Look at the sun that radiates on planet earth. Does it hold back it's light from those it judges that don't live accordingly? No, *the Sun shines unconditionally and never expects anything in return.* In other words it sends it's light to all people *without attaching conditions to how people should receive its gift of light.* For the truth is that the Sun finds its true fulfillment, its true joy *when it radiates it's light. It is what goes out from it's being that is the source of fulfillment, and not what comes in.* God is the same. He never withholds His light and *He does not just shine on a certain group of people.* When you understand this then and you know you are made in His likeness, *you realize that judging others and how they live only brings upon your own judgment.* You are *designed to let the light* of God flow through you. You also have the ability to direct God's light into specific conditions on earth, *which can transcend their current imperfect state.* You are here to bring healing and light to the world and to help everything on Earth become more and in so doing, you will become more. Giving of your light is what brings your fulfillment. Many people have the attitude that if someone isn't nice or someone doesn't believe as I do, I will not give of my light or my friendship or whatever. Conditions in this world are set up everywhere. *Many religions "say" they love all people but when someone doesn't believe the way they do they often won't have anything to do with*

them. People set up conditions, which say that if people do not treat me a certain way, or if people do not give you the return you want, or if they don't believe as I do, you will shut off your friendship or light from them. *What you do to others, you do to yourself* and so if you shut off the flow of light through yourself to others, *you also take away your own sense of fulfillment.* And if you shut off the light completely, you end up feeling very empty with no sense of fulfillment or purpose and your life becomes a continuous struggle.

The abundant life that God wants you to experience in this life is the light of God flowing undiluted and unhindered through your being, *magnifying everything it encounters.* You will *not be waiting to receive abundance* from somewhere outside of yourself but you *will be actively producing abundance* by letting the light from above accelerate everything you encounter. *You will ultimately be multiplying your talents by letting the pure light of God flow through you. This is where you need to remember you are what you think you are and you receive what you send out.* So if you want abundant life you have the power within you to experience it by letting God's light flow through you. Many people have dualistic beliefs that define conditions for their giving but in all reality *they are only hurting themselves* and feeling more and more empty.

There is another aspect of allowing God's light to shine through you. When you shut off the flow of God's light through your being, you are not sending light into the cosmic mirror. The cosmic mirror is another way of expressing Karma. *You reap what you sow and if you don't send it out you cannot receive it.* The cosmic mirror simply cannot reflect the abundant life back to you in the form of physical conditions, because it hasn't received it. Remember the mirror and what you reflect in the mirror, is what you see and what is returned to you in the image. To change an image, you change what is reflected in the mirror, simple as that. *Sometimes it doesn't return right away but don't loose heart for it will return.* The only way you can manifest a materially abundant life *is to first reestablish the spiritually abundant life* that you were designed to have. So the truth is that when Jesus said to seek first the kingdom of God and his righteousness, meaning the right use of God's energy, all things will be added unto you because the material universe has no other option but to reflect back to you the abundance that you are sending out.

When I talk about how change begins with yourself, I really want you to know that the key to changing your life is only possible when you pull the beam out of your own eye first. **God created the universe as one interconnected whole**. This also means that your life is connected to all of life on earth. You can have abundant life but you must first open the door for it to happen. I want you to realize you have the power to change your own life. Only your life, can you change. When I talk about "being the change" in this world, this means that you must first take control back over your life and make the necessary changes that will help you in your life before you can help the world. Jesus was our "example" and not our "idol". He came to show us how to live and His example is to show us that in taking control over our lives, in using our free will to experience life on this planet and to learn by our choices, we can grow and mature as human beings.

I want to help you understand that there are many self-help processes in this world today that can bring about a certain amount of change in your life. I understand this kind of philosophy and there are many things available in our world that awakens you to know you need to better your life. Sometimes it takes a personal crisis that opens your mind to discovering that **there is more** to your life than what you see it as right now. These self-help, motivational **"onramps" to finding your spiritual self**, sometimes are blessings in disguise. The important part is to remember that they are not the only path and they are not **all there is** for you to reach your real identity as a spiritual person. They are necessary for you to take the next step in finding your true self. In all things in this life, we need to keep in perspective that **not one thing** holds the entire answer. We need to **not become attached** to a method or a teaching that has helped us on the path and **think it has all** we will ever need. God is always growing and He is always becoming more. We also are always growing and becoming more. Any organization or technique that teaches **that this is all there is, is false.**

Every person is on an individual quest to re-connect to his or her real self and the spiritual path is a ***highly individual*** process. Each person is unique and needs to go through a set of ***personalized steps*** in order to complete his or her path. The spiritual path is a process with several stages. ***Change begins with loving and honoring yourself and your spiritual mission on earth***. Don't get anxious if things don't happen fast. Just take a step at a time and learn. Remember your school years. You didn't get from Kindergarten to Senior year in a blink of an eye. You took each year and grew. You took summers off, and you found times when you didn't learn so quickly. Eventually we do learn if we keep trying. Some subjects we never get and others we master. Remember that Y-O-U and your spiritual teacher uniquely design the spiritual plan you came here with. This alone can give you the assurance ***that you will arrive at an understanding if you continue to walk the path***. Don't get overwhelmed if something comes your way and throws a curve ball at you. For many people the path can seem overwhelming and long and this is when they ***need a lifeline to get them anchored on the path.*** The best way to overcome the sense of being overwhelmed is to select a teaching and a practical tool that becomes your bread and butter. You need something solid and practical that you can use as a foundation on the path. This isn't something that you will always stay with, but it will give you the foundation you need until you are ready to move forward on the spiritual path, or until you have completed something on the path. I ask you to not be afraid if you grasp onto something for a period of time but remember you are in control of your journey. ***Don't give your control to someone else***. When you are ready you will branch out and away from what once served you in staying on the path. The true foundation for your growth on the Spiritual path is that you must ***increase your understanding of life and attain your own personal revelation*** about each level of life you encounter. Find for yourself the need to increase your spiritual growth by studying a variety of spiritual teachings. Don't limit yourself. You are a co-creator and you need to expand your awareness so that you can come to your own understanding. Remember that as you begin the walk on the spiritual path; use both of your legs. Both legs will carry you forward on the spiritual path and *keep you in balance. Balance is the key to life.*

Jesus rebuked the lawyers saying, "Woe unto you, lawyers! For ye have taken away the key of knowledge: ye entered not in yourselves, and them that were entering in ye hindered: (Luke 11:52) What Jesus was talking about was that men were discouraged about looking beyond what is known on earth about religion. *The churches discouraged anyone from finding further knowledge.* But if you look at the pattern of mankind, you will see that the tremendous amount of progress and the driving force behind it *is that in every generation someone dared to look beyond what was presently known and reach for a higher understanding of a particular aspect of life.* This drive for understanding, this curiosity within all of us is a reflection of our Spiritual Being, that is a co-creator with God and has the potential to take what God created and bring more to the earth. This is a very critical part of your growth. *Don't beat down your curiosity and zest for knowledge. Understand that this is a key to helping you go beyond your current understanding* you have of your life today. This is what will begin the change you need to take for the next step in your progress and the steps in the future. If you silence your curiosity and you don't make your own choice to further your knowledge about everything in life, *then your inward curiosity will be like background noise that can never be silenced completely.*

When a soul matures and is ready to embrace the spiritual path, its curiosity is usually let out of the cage. This is when the soul eagerly studies new teachings and opens their mind to new possibilities. This curiosity is actually a thirst for a higher understanding and is the fuel that drives your growth to new heights. *Your search for understanding is the driving force behind the path of spirituality or Christhood.* Remember we never stop learning, even after we reach Christhood. We need to *keep a pattern that is for constant growth, constant self-transcendence.* Attaining Christhood or Christ Consciousness doesn't mean that you stop learning but it means *you gain access to the mind of God. The mind of God is infinite and you will never know all there is of the mind of God.* Again I repeat myself when I say that learning and growing is what Humans naturally know to do, so believe that this is what you are to do. When anyone tries to stop you from transcending or growing beyond what you currently understand, by telling you that you have the final truth, you *must not believe them*. There is always more to learn, even after you reach the spiritual realm. Many honest people fall into the trap of thinking that they have now found the one true religion or the ultimate philosophy and they simply close their minds to anything beyond its doctrines. *Once you have this belief, your spiritual progress comes to a crawl and sometimes to a complete halt for the rest of their lives.* I want to prevent this.

Even this book is *only a tidbit* of the knowledge there is to know. There is far more you can learn beyond these words. Spiritual growth is the only way to begin to change yourself. Spiritual growth is an ongoing process that can continue indefinitely and you should never stop looking for a teacher. There is more to learn constantly, and teachers come in all forms. The Spiritual path you need to walk comes in a number of stages. Think of a mansion and how there are many floors. When a person discovers the spiritual path, that person is on a particular floor or as the Bible states, "My Father has many mansions", so in essence that person is on a particular mansion in our Father's house. The person now has become aware of a staircase in the form of a spiritual teaching or organization. The teaching presents a series of smaller steps that allows the person to ascend to the next floor. When the person arrives at that floor, they will feel as if an entirely new world has opened up to them. Naturally some will want to explore this floor and *yet in doing this they could possibly fall into the trap of thinking they have reached the top floor and there is nothing beyond this floor.* How do they get the mindset that if they stay on this floor for the rest of their lives, something magical will take them to heaven in one giant leap? When they get to this closing point, this is when they have closed their minds to the existence of a path that leads from floor to floor until they reach Heaven by their own efforts. The Bible says, "There is a way which seemeth right unto a man, but the end thereof are the ways of death" (Proverbs 14:12). The dream many live, that a particular outer religion or philosophy can guarantee your entry into Heaven *is the way that seemeth right unto a man.* Just as Proverbs says, when you stop growing, this end is the way of death.

Never stop searching for a higher understanding. Change begins with yourself and you must keep growing so that you can re-connect to the spiritual person you are and in turn you can fulfill your mission in this lifetime. My Father's house has many mansions, many floors. Remember to enjoy each floor for only a time and remember there is more to see on other floors. Don't stop and take on the belief you have reached what you are looking for and there is no further to go. Stay on the floor to learn that level of understanding and *then look for the staircase that leads to the next floor.* Any person, doctrine, or religion can never monopolize the key of knowledge. *No human authority will ever attain a monopoly on "truth", and I mean NEVER!* You can never define truth by an outer human teaching or doctrine. You will find truth in only one place and that is God's kingdom. Remember the Kingdom of God is within you!

As change begins in your life and you find new growth be careful to *not become emotionally attached to the tools you used to get there.* Try to remain in an understanding that tools are used to reach new levels and when those levels are attained sometimes the tools you once used are not useful anymore. Don't become attached to a particular level but be willing to see it's usefulness and move to the next level. *God wants your growth to be a continued transcending experience and only you can heed the warning of getting trapped on one floor.* The truth is that you have something new waiting at each level, and when you have the faith to believe there is more with each level of understanding that is when you will begin to set up a pattern of growth. Jesus has learned by walking this earth that the very tools He gave to help people climb the path of spiritual enlightenment and to help set them free, became perverted into becoming tools to imprison them even more firmly in the dualistic state of consciousness. *Progressive revelation should be an essential element in all religions but it isn't the case.*

Jesus gave a promise to us in Matt. 7:7-8. "Ask, and it shall be given you; seek, and ye shall find; knock, and it shall be opened unto you: For every one that asketh, receiveth; and he that seeketh findeth; and to him that knocketh it shall be opened." Jesus knew the ways of man and He knew that one of the laws that guide spiritual growth states that if you seek understanding with an open mind and heart, you will always find the true understanding. ***When the student ready, the teacher will appear.*** When a person *is ready to embrace a higher understanding of a teaching, that person will immediately be given a way to attain this understanding.* I haven't spoke alot about those that are keepers of the flame and I will in the last chapter. But the truth is the keepers of the flame of God, the eternal love that God holds in the universe, are the Ascended Beings. Those that have ascended to the spiritual realm and want to help all of us to attain the same goal they have attained. They are not looking for something for themselves but they long to give what they have to you. ***All you have to do is ask.*** The truth is that the Ascended Beings will never leave any soul alone. If you have ever felt abandoned by God, God has not left you and He has given you a spiritual teacher to remain at your side and that teacher is always seeking to give you a teaching that can help you grow spiritually.

There may have been times when you have felt no answer has come to your prayers. Let me clarify what happened in those times. Jesus loves you and he is always with you, because God and the Ascended are always with you. Jesus is a spiritual teacher and longs to help you rise above the pain you feel in this life. He knows you will understand many things if you connect to your spiritual teacher. The reason so many people feel that their prayers aren't answered is that ***they are not able to see the teacher because they are not looking for the teacher.*** Let me give you an illustration. Let's say that you are going thru a very difficult situation and you are crying out for God's help. Let's say you feel that your weren't responsible for what is happening in your life and that you are simply caught in circumstances beyond your control. Remember that the universe is a mirror and that your situation is a reflection of your state of consciousness. The only way that you can escape your current limitations is to help yourself rise to a higher level of consciousness or a higher level on the spiritual path. God hears you but you might not hear him because you aren't listening from the right level of consciousness. He will give you an understanding that will help you rise. *Sometimes we are so burdened by our life's situation that we cannot hear God but he sends someone to be a messenger to keep us going and believing that this isn't the end of our story.*

So is there any place for religion when climbing the spiritual path? Yes there is a place. *Sometimes people are just not able to tap into what is within them.* Many times this is the hardest obstacle from one level on the staircase to the next. This is where religion becomes the only avenue in which spiritual teachers can teach. Many people don't recognize the spiritual teachers and so religion at least opens a door in which *something can begin them on the path.* The problem with religion is that it often becomes a dead end in which you cannot grow beyond their limited beliefs because they lock you into a box and teach you that theirs is the only way to God. So they can help on one end but eventually if you don't take the initiative to get out they can end your growth. This is where you need to bring balance into your life. So if you feel lost and you choose a church to help, then realize it for what it is. *It was your help and you may need to leave when you get on your feet.* No religion can save you and there are no exceptions. The reason for this is because it is essential that you become spiritually self-sufficient. *You must be able to get understanding and direction from within yourself.* When you attain Christ consciousness you establish a direct connection to your I AM presence and the mind of God. When you receive this connection, the answers to your questions become readily available and you no longer desire outer spiritual teachings. Until you actually receive this connection you will still receive direction from the source inside of you, in the form of intuition.

Keep in mind even the words in this book can do nothing for you. Intellectual knowledge is all around us but it cannot empower you to change your life. To produce change, the knowledge you gather must become internalized. Continue to learn and grow within by keeping your intuitive connection, growing. Often we hear of the still, small voice within. This voice is not the voice of conscience that puts fear and guilt into your mind. *This voice is an inner knowing that something is true, even though you might not be able to give an explanation for why.* This voice can also save from danger when it senses you must turn in the direction you are going. Get in touch with your inner voice. Watch what it tells you and begin to trust it. As you begin to trust your inner voice, you will find an open door to your spiritual self and this alone will help you progress on the path much quicker. Developing a listening ear, will cause you to go within and trust what is within you. Intuition comes from your heart center and this is how your Christ self and your spiritual teachers give you understanding and direction. Some people have experiences in finding a book or seeing a teaching stand out in a profound way. Some find people suddenly appear in their lives giving them messages they needed just at that time in their path. As you grow on the spiritual path, you begin to experience these situations and you no longer believe they are coincidences. You find they are messages and every situation you encounter is an opportunity to learn. ***Next time something like this happens and your intuitive feelings surface, look for the hidden message and for the teacher in disguise.*** You will be amazed at how many of the Ascended and unascended surround you on a continuum. You will realize you are not alone and never have been. The reason you feel alone is because you are disconnected from your source, from the Spiritual being you are which is directly a part of God. You feel alone because of how you see your world. When you begin to see your world differently, you will never feel alone again.

As you begin the walk on the spiritual path you will also develop the willingness within your own being to look beyond your current knowledge and beliefs. Never stop learning and remember when you make yourself ready for new teachings by opening your mind to a higher understanding, ***the teacher will appear.***

HOPE BEYOND THE PAIN

So many times in life we hear of a good way to re-look at our lives and it sounds like it makes sense but when we apply it to our everyday circumstances we don't find that it is as easy as it sounds. Many times re-looking requires mechanical ways to heal by writing, by talking, or by constant therapy to overcome traumatic circumstances. These things can somewhat help but the greater tool to help you rise above everything that hinders you *is to see why they happen, learn the lesson, and then you are free to move on.* Life is classroom with many lessons to learn. Life's experiences are simply tools in which we have the potential to become more aware of who we are and why we are here. When we go thru life's experiences *we take them personally* and don't see them as a classroom lesson to learn something from. This is critical to understand. When you take something personal, you attach it to your "emotional identity" and you live with it but don't grow from it. You live the emotion over and over but all you feel is the pain from the experience. Life continues and when *our experiences don't make sense to us, the path becomes harder.* When life becomes a hard road ahead we take on *a sense of hopelessness.* You are not alone. This is a *part* of your journey. It is a "part" of your journey *but not everything and what I mean is there is something even better waiting on the next step of ladder you take. Don't give up, keep going, and believe like never*

329

before. Each experience is like a stepping-stone to help you be ready to learn something MORE. What you are feeling when you do begin to apply certain understandings to your journey, and new methods of seeing things, is a very important part of your experience in life. *What I am saying is there is no magic bullet because if there were, you would not see the deeper things that you need to still overcome.* If God always gave you everything you prayed for, you really wouldn't be happy. Happiness is found on the journey and in the things you experience. If you are going through very hard times, remember there is something you can still do and it might simply be to show courage and an attitude of hope. Something can come from the worst of experiences but that something might just be courage and determination. You will know your options. Look at them and then find what you can do to bring joy.

⁓When times are difficult it is then that others are watching. It is then you can shine.⁓

Throughout my life I have experienced as much struggle, pain, and sorrow *as anyone else. I am not different than you but we share a common understanding about life and what we encounter.* Yes, it's about us but more than that *it's about what we become in our own journey and even greater how we help others in their journey.* Many times we, as humans, set goals and plan our lives to achieve a certain destiny we hold in *"our minds"* that we *think* will bring happiness. God knows that when we make these plans, we take what we know at that time, and we empower the plan by our own choices and ambition, and *through this HE Gives us power to Become the Sons and daughters of God.* The path of your life is not set in stone because God wants us to achieve the maximum growth we can achieve in this lifetime. You are never alone and angels, spiritual beings are waiting to assist you. I have learned how ready they are and when I send my love and light to them and commit to the greater purpose, the comfort and the assistance brings to my knees. You *do not understand the help available to you right now* in your journey. It is incredible and I have experienced it time and time again. There is no doubt it is the Ascended Host, who are truly the keepers of God's eternal flame. Call out to them in love and they will assist you.

As you journey, you often find decisions along the way that must be made. Each decision is a path opened unto you, like a door. *Each path you choose has the same potential to manifest your divine, spiritual plan. Not all paths are created equal* but you use the knowledge and understanding you have at the time in which a decision is to be made and you choose the path you desire. *There is no right or wrong in God's eyes.* Even if the path creates destruction and God mourns that you had to take that path, it was the path you needed to take. *God doesn't want you to suffer but He loves you with a love that is so GREAT!* When you understand that your decisions are for your growth and your growth is necessary to become fully empowered as a Son or Daughter of God, then you begin to see life's decisions as lessons in a classroom.

My oldest son shared with me a story years ago that I wanted to share with you. In seventh grade he was sitting in math class, struggling along with a classmate, with math problems. In his frustration he called the teacher for help, and told him, *"I just wish I had all the answers."* As a mother, this story caused me to feel for a son struggling but as a spiritual being, I saw a glimpse of the greatest struggle of mankind. *The teacher said, "If I gave you all the answers would you be happy?"* My son came home and told me but it wasn't until years later that he saw the higher understanding. He told me when he was 26 yrs old that he never forgot that conversation. Think about that for yourself. Are there things that have happened along the journey, that are kept in the long term memory of your mind and you haven't understood the higher understanding of the struggle? We all have these truths to teach us and they are within us as teachers. *When the student is ready the teacher will come and the teacher is within you, the part of God that lives in you every moment of every day of your life.* What my son told me later was that "if we always had everything given to us then we wouldn't have experienced the journey of the struggle and we wouldn't appreciate it." And then he said to me, "Mom, once you loose appreciation of things in life, you loose everything." What truer words can be said. This is an example of how it takes time to learn but when we understand, it is then we can move mountains. ***Do we really understand the value of the journey? Are we always focused on the destination?*** The truth is, it is ***in the journey*** that we find what life is about and if we never find what life is about then we will never be able to know the greatest abundance waiting to manifest within our selves. You see if you don't have an appreciation of things in life, it is then you are empty. ***What we have in this world doesn't last and isn't ours for very long but it is given for us to grow from and find a deeper understanding.*** "Life happens while your looking for something else." Every experience is an opportunity to go within and find more of ***who you really are***. Whatever path you take has the same opportunity to teach you as any other path. Yes, some paths are harder but in reality each path has the ability to create growth. Notice I say ***has the ability***. It has the ability; the potential waiting but only you can grow from it. Only as you experience the journey and find the jewels, hidden, waiting to unleash a deeper part of you, will you grow.

~*Every path, although different, can still bring you to full manifestation of your divine plan.*~

Choices we make may not be in our best interest but we choose for various reasons. I want to share a detour I took from the path I was on and how the detour, although painful, ***was my choice and my need to learn something.*** I grew up with one parent who was an alcoholic. My spiritual awareness of my being was very great even as a child but it didn't keep me from making choices where I would travel down illusionary roads that ***I created by the things I allowed to manifest***. In my early years of a marriage I would have differences in doing things from my husband. I loved so deeply and wanted to please. Our arguments often were of our differences. He knew of my alcoholic mother and so he would accuse me of blaming my mother for my problems. Keep in mind that although I am not married any more, ***my ex husband meant well in trying to help me.*** My point is to help you see how your choices make your own path but it is the path we need to go on. *We choose because it really is something we must get past and so the journey begins.* That's why it's *no ones fault* but your destiny to find the higher self. *You can accept responsibility for taking the path, but don't blame yourself.* You needed to take this journey. If you go down the "blame game" road, then you have to overcome other emotions, just don't go there. He blamed me for my inadequacies by saying I was using an excuse of my behavior because of my mother. I, in fact *did* use those words because inside I knew there had to be a reason for his unhappiness and my inability to make him happy. I chose to take the blame. This is the road I am trying to keep you from, the blame game. The truth was we had lots of differences and they were *not* because anything was wrong with me or with him, we were just different. Because the self-help world focuses on connecting our problems with our parents and those around us, *I used that mentality to explain my problems and my level of understanding was in direct connection with that teaching.* If we spend countless hours explaining why this person did this and it causes me to do this, etc, we simply go in circles or we take on a new challenge. The truth is God made us different and what is good for one isn't always good for another. Just accept that it's ok to be different and when something doesn't work, try to come to a compromise where both are trying to make things work. If nothing works then move on.

~Don't go in circles. Don't try to fix something that isn't broke.~

Just because you don't do things as others do doesn't mean you are wrong. So for myself I choose this path and this was the road *I needed to be on* in order to learn something. What I learned was we cannot take blame for something that isn't ours. *We must stand true to who we are no matter what.* I call it a detour but maybe it was just the road by my choice I took. Was I aware that I was creating a continued problem and that the road would only get better if I took on a different understanding of our problems? No, I wasn't aware. *The value of the path took years to understand but when I did I also had to confront our differences.*

With growth there is great relief and comfort but also it can create a new decision. Through the years we had a family and because I had made that statement of my mother, he took it as I was blaming everything in life on my mother. He told the kids the same and they grew up thinking along those lines. However, I went on to become wiser in understanding and more spiritual. I didn't correct things, because they became too big. My focus became in raising my kids and that was all that mattered. But because of what I sent out, as an excuse so long ago and I didn't take back my power of knowing that had nothing to do with our differences, I kept walking on a path that strengthened his case. *This isn't about he was wrong and I was right. NO!!!! This is about understanding how our journey takes us down paths of our choosing and the only way out or the only way for change is when we choose differently and by that it means taking back our own power to walk in directions best for us.* Now you know why he said what he did. *I said it first to make excuse.* He simply reflected back what I said. Karma is our saving grace because it helps us grow. Karma returns to us what we send out and in order for us to receive something we have to send it out. And if you send something out with the wrong attitude then you will receive something back with the wrong attitude. I sent out a lie about myself and although I was taking the blame and trying not to put it on him, I created more problems for myself. Our actions and our attitude or what is within us, what makes us who we are, are directly related. *For me, this is what happened*. I used that excuse because I feared he would leave me and so I took all the blame of our differences to keep him happy. I feared he would leave me because I had within me a fear born from early childhood that came as a result of my life with my mother. So in some sense of the word *it was my fear that kept me from being who I was* and that caused me to make up an illusion that the reason he was unhappy was because of my mother. I knew it wasn't true. I knew we were different and he had his own struggles. Because I took the blame early on in our marriage, he thought it was true and in turn he explained my inadequacies to family and our children this way. I struggled to keep my own inner sense of identity for years based on this belief. Who created the struggle? *I did. I allowed myself to make an illusion of who I was so I could keep peace and keep a family together.* It was my survival skills that choose this road. Was it right? Well, it wasn't right for myself, because I simply lied to myself about the real me in an effort to preserve my security in my family. *But it taught me a wealth of wisdom I could have never learned any other way.* You see we create the path in which we choose to walk *by our sense of understanding at the time we intersect with certain roads.* This is about how I became my own worst enemy. I would have to reclaim my identity and only when I did that, would I really understand the value of the journey. My ex husband has his own journey and his own rightful reasons for what he did. *I blame nothing on him because in all actuality his reactions were trying to wake me up even though he didn't know it.* We are spiritual beings and our higher self resides in the higher realm. When situations arise such as mine, the higher self knows we will take the path that will bring the optimum growth and, *so no one is to blame.* It was suppose to be this way so I could rise over an obstacle, a belief I carried in my being and have victory. *I was drawn to these circumstances to help me have the most optimum growth in my journey.* After I realized the higher understanding I had *no reason to blame anyone including myself* because it now appeared to me to be *God sent in my best interest.* I rejoice for the path I took, and I feel no sadness. The journey is meant to be, so that we can be more of who we are and know why we are here today in this lifetime.

~The important part here is to see our responsibility in our path in life.~

And to see how we all are a part of a greater picture. We walk roads with people in life whether they are family, friends, co-workers, or anyone else so that *we can all grow* in our own journey. If we spend time focusing on what others do to us then we have created another path in which we obviously need to go down and learn something from. *To blame anyone, even yourself, is going to attach emotions to the journey and when that happens, we don't see clearly.* Emotions cloud our vision because they create an attachment to the people we are blaming. When you blame someone you create a karmic attachment to that person and until you resolve what keeps you attached you may even return in another lifetime to the same soul to resolve it. Why? Because there is something deeper within you that created that attachment that must be resolved in order to move to the next level. Your life on earth is about your ability to spiritually grow. So if you have emotional attachments, then ***instead of getting more emotional over it***, begin to find a way to detach from it so that you can see the real problem.

~Try to pull yourself "out of the picture" and look at it from a different viewpoint.~

When struggles come in life, try to have the attitude that you are going to grow from it and that you will live through the struggle and become more understanding of everything. We are put here on earth in many different lifestyles and each has the opportunity for growth. Every path in life can potentially manifest the best possible growth at that time in life and at the level you are at. God knows you cannot have all the answers right now because it is ***by the struggle, and the journey that you become what you become***. Take responsibility that maybe your life is the way it is because of your choices or maybe your life is the way it is because of something you need to learn. ***Step away from the picture and look at it differently. You just might find a clue.*** Instead of getting emotional, try to see what you could learn from it or better yourself from it. You might not see it right away, but just give it time. Don't give up. ***Don't start telling yourself you messed up or whatever in an effort to justify why you chose what you did.*** You want to have the attitude of gratitude for the path you are one. When you take a different approach and ***don't beat yourself up and anyone else*** then this mindset will send out into the universe a reflection of what you want. A door will open and you will be ready to walk thru it because you have a higher level of understanding.

One of the keys to life is in giving but the other important and ***critical key*** that most people don't always value as highly, is in receiving. Anyone can give and it doesn't have to be monetarily. However if money is involved it is an even greater obstacle. God created this world and everything in it to become abundant through ***BALANCE***. God is both masculine and feminine and ***it is this even exchange*** of breathing in and out that has the ability to create balance.

~*All of our problems on our planet are due to imbalance.* ~

Let's simply look at giving and receiving and then begin to apply this understanding in everything in life. You will eventually begin to see that Balance is the key to abundant life. Many times wealthy or influential people reach the top and find there's no one up there. There is loneliness unlike any loneliness you have ever encountered. It becomes more profound because in the journey you encountered a lot of people but the problem is you have now found an imbalance in life that you don't know how to get rid of.

~*This road is given to you to find the balance again.* ~

It's a major challenge. You can't change what is, so the key is to find an open door where you can quietly make change from within. Change comes within yourself first and then you become creative and find ways that you can help others without drawing attention. For some, their very appearance will always be a problem while alive but life is more than appearance. For these people they need to begin to build ***a new internal foundation, where no one can hinder their growth***. They must find ways in which they can enter a part of their world, ***unnoticed***, where they begin to help. Giving out of themselves in some way, but when they do that they are creating an avenue to receive something in return. For you, ***being the giver you really want to know it made a difference and so when someone gives back with the same intention, even if the gift is far less than what you gave, they need to have the same appreciation for their gift***. If you don't allow others to have the same experience by giving back to you, ***then you are being selfish***. This ***critical exchange in life*** can literally ***change the atmosphere on this planet***. Just think if you go to a poor country and give, then they will receive and nothing more might happen but *if you give them the ability to give back, then you help them believe they have something to give and to make a difference with.* If you *give them the tools to build a better world then you have saved the world.* To take things by force in war only creates more of the same. But to understand we are different and then to reach into their world and allow them to build *according to their dreams*, will send back unto you the greatest sense of oneness with God. *Balancing something takes a conscious effort* to see the lack and to help another know they have the ability to be the change in their world. It's so easy when we stop doing things from the intellect and start doing things from the heart. It's not our actions that are as powerful as the reason for the action. *The power of change comes when you change within how you see things and then understand and encourage another to believe* and to know their gifts to all are so appreciated. Sometimes I see into the Middle East conflicts a deep yearning in the *hearts of the people* for peace and understanding. They long to move past and really stop looking at war and focus on their future. Sometimes we loose sight of why we don't agree and we waste years *on conflicts that cannot be solved by the same method that created them.* Taking things by force will only create a reaction of the same. Why is it that leaders believe we have to force our beliefs on others? Sometimes terrible things happen in countries *as opportunities for healing by taking the time to hear why they did this to us.* Sometimes when we don't respond with violence we find we awaken the loving hearts within others that simply want to be heard and understood.

~Take time to know why your brother hates you.~

You just might find out something that can help you both. When you forgive others, you heal your own heart. *When you hear others, you help them to hear you.* We must stop trying to solve our problems on earth with the same method that created the problem. Instead of reinforcing the divisions we have, let us find the common ground *and BUILD ON THAT GROUND instead.* Do you know the strength mankind would have if we worked together instead of always reinforcing our divided philosophies? *There is no limit to our power as human beings when we become one people under God and we are unified.* Remember that Balance is the key. Bringing balance and becoming unified is the hope of the spiritual world, for us. The energy we exert to *keep divided* whether in personal experiences or in war, is an equal output of energy. *The more tension that is generated, the more one's energy is depleted. NEITHER ONE OF US WIN.* But if we work together we all win. We must take a new road. If we don't pull together on earth, we will experience a "collective failure". We must believe in our brothers and sisters and in turn help them believe in themselves. If we change our opinion of something and instead of trying to sway them our way, we focus a deep desire *to really understand why* they feel this way, and we may possibly open a door where they choose to stop fighting.

The journey is *layered with many levels*. The more willing you are to allow yourself to walk through *each layer and learn from it* beyond your understanding right now, the higher your understanding will become. This is about you and your potential to rise higher and become united with your divine plan. You have the keys to unlock your greatness but with greatness comes opposition, *expect it but don't allow it to create fear or stop what you are doing to grow.* Whether the opposition is obviously seen from others inflicting difficulties or not, *the true opposition is not about them but is your own struggles from within.* The people that have entered your own personal journey are like lessons in a lesson book. They are real and they are supposed to be real. *Think of your life on a movie screen and how each scene must occur in order for the next scene to make sense.* Yes, you could leave out some of the scenes but the ones next in line would have a lesser impact when they happen on the screen. God wants you to be able to really grow and experience life in its fullest so that your ultimate goal, *your spiritual attainment at a higher level, will be given to you because you are ready to receive the greater light from God.*

As I have tried to explain to you about the light, the pure light of God, let me refresh your memory of this. You are a spiritual being and you have come to earth in an earthly experience. Your goal in coming is to be able to have a greater amount of God's light in your being but *in order to do that your being must be able to receive it.* Think of a clogged drain in a sink. The water cannot flow but only stands at the top of the drain. The water has no way to penetrate but it's *not because it doesn't want to flow freely. It can't flow freely because something is blocking it.* In order for the water to flow, *you must unplug the drain. There is no way around it.* The same goes for God's light. All humans *can receive God's pure light* but the reason they don't receive it is because their vessels, their spiritual beings still have something blocking the ability for the light to flow into their being unhindered. We want God's light so much because we have a taste of how it fills our being with wholeness unlike anything this world can ever give. The reason we come to earth is so that we can become more of the spiritual being we are. *We come to earth knowing that we must unblock certain passage ways in our being, that have been blocked in other lifetimes, in order to receive more of God's light.* We come to earth on a personal mission of bettering ourselves. Yet when we come, we are engulfed with the human drama of life on earth. Some of the drama is a personal choice we made to enter into when we made our spiritual plan. We knew what we needed to overcome so that more of God's light could flow thru us and *so we chose, on our own, to enter certain circumstances in which the challenges would give opportunity for optimum growth.* Other dramas, or difficulties we would experience would come from the "collective whole" of what is occurring on this planet at the time we arrive. To tell you the truth when we look at the reality of why we are here, we must come to the conclusion that *human beings are incredibly courageous and strong souls.* Why in the world would we choose to come into a world that is so confusing and on top of that into a personal setting where we would have to endure and overcome other difficulties.

If you have ever felt defeated, hopeless, and just tired of life, *you are only experiencing a separation from the reality of your spiritual plan.* The reason we feel these desperate feelings is because we are suffering and the reason we are suffering is because we have lost our *ability to see* who we are and why we are here on earth. That is ok and today I want you to understand that your feelings are justifiable but *you must see beyond them in order to move ahead. Knowledge is power* when you realize that your understanding of something can take you to a new level of growth. Keep in mind that *knowing something doesn't really change it. It "is what it is" whether you know it or not.* Knowing something is a gift that is given to you so that you can now have the potential to grow. But why do we as humans tend to get stuck when we find somebody that really hears us and empathizes with us. Why do we get caught up in our own drama and simply sit and wallow in it for years? I honestly feel it is because *we feel alone and we feel cheated with life.* This feeling of being alone is because you have separated yourself from God within you. As I have already explained God is in you and you have Him always, so **you are never alone.** This will be something you need to remind yourself about until it becomes a living presence within. You are so use to thinking of God somewhere else that it will take some time, if you are willing to work towards this new understanding, to feel God in you. *Pray to Him, let Him hear everything about your day, talk quietly to Him always and you will begin a relationship that will become such a comfort, and the love will flow thru you as God longs for it.* This is where when you understand why things happen to you, you will be less likely to sit for too long when you find someone to understand you. Like I said just because you know something doesn't mean it will necessarily change. *Change comes when you look at it with a different perception* and you are willing to see the lesson and move on in your life. Don't stand still; *don't allow some experience to be your whole story.* Don't set something up as an idol that never changes. God is always becoming more and you are to do the same. *The experience doesn't define your life but it has the ability to greatly bring abundance to your life by what you learn from it.*

We get stuck sometimes when we back up and look at why we have been hurting for so long. We get stuck because as we look at it, we see how bad it was. But if you could step out of the box, and look in from a different perspective you would also *see it differently.* When a friend tells you their story, you are not usually as emotionally attached to all the details as they are. Yes, you feel their pain but when they repeat it enough, *it becomes a thorn in your side.* You don't like what the experience has done to them and you don't like hearing about it all the time, because you realize no one can undo what has already taken place. But the person telling the story is reliving it as if it is happening right now because they are so *emotionally attached that they cannot move away from it.* I guess somewhere deep in our consciousness we attach to terrible situations *in an effort to heal from them but most of the time, they drag behind us like a ball and chain. They keep us going in circles.* We know deep inside we need to see it, but *then we attach to it* and that becomes *all we see.*

The hope beyond all that you have felt pain from comes when you understand your mission in life. Let's begin to see a greater purpose, a greater overall vision you have in coming to this earth. Step away from your life for a time and look in as if you are above the earth. See yourself as a spiritual being that has lived many lifetimes. This lifetime you planned for your own overall growth of the higher spiritual being you are but it is a part of the blueprint for your entire sojourn in the material universe. You are far more *than the part of you* that chose to enter the material realm of earth as a human.

Let me try to give you an idea of what happens when you decide to come to this earth into a physical body. The conscious you begins this descent and it first integrates with your long-term mind, which is best known to be the mind that you carry with you from lifetime to lifetime. The Conscious you sees what is in the long-term memory bank you carry but as it descends into this world it also sees what is in the short-term mind that is centered around your current physical embodiment. So *you carry both memories with you* but the long term memory that enables you to see your true identity as an immortal spiritual being can easily be forgotten because life on earth has it's own expectations, desires and ambitions for your current embodiment and *your true identity can easily be put aside and quickly forgotten.* The experience on earth is where you grow but it also comes with certain drawbacks that create for you a greater struggle. For instance if your expectations, desires, and ambitions are heavily influenced by family or society they might be in direct opposition to what your expectations are in your long-term mind. ***They actually might be out of touch with what your true potential is.*** This is where a ***division occurs*** in your being. Before you came into this embodiment, you met with spiritual teachers and created a detailed plan for what you want to learn. You wanted to experience certain things in order to overcome your past karma imbalances from other lifetimes. ***In the spiritual realm you are not weighed down with ego or the carnal mind and you can see the greater picture with ease,*** but when you come to earth you loose that ability because you enter into the material world. It's part of the experience of coming here but it is also somewhat of a challenge. This is where it is possible that your outer expectations, the ones you have built based on the programming from family and society are possibly out of alignment with your spiritual plan. This is where Jesus said we are a house divided against ourselves.

> ***"It is to our greatest advantage to clear our mental body so that we can have a clearer vision of our divine plan."***

To put it simply, our mental body consists of certain beliefs about you, God, and the world and can be influenced from family, and society. They are a result of a dualistic way in which we see life and then ***we believe it's the whole truth.*** To clear this out means we will put on the Christ consciousness and see our life from a higher understanding.

> ***"Your greatest joy that you can experience while still in this life is to know that you are fulfilling your divine plan and that every aspect of your life is in alignment with that plan. This is what Abundant life is about."***

As you descend to earth it is highly probable you will forget this plan but there are people who are very spiritually aware and have a strong intuitive sense, even as young children, that know what they are here for or at least have some idea. But even they have to reconnect with the divine plan they came to do. ***However, the higher self that resides in the spiritual realm has full memory of who you are and that is why it is critical to reconnect to your higher self.*** What I want you to understand in hearing all of this is that you don't need to panic or blame anyone, including yourself if you have no clue as to why you are here. What you can do is ***simply begin to walk and make a determined effort from this day forward*** to observe and to listen from within to your intuitive voice in an effort to rediscover who you are and why you are here. Just be patient and take each day as a gift. You don't need to worry that you are going to miss something because when the time is right you will know and you will be ready. ***Just do what you can and grow as life continues on.*** To reconnect to your divine plan you will find a greater peace within you and a deep sense of meaning to your life. This is what my desire for you is in writing this book. ***I want you to see how special you are and that your life is not a random act from God.*** It's not an accident but in fact through whatever circumstances you were born into, ***the truth is that you came here on purpose, with a very important mission to accomplish.*** The avenue from which you came and the reason for your conception is not as important ***as the fact that you came through "someone" who brought you into this life and you have something to do.*** Don't see your circumstances as attachments that weigh you down but just see them for what they are. They are not about who you really are but they define a certain place in this world with which you came through.

Your divine plan is how you can manifest God's light by bringing it to earth but also it's about something you want to accomplish which is in direct relationship to who you are as a Spiritual Being. In the spiritual realm there are a number of God Flames. The best way to explain a God Flame is to just see them as a "particular quality" of God's nature. God is vast and complex but all of God is reminiscent of all of His creation. For instance there is a flame of God's Will, God's Wisdom, God's Love, God's Peace, God's Mercy and the list goes on and on. We as humans are aware of the positive qualities we can have and these are the qualities that make up the God Flames. ***The reason you are here is to bring forth one or more of these God Flames so***

that you can bring light from the kingdom into the material world. Now to understand a greater teaching about the God Flame I want to introduce you to the two sides of God. I have briefly touched on this earlier but the two sides of God are the Masculine and the Feminine. The expanding element of the Father and the contracting element of the Mother. The Bible mentions it as the Alpha and the Omega aspect, in Revelations 1:8. To better understand this, think of the Alpha aspect of your God Flame as the *masculine aspect out of which you sprang.* The *feminine aspect is the gift you are here to bring to the world.* An example might be that you came out of the God Flame of love, but you chose to come to earth to bring truth. What this means is that in order to bring truth you have to bring truth *in a loving manner.* Or maybe you are out of the God Flame of peace but you are here to bring direction. So you must bring direction that helps people attain peace and will express the unique quality of peace. Before I continue I want to share a poem my daughter wrote. She said she didn't understand what she was writing but she just began and it all spilled forth. After I read it I realized with tears in my eyes that she was writing about the Feminine Side of God, *the part of God that is THE GIFT we are bringing to this world.* We, God's creation represent the feminine side of God.

She Knows the Way

One thing leads to another,
This is what I have discovered.
We're taught success is built upon planning,
On writing down our dreams
And clearly identifying what this means.
I boldly confess this is wrong
This is not where our dreams belong.
We should trust in a high power.
The same higher power that flows in us and through us.
We should not try and plan it all.
If we do, this will ultimately be our fall.
There is order in this chaos

If we tap into the connecting force
We'll see that the path we're on belongs to many
It is a path that is connected to infinity.
To plan our lives disconnected here on Earth
Will cut us off from the source of energy we knew at birth.
We should plan to GIVE,
To GROW,
To LIVE,
To LOVE and FORGIVE.
We should plan to be part of the bigger picture.
Plan to share our God given features.
This should be our prayer.
Self-centered success brings home only an empty nest.
Live your dreams always thinking about the bigger schemes.
We're connected at the heart
Our life giving energy will never allow us to be apart.
Our creator connected us together
So we could give, we could love, we could grow forever.
Think of your life
As a stream that flows into the bigger ocean.
What you do
Should not be about your name
Nor about attaining fame.
What you leave will be based on what you were able to perceive.
Your perception will have been made
Based on the amount of love you gave away.
Your planning is intelligent
Your goals are honored by the successful
But do this world a favor
And dare to uncover the magic behind
A life of loving and flowing
Being connected to the realm of infinity.
Let the universe take you on your journey.
Trust that it knows what you need to be.
The business realm advocates to live intelligently;
To plan out your life.
Well, the universe is intelligent,

It knows where you need to go.
So, I ask you,
Just to let go.
Trust in the possibilities of truly living an abundant life.
Witness the energy that flows when you live a life without strife.
When you trust her to guide you on your journey
She will meet you with opens arms at the gateway.
Her profound love will take you away.
She truly is the only one
Who FEELS your presence
And if you dare to take her hand
Your life will change
For her energy always remains.
She is the one and only
Who knows
Who feels
The way.

It is hard to know what flame you are until you clear out the debris of your mental body. But you might already know by just thinking *of what is dear to your heart*. What things mean a lot to you and have always been important in life? It might even be wise to see the certain problems you often encounter in life that seem to weigh you down and create havoc, *maybe they are pointing to who you really are. Maybe the reason for all this trouble you have encountered is that they are in opposition to your God Flame.* In other words *you are here to let your God Flame consume them, which means that you attract them to you so that the fire of your greater Being can consume them.* This is the benefit of not becoming *emotionally attached* when certain experiences weigh you down, but *simply allow the fire of their presence to pass through your inner Being.* Learning the skill of being *"non-attached" will prevent you from magnifying the negative qualities with your emotional body.* Keep this in the back of your mind so that you can be empowered when these situations take place. *Remain non-attached, be the observer, step away from the scene, walk out of the picture and look back in from a different view.* When you are able to see life as a lesson in a classroom you can *then begin to see what you are able to bring to the lesson.* In a classroom when you are learning something, there are others in that room learning, too. When you are able to see something with a higher understanding you will not only be able to help yourself move beyond the experience but you will help others looking on. Your life has a divine plan but it is also connected to many around you and you can potentially help them with their lives. *If we could stop becoming so emotionally drained from our experiences we would clear the way for us to see the higher purpose with which we came to this life for.*

Let me try and explain to you the problems you will encounter with the mortal self in your identity. Your mortal self has *it's own definition of what your life is about* and it defines it by the views it has of life in this lifetime on earth. Your mortal self will do what it can think of to prevent you from acknowledging your divine plan. It is very controlled by the dualistic view of life you have thru the ego. It will try to make you so attached to the expectations you have built in this lifetime, expectations that your mortal self has programmed into your mind that *you simply will not look beyond.* In other words your mortal self will want you to become so attached to temporary desires and pleasures of life so that you will ignore the true desires you long to fulfill. This is where you have to see what is happening and *be willing to intentionally give up certain expectations or emotional attachments that you know aren't in alignment with your hearts desires.* An inner knowing, a consciousness that penetrates in your soul is what can put up the red flags and you can begin to grow faster when you listen and respond to the warnings you hear inside. Jesus described that we cannot serve two masters, that we cannot serve God, which is representative of your long-term spiritual goals, and mammon, which is representative of your short-term mortal desires and expectations. *For the truth is when you are pulled in two opposing directions, you either wake up or you give up your greater plan.* The mortal self is quite capable of creating an illusion projected on the picture of your life and *it will take a conscious effort to go in another direction. Your own act of WILL can save you if you are willing to listen to the truth within*

and change the path you are on. When you come to peaceful terms with the knowing of a divine plan, you will then no longer be a house divided against itself and you will reach beyond the mortal desires and expectation for what your life should be like. Jesus spoke about loosing your life and this simply means to loose your attachments to your dualistic expectations of life as you see it.

As you begin to find avenues in which you feel intuitively what your divine plan might consist of, keep an open heart and mind because **this is a gradual process and when you begin, what you see is only parts of it.** When you are faithful over a little, you will be made more aware over more. As you begin the process you will find the first **step is to decide you want to know** and then as you are faithful over your intuitive revelations, **you will prove yourself worthy to grasp more details as they are revealed.**

I have spoken often in this book about your perception and how you view things and how important it is in your healing. It is critical to have the understanding of the power of how your attitude of life can help you or hinder you. It is extremely important that people **don't take on the belief that they are a victim of circumstances that are beyond their control.** If you believe that life is throwing circumstances at you that are very difficult and often overwhelming, then you are one that is always trying to cope with it. Often you feel there just isn't any more that you can handle but this is a result that you are really carrying way too much of a burden. **Not attaching to everything that comes your way will help you begin to breath more freely and shift your attitude of life away from the sense of being a victim of circumstances beyond your control.** You need to remember that everything in your life happens as an opportunity to grow and eventually all of this can help you see who you are and your divine plan. The truth may be that you chose to enter certain circumstances in this life so that you would have an opportunity to rise above your dualistic beliefs and your karma. So no matter what circumstances you encounter in your life, you can assume that they can ultimately help you. The entire purpose for this plan is to put you into circumstances where you have the best possible opportunity for coming up higher, for taking another step up the spiral staircase, by overcoming a certain dualistic belief you hold within your body. Don't see yourself as a victim of circumstances beyond your control but *see yourself as a person who is constantly in the process of learning your lessons in life and becoming more with every victory.*

Your perception of your life can empower you but in order to have a greater perception I am trying to give you an understanding. My prayer is that whatever you are going through in life, you will not throw in the towel but take a step out of the picture and look back in from a different viewpoint. If you really see that life is about learning and becoming more then you will put away the illusion that life should always be easy. This is a lie and contradicts the very act of coming to this world. You might have an easy life but life is about learning and growing. The skill is found in understanding and when you take on the attitude that there is something you need to go thru and move beyond, *you will not fall victim to everything that comes along.* You will begin to build a realistic picture that life is an opportunity for growth and that life should put you into situations where you have to overcome certain limitations. When you reconnect to your divine plan you will see that all of the experiences to move closer to the abundant life. Furthermore when you look at life, as an opportunity to grow it will become *easier to detach from the emotions that used to weigh you down. Instead of falling into a trap of running away, and of not being willing to look at a situation, you can begin to question what it is you need to learn from this situation.* You will then be taking an active role in which you become in control of your learning and your destination. No longer will you feel the whole world against you or out to get you but you will see that you understand what is happening and God will help you through everything. No matter how much you understand you still will know you have a loving Father that will assist you in every aspect of the challenge. God is in you and He is experiencing what you are going through as you go through it. Keep in mind that when you keep an open mind and heart, you will receive an answer when you ask you're Christ self, within to help you learn the lesson behind the outer situation. When you learn the lesson I can promise you your situation will all the sudden change. In some situations *you will no longer*

attract specific outer circumstances. But there could be certain outer conditions that might not change but your understanding of them will have changed in an incredible way. Either way everything will take on a new view of life.

Let me give you a little more understanding of why sometimes you attract the same over and over in your life. I think this is a critical part of your experience that you need to fully understand so that you are clear why certain things happen over and over again. Everyone is different so we will just take an example. Some people have one failed relationship after another and they can't figure out why this keeps happening. Every time they move out of one relationship and into another, they seem to attract the same kind of person and have a similar problem. Most people aren't sure why they keep attracting the same circumstances over and over again. I would guess that most people think there is something wrong with them and eventually they become fearful of another relationship. However, there is a reason and it is because their divine plan specifies that they need to learn a particular lesson in this lifetime. If they do not learn that lesson from one situation, the cosmic mirror will give them another situation that out pictures their beliefs, and **they have another opportunity to see those beliefs and let them go.** This is why when you look at the reality of what you are going through and why; it is then you can take hold of growing and becoming more. If you always think you are a victim or not loveable or whatever, **the cosmic mirror will keep sending you the same** and you will feel your life is just full of misery and bad luck. So what you feel is attracting more of the same to get you to move on, but you can't move on until you learn what you need to learn. Once you learn the lesson, there is no longer any need for you to experience these kinds of situations and **all of the sudden, you will see that problems which might have followed you for decades can be resolved overnight and you will not encounter them anymore.** You are in control of your destiny but how you see yourself will determine whether you take control or remain a victim.

We often see our lives through filters in which **we have projected certain expectations for ourselves to live up to.** Whether family, religion, society or even your own idea of what life is about, caused those filters, they are not serving you but in fact are hindering your growth. You can hang onto anything you want, including your emotional ties to things and people but really in order to be true to yourself, you owe yourself a chance to experience the greatest abundance in life. You experience this when you free yourself from everything that ties you down and keeps you from seeing who you are.

I would like to share a couple of other beliefs that we carry in our minds that keeps us in a "stuck" state. Sometimes we get to a place where we know we need to do something to correct our lives, but we don't think we can do it. We feel we can't possibly overcome something because inside we have a belief we can never move forward and overcome our situation. *It is a mindset, an illusion* because the truth is that the other belief that we need to carry is that we are *never in a situation where we are facing a limitation, which we cannot overcome*. Your spiritual teachers along with yourself designed your divine plan and *the entire purpose is to set you free from limitations.* You might have many limitations that you need to overcome and many might *seem* impossible by the way your level of awareness is at this time in your life. But only those that you can overcome at this level of awareness will you need to address at this time. When you learn the lesson and move on, you will attain a higher level of awareness in the journey and *it is then that new limitations will be presented to you when you are ready*. Your divine plan is designed based *on a realistic view of your current level of spiritual awareness* and *you will not be presented with challenges that you are incapable of overcoming or cannot learn.* The point I am trying to make is that whatever level you are at, you will be presented with circumstances that will challenge you and require you learn the lesson and move on but in order to overcome the limitation, you must be willing to do what seems impossible with your current level of awareness. What I am saying is that you need to understand *that the sense that something is impossible is the actual problem and is what you need to address by believing it is possible.* Let's look at an example. You are in a relationship that is difficult and you have this belief that it is there doing and they need to change. It is easy to want to blame someone else for the problems when it isn't always the case. So you begin to believe that if the other person would change then everything would be solved. However in reality, the key to any improvement of your personal situation is that you must change. You need to find the desire to go within and discover the lesson that you are meant to learn from that particular situation. **When you learn the lesson, the outer situation will change.** Now keep in mind that **the other person may not change,** but the very fact that your attitude toward that person has changed will bring about drastic improvement over the relationship. Also the outer situation shows change because you see things different and therefore some of the problems are not problems anymore to you. The truth is if we want to be free of a particular challenge in our life, **that might have followed us for eons, we need to look beyond the outer circumstances that appear to be the problem.** When you look within, to the inner circumstances and change what is within, you find your whole life changes. You need to look for the hidden lesson and **realize that the lesson you need to learn relates to a certain belief you hold in your mind to be true.** Part of this belief is that you think it is impossible for you to overcome a particular limitation. So if you believe you cannot find a partner with whom you can have a positive relationship with, then there is some lesson you have not learned and **so you keep attracting to you the same kind of people and this is to force you to confront the lesson.** However if you hold the belief that it is impossible for you to change, and you keep running from every situation you come across, you will not learn and grow. **This is where you put yourself in a catch-22 in which you keep attracting the same situations that force you to confront them but you resist doing so and you never learn the lesson and therefore you create your own life of suffering.** Do you realize there is so much more to your life than this one obstacle? You need to understand that finding your divine plan takes time and only when you stay on the path and keep growing will you find it. But if one problem stops you and you don't go any further, you won't experience the greatest life you could ever have. Take the courage to be who you are. Face the challenges and learn and move on. I promise the life you will finally see because of your persistence will be the greatest life you ever dreamed.

Many say life is a school of hard knocks and yet I would like you to see it as a school of learning how to reach within and find the God within you to overcome anything you encounter. If I remember right, Jesus said He could do nothing of himself because he said, "that with men all things were impossible but with God all things are possible." To keep the power of God's light flowing undiluted through your body you need to let go of the things that keep you from believing that you have purpose in this life and that purpose is the highest vision of God. It is our beliefs that we carry in this lifetime that have no truth to them and put us down, that keep us from manifesting our potential. We have nothing to fear but fear itself and that is the truth. Our fear-based beliefs that cause us to accept certain things as impossible, *will be the very things that will keep us in a catch-22 where we cannot begin to see the abundant life waiting for us to embrace.* When I say we have nothing to fear but fear itself, what I mean is *that the problem with fear is that it makes us unwilling to look at our beliefs, which in turn keeps us from identifying our illusions.* Think of it this way. You feel trapped in your life as if it were a prison cell, *but all along the door has never been locked. You have been allowing your illusions to make you afraid to try the handle and open the door. The fear is what is keeping you from taking a hold of your life and not the circumstances.*

Let's look at the life of Jesus for one moment in our understanding of divine plans. I think His life is a great example of how some divine plans are connected to a planetary purpose of raising the collective consciousness of human kind so that God's abundant life can become a planetary reality. Many spiritual people that have raised their level of spiritual awareness will come to this earth in an effort to help the whole of mankind. You might be one of these people. If you have a natural tendency to be able to rise above situations and still have so much love in your heart for others, you might have a greater purpose than to just help yourself in your walk. Many spiritual people who are of the Ascended Host have observed humankind and the problems they encounter. This has caused many to volunteer to take on certain burdens that are aimed at not only raising their own level of consciousness but also raising the collective consciousness. This can be done only by transforming mis-qualified energy and by resolving blocks in the collective psyche. When I talk about "collective" I am talking about an accumulation of many who create the whole. When the planet has accumulated a certain amount of negative or harmful emotions and actions, this drags down the ability to rise out of it and *sometimes the effort of a spiritual being to help overcome the negative downward pull is what stops it dead in its tracks and finds a way out of the downward pull.* In the life of Jesus we know to some degree he carried the sins of the world, meaning the karma of the world, *in order to give humankind a reprieve in which they could rise to a higher level of consciousness without being so burdened from the negative energy of their past.* I have tried to explain to you that life is about learning and so if Jesus took on the your karma permanently, and you never had to deal with it again in your life, *he would have done the greatest injustice to you ever. He would have ultimately hindered your ability to learn and grow and that was never Jesus intention.* Jesus came to help you and to bring unto you a path, a pattern, and an example that *you could follow so that you would have victory.* Religion has created a picture of Jesus in which he supposedly took upon himself not only the sins that were committed in your past but in your future, and in doing that they not only lied about his deep loving commitment to help you *but they took away your power to help yourself.* When you believe just this lie, then you stop taking responsibility of learning for your own growth. *If Jesus had done this then how could we ever take responsibility and learn the necessary lessons in our lives?* The reason for the troubles, the sins if you want to call them that, is because the universe acts like a mirror and reflects back what we send out. It is in the experience that comes back to you that you have an opportunity to learn a very valuable lesson that ultimately can take you higher on the your spiritual path. *Why would Jesus want to take that from you?* Just so you know *he didn't intend the interpretation of his death to be the main obstacle that would keep you crippled from taking control of your life.* Jesus abhors this teaching and I believe with all my heart and soul *he desires right now that you know he never meant for this to happen.* This is another example of how religious teachings have created illusions around the loving life of one of God's sons. So when a number of more spiritual beings choose to come to earth, volunteering to take on negative karma or energy that is collectively burdening us, ***it is done to lighten the burden so we are not so overwhelmed but it is also to give us an opportunity to make spiritual progress in this lifetime.*** Many times they carry the burdens whether it is of poverty, sickness or disease or even injustice towards humankind, to help demonstrate to others that they can overcome such burdens by taking a more spiritual approach to life. If you are one of those then please hear my heart to you. I love you so much for being willing but keep in mind that the purpose of your life ***isn't to be overcome by the burden forever and you will experience the joy before you leave earth.*** The purpose of your life is to ***demonstrate the love you have for others*** in showing them they don't need to be overcome by their burdens. I thank you for giving us a vision of God's higher vision of life on earth. By your willingness you have loved enough to show us how to love others. We cannot know all of our spiritual plan instantly but ***we can recognize along the way those who have been an inspiration to us in our walk. Never think your life isn't important.***

To remind you that there is hope beyond the pain you have suffered in your life is to give you back the power of your own destiny. Life is not a random game of chance or even the punishment of an angry God. Life is not a chaotic process that seems to have no meaning or direction. ***Life is a chance to become the change that will not only empower you but also encourage others to be empowered.*** God put all of us in the River of Life that is ***unstoppable, always moving forward.*** We can live by our choices in life and slow down the process in which we grow but ***we cannot stop the river.*** We cannot stop the process in which we are growing. ***Progress is unstoppable and time is unstoppable.*** Life goes on whether we choose to go on or not. The wonderful truth about life since the days of Jesus is that we have indeed become more aware of our spirituality than ever before. So many religious people speak of the world getting worse and of conditions so bad that God will return and punish everyone. The sad thing is that ***they see this in their minds***

illusions. The truth is that the reason God will come is because the level of consciousness in man's awareness will bring it here, because it has risen higher to accept it. It's because our consciousness will be linked to the Christ consciousness, which really means that we have come along way. ***To understand the reality of life today is to know that we have indeed progressed to a much higher level of awareness and to a greater understanding of life.*** The Bible says, ***"Wisdom is the principle thing; therefore get wisdom; and with all they getting get understanding:" this is our highest goal for getting past the mental images we hold as illusions in our mind.*** When we clear our mental body we will come to understand the laws that God used to design this universe. We will align ourselves with those laws and this will fulfill our role to bring the Kingdom of God into manifestation on earth.

The religious world is motivated with fear tactics, which actually keep us in a "stuck" state. They use what they know to be all there is to know, and then they condemn the rest of us. ***This is not God's love. I don't care what their argument is*** because many times when I hear them condemning others to death with their sermons ***they are simply confirming that they don't serve the loving God that created us.*** They serve their own idol they have created in their mind, of God. It is sad indeed. ***But we must go on and we must not allow them to hinder the work we can do.***

Keep in mind your connection to the WHOLE of God and all that ever lived and are living.

⁓*When we hurt another we hurt the whole and when we love another we love the whole.*⁓

In knowing this let me remind you of the cosmic mirror again. When we see life with limitations we project it on the cosmic mirror. In order to rise to a higher state we need to begin to understand that life is an opportunity for growth and ***not an endless sea of limitations***. When we raise our level of understanding and in turn raise our consciousness we no longer project on the filmstrip in our minds ***imperfect images of life***, which in turn is sent to the cosmic mirror.

~It is in our ability to raise our awareness that we actually uncover the filmstrip of our higher vision and divine plan.~

So when we begin to project perfect images into the cosmic mirror because we see life differently due to our higher awareness, the cosmic mirror will reflect back those images in the form of perfect physical conditions on the planet. This is how the earth can, not only return to its current state of purity but even move beyond. We might have a hard time grasping this possibility but as you continue on your own path in life, you will begin to see a vision beyond what you have ever dreamed.

~It is in the journey that we awaken and begin to see God and His magnificent plan for our lives.~

It is in the journey that we grow to a higher understanding and with each level we attain, we become more of the Spiritual Beings we are.

~The hope beyond your life as you see it today, is something you attain in your understanding.~

I want you to know that life on earth is to lead you to a path of Oneness with God and all of creation. There are many who have already attained this and they are ready to help you because it is their greatest desire that you become one in the River of Life. **When you become one with your higher self, you add to the whole and the Whole of all of God's creation is magnified.**

Change begins when *one person has a vision*. When one person takes hold of what there divine plan reveals they are to do, *they begin a force* of God's Abundance and many will begin to walk with them. Not because it profits them financially but *because when you see for yourself the wondrous abundance of something you see with clear eyes how you don't want to be without God's abundance.*

When God says He won't do it all for us it is because He wants us to be the co-creators and when we see the power of what we can do for the good, *we are glad that God didn't take away our victory for the moment.* God wants to help us but also wants us to do the creating because.....

~...He wants us to experience the incredible feeling of what we can do. ~

He knows it will help us to become more. When life is hard and you find that many roads are blocked in your journey, it might just be that way because the key to change for you is simply to take hold of your life and make different decisions. And all of this blockage may be due to your *emotional attachment to the situation.* When you are emotionally attached you see things in an illusionary fashion, like that mirror at the State Fair that warps how you look. When you are emotionally attached you need to be, *so that you can now make a conscious effort to stop attaching this way.* You need to feel its impact so you know it's *not in your best interest* to keep allowing its power over you. It's for *you to let go of* because if you see it blocks your light of your higher being from flowing to your mortal being, then you will let go of it. You must be willing to look at the problem and understand it, *so that your prayers to God will be more affective. You must be willing to take action on your part, so that you let your light shine and this is what Jesus said, " to bear witness of the truth."* You become *one solution* to the problem. *The power of your light is greater than you think.*

~I believe the reason that there is evil often winning in many situations is because the good people tend to sit back and do nothing.~

They can tell what they don't like but action isn't very often what they choose. ***Actually this is something that is very necessary to change.***

~If our world is going to change we need to call forth those who are of an honest nature who do not like evil in this world, to come forth and become an active voice of change.~

The world is ready and I believe that if a few brave souls, who really are aware of what needs to be done in our country and in our world, ***would speak up and take action, others would join in.***

~Sometimes I think what keeps us quiet is that desire to not be involved but if we aren't involved then how can we complain when terrible things keep happening in our world?~

A lot of the wrong doings around the world have ***no logical reasoning.*** Why someone would waste time on things that only hurt themselves and the world around them is simply because of why they do what they do. Recently we have heard how large corporations have hurt honest hard working investors because of selfish desires. Wouldn't it be to their advantage in the long run to support the people that make their companies what they are? ***Wouldn't it make more sense to spread the wealth among all of the shareholders and not just a few so that a greater market would come as a result?*** Think of the logic when a government allows large companies to pollute the land, which in turn affects our natural resources and our population as a whole. All of this is for profit? ***But for how long do we profit from this foolish decision? Don't we suffer as a whole on the planet we love so dearly, the only home to humans? What's wrong with us?*** We might see a short-term profit but overall these kinds of choices affect the long-term and make no sense. ***There are ways to have abundance in life without taking from others and without destroying our natural resources*** and all that surrounds us. *Abundance was never one sided where one would gain and the other would be lost forever.* Abundance comes with balance. Balance in nature, balance in understanding, and balance in everything. *If we don't stand up, speak up, and take hold of some of the foolish choices we make in an effort to create more temporary abundance, we are going to loose it all. What I want you to understand is that humans tend to make choices that have no logical reason and can never benefit anyone*, whether on a personal level or on a worldly level. Violence, murder, molestation, rape, organized crime, and war, all take us down more roads in *which we have to get past in order to get back to square one.* The mindset that chooses to do these things is self- centered and is the Carnal mind Jesus talked about. *It's why we do what we do that awakens our awareness and in turn has the ability to re-look, re-think the situation and make change.* Change comes when you understand the problem and only then can you begin to work on a resolution.

No "one" President can fix something *if the people are always battling him.* What happens when the people become a voice *that only stirs up the pot instead of looking for a resolution* is *the sense of struggle becomes the struggle.* In other words we are just going in circles because **we want to do it our way**. We create a greater struggle when our mindset is focused on pride and selfishness. The President will *then have to focus on getting the people to trust again* he is working in their best interest, instead of working on the problems. *He will be forced to put more energy in places that don't serve the whole because the whole wants to allow emotions to rule.* The people, *because of the mindset* have gone down a road *that takes on a whole new problem. That is why many problems never get solved.* We need to stop emotionally attaching for whatever reason and really work on what is good for the whole. Emotional outburst, signs of mockery, name-calling, and the list goes on and on, *is the problem.*

~It's our pride and emotions that keep us from ever seeing real change.~

I have watched many spiritual men and women descend to this planet throughout the pages of history and many were lost before they got too far. Why? ***Because the people focused on the wrong things and the good that was intended, again was lost.***

~The real problem isn't the problems, but the mindset that gets going in one direction and before you know it we have taken on mountains of problems that have nothing to do with the issue.~

Get your eye on the "problem" which is not the person trying to help you.

~If Americans don't take hold of the way they see things, we will be no different than those who have warred in other countries for decades. ~

We may not be at war like that, be ***we are at war*** in many other ways. ***We are destroying ourselves from within just like you can personally destroy your own self from within. It's no different.***

~Let us return to the great country we are that sets examples and has a focus on freedom for all.~

In our racial slurs, our emotional outbursts we are taking, the world is confirming that although we chose a president that reflected we are not divided by color anymore, ***we have not changed within.***

~We still have the old mindset of separation and a dividing rod we hold in our hand is the reason why we cannot make peace and understanding with those in other countries. ~

It's not our leaders problem but ***our problem***. It's going to get worse unless we as AMERICANS see, and remove the beam out of our own eyes. WE have the potential to grow from this situation but if we don't we will experience more and more in times to come. *It's because this is a lesson in a classroom and until we learn the lesson and change from within, we will receive more lessons down the road*. God want's us to know that this problem is *blocking our ability to receive the light* and to experience abundance. America's future is in our hands. *WE talk about saving our environment but saving our unity, as ONE NATION is even more critical*. Step away from the picture and see *the real problems*. Learn by changing *your mindset* and embrace all of Americans as ONE PEOPLE.

~When enough light is present, those that choose to remain at odds in the darkness, will be overcome with the pure light of our BEING.~

Don't battle everything and focus on the battles raging, but focus on your own change and just become the light, just become the change. Stand up and speak up for unity and *get off the paths that only take all of us further from the solution*. We are basically good people but we take on incredibly bad decisions for different reasons. *Let's get down to really looking at what can help us and get rid of the things that only take us further from a solution*. Let's remember that when we face why we do things, so many times our answer is "We don't know why." Should that alone be an alarm that goes off? *If we don't know why, then let's not do it*. However, if you really want to waste your life and take a chance that you could loose your identity forever because of the messes you get into, then that is your choice.

~I am calling forth for a few people to stand up and speak up. Let's become a voice of change.~

Through out this book I have spoken a lot about the mind and it's perception, the level of understanding and the way to increase it, and our identity and it's power. I think that you have come to somewhat of an understanding that *life is more than how we perceive it and interpret it.* Life on earth is seen through the energy level that exists in the material universe. There have been many thoughts on perception and reality, by many people over the course of time. *Just this should tell you that how they saw life wasn't enough and so they increased their awareness by learning and experimenting.* Just think of what I have already spoken about in your identity. You see things thru your own personal attachment to life or in a worldview of life on earth, to the best of your ability. But *you have a greater ability to see more* and this is what I want you to work on. *Increase your awareness, and your understanding and remember how you see something now, is not by any means all there is to see.* Know there is so much waiting to be revealed to you in everything you see in life or in the mind. Many times I have mentioned that there is much more to learn about everything and there will always be more. Learning about what others have experienced is wonderful but the power lies *in your own perception.* What I mean is that when you *personalize a particular teaching and apply it to your life*, to your divine plan, and see clearly how it can help you, *that is when you empower your own life to become more.*

Aldous Huxley, a well-known writer, brought to us his understanding of the doors to perception. In his writings we find enormous depth but do you know that his greatest personal, physical struggle was his *eyesight*. How ironic because we often relate perception with eyesight. The truth is our eyes have something to do with our interpretation but even if you were blind, you could see through perception. Here was a man that revealed in his writings that when you force your perception of something on others, *it kills their potential to see from their own ability.* He struggled with own ability to see physically *but it never stopped him from looking beyond the physical and the material universe.* What fascinates me is his desire to see more than what is seen in this world. *That is they key to our own growth.* We need to understand that in the spiritual realm, place, time, and distance *cease to exist.* The physical objects of our everyday world seen from a spiritual realm have little substance, little importance. In all actuality I believe that when you see from the spiritual realm, reality becomes different light waves and what your brain normally speaks to you in terms of material objects seen, is shut off. For instance the chair that is at your desk where you write, isn't seen in the spiritual realm the same as in the material realm. *In the spirit world you see things differently because you live differently and what you needed to see in the material world becomes no longer important in the spiritual world.* An example would be that in the spiritual world you see the "nature of things" but in the material world you see things as to there worth or value in the material world. In the material world the same object takes on a different meaning because it has a different purpose. *This is where attuning your perception to the spiritual realm will help you to get a hold of your real identity and the purpose of your divine plan.* It takes time and a willingness. *If you could see how unimportant some of the things we live for while on earth are in the spiritual realm, you will be able to make a clearer decision of what to keep and what to throw out.* In attuning your perception to how important something really is in the overall view of your divine plan, you will find a sense of freedom and not a feeling of being a victim* and this will help you realize that *you are in control* of your destiny. The control panel is what is within. When something bad happens and it seems your world is falling apart, if you could see that what you are going through is "temporary", and learn how to grow from the experience, you will have greater confidence that things are happening for a reason and they will eventually work out. As I have already covered, keep in mind that *your divine plan is mixed with your desires to heal on earth,* whether it is in relationships or bringing knowledge or growth to the planet as a whole. So if you feel you came to earth to bring knowledge and understanding but you feel cheated in relationships, then *the mixture of both needs are meant to be fulfilled.* Together they bring wholeness and balance to your experience and *they are both a part of what your divine plan needs to fulfill.* What I'm saying is that often we feel God's will isn't our will. *The truth is God's will is our will.* We are a part of God and God is in us and so if you desire to find love in a relationship on earth, God wants you to fulfill that. But because there is more to your divine plan, you need to also fulfill the other part of bringing spiritual understanding to earth. ***God's will for your life has never been in opposition to your divine will for your life.*** As I have said over and over, You sat down with your spiritual teachers who are also of God and you explained things you wanted to heal from, to grow from, to experience in life on a personal level, but because you are a spiritual being and you want to become more in understanding and closer to God, you also wanted to bring to earth, at the same time, a quality of God's pure love. ***Together these desires are very much your plan and they do not oppose but attract to each other.*** God desires that you become all that you can become. When I say that I am saying that God loves you so much that ***He wants to hear what you need and He wants you to experience the healing and the fulfillment you need.*** When He sees you healed and your longings fulfilled it heals Him and fulfills Him and it gives Him such a joy beyond what we can imagine, to see His Creation ***MORE than He created***. It brings great joy to God to see the fulfillment of His desires. His desires are in seeing us become successful in achieving ***what we need*** to be as the co-creators He created us to be. ***He also loves to feel a oneness with us by our desire to draw closer***. This is where praying can help. If you pray for God to grant your every wish and bring abundance all at once, He can't do that because it is against His own laws. When you pray for growth and understanding, it comes freely and in alignment with His laws and in turn you grow closer to Him. ***You begin to understand you are both on the same team and working together.*** Your victory becomes a joy for you and He experiences it through His creation and it becomes a joy for Him, too.

~When you learn and grow you add to creation more power of God's light. God is not in opposition to your divine plan.~

We draw closer because we fulfill our plan and at the same time rise to a higher level of the spiritual realm. When we are fulfilled, we fulfill the entire plan of God and it's as simple as that. ***That is why believing the lies of God being angry and judgmental are the greatest injustice not only to God but also to you.*** The potential to fulfill your divine plan is waiting but we must begin to pull down the lies of deceit that keep us from starting out and finishing everything we desire.

Before I leave this chapter my heart wants to share a personal message to you. No matter who you are and what you've gone through, everything is for a reason and that reason is for you to rise and shine. Through out my life I have found myself being very misunderstood. I have noticed that forgiveness and acceptance go hand in hand. I have always been one that accepts my responsibility for the path my life is on. When I do something that affects others in a bad way, I accept that I have caused them pain. I respond with a quick and sincere, "I'm sorry" because I am sorry that my choices have inflicted trouble for them. I knew the value of my choice but it affected others and I wanted them to know I understood. We talk about war and the greatest gift we can give our brothers and sisters who disagree with us is *our understanding*. I have learned to re-word the "I'm sorry" to "I understand" in many of the situations because in taking the immediate blame it isn't always good. I have mentioned already to not blame yourself for your path because it was necessary. If you had not taken "a path" you wouldn't be growing, in fact your wouldn't be alive. All of us must take one path or another and all paths are to teach us. So telling someone you are sorry all the time, simply takes away from you what you need to grow from. *It attaches you to the emotional part of the experience and that emotional part takes you away from the lesson needing to be learned.* Many wonderful guiding friends have pointed out to me that I shouldn't say I'm sorry over something that wasn't my fault. They are also keepers of the eternal flame. In my life I have learned to take blame in order to survive and because of my great love I have survived very well. But taking blame is taking on someone else's responsibility for the situation. It takes away their power to grow. We talked about Jesus and how he never wanted to take away our power to grow. But because of the life I lived in "survival mode" and because of the religion I choose for many years, I found that there were certain self talk statements that came full center in my journey out of a lower mindset. One of them was this of always taking blame. There is nothing wrong with saying you're sorry when indeed you need to, but to always say your sorry is not healthy. And when you say it, let it have power in the first time. In other words you really don't have to say it over and over. They may accept your apology but if you have to repeat it because of an ongoing drama, then this is when the responsibility of your side of the equation must be laid to rest. You must remember you did your part with a sincere effort and leave the receiving to them; it is there problem now. Let's look at the definitions of "sorry" for a moment. One definition is "feeling distress, especially through sympathy with someone else's misfortune". An example statement would be "I'm sorry to hear about what happened to your mother." Another definition is "filled with compassion for". An example would be "He couldn't help feeling sorry for her when he heard how she'd been treated." Another definition is, "Feeling regret or penitence." As in the statement, "He said he was sorry he had upset me." One of my sons, at a very young age taught me enormous wisdom through the verbal fights we would get into. *I learned by his "old soul" that giving and receiving had to be balanced.* Although during the experiences he may not have understood his wisdom because he suffered too through our arguments *but he taught me with what we endured together.* This is where growth for each is available. Even when we are different in age or understanding, every confrontation is for our good. *The path we are on doesn't need to be apologized for because it is suppose to be the path we are on.* And if something really hurts another we need to understand and *help them continue on their journey.* Sometimes this means we say we are sorry or we understand but *we cannot focus on blaming ourselves.* We need to stop saying we are sorry for the experiences because in fact it is *by the experiences we grow.* They are the opportunities and so why do we need to apologize for our journey to self-awareness. *WE DON'T'!!!!!* When someone says they are sorry, it's as important to accept their apology as it was for the other to give it. It wasn't that I didn't know this and it wasn't because I didn't teach it but when I found my life was going so far down a wrong road, I chose to take blame to survive. But this was wrong to always take blame. You see we need to be easy on ourselves. Understand that what you are going through *has attached to your emotional identity and that attachment brings with it a clouded view of who you are.*

~You are still who you are but because emotions take over you begin to go into survival mode.~

This is where you are trying to keep going, simple as that. It's not something you should feel bad about because it is your saving grace at this time, in this level of your awareness. Recognize it for what it is and begin to remove the guilt and regret by forgiving yourself and accepting your forgiveness. Also, don't totally take the blame. When I say forgive I mean forgive yourself for allowing yourself to go down a road that separated yourself from the real you. **But that is where the black top ends.** Accept forgiveness from yourself and move on. What happens when we "get stuck" is *we don't grow from anything.* The truth is "I'm sorry" is an opportunity for you to grow and for others if this is necessary in their journey. **But flinging those two words into the material realm, too much, takes away their power when needed and takes away your power of feeling in control of your life.** Your internal voice begins to feel defeated and you begin a new struggle of believing in your potential. **Flinging guilt at yourself all the time, takes away the power of the purpose of your path.** God wants us to take these paths to learn and to grow and in appearance they don't always seem very beneficial but **they are to teach.** If you were working a math problem on the board, and you derived at the wrong answer **wouldn't you focus on just redoing the problem and even more on the method you took to get that answer?** Wouldn't you be more focused on learning so that next time you would get the right answer? In math if you don't understand the methods, you can't do another problem. In math there is always another problem **and if you focused on the failure of making a mistake on one problem, you would never be able to see beyond the mistake so that you could get the next one right.** My point is that in life why we do what we do is very critical. If we have focused on our failures as humans, then we will never know how to really grow and we will never move on to the next level of our plan. **If we focus on always saying we are sorry when in fact we are just learning and growing,**

then our mindset will be the most crippling of all of our problems.
In religion they want you to focus on how unworthy you are and how
you can never match up to the life of Jesus. **This is where your growth
stops. It stops in the mindset, how you see things and how you see
yourself.** Look at all of these scenarios and see how all of the pieces share
a common denominator that has to change if you are going to grow.

~It's not so much what you do but WHY YOU DO WHAT YOU DO that is as important.~

What is within must change; it's as simple as that. You are
on a journey and you will encounter choices that will affect you and
others. But remember anytime you feel you have made a mistake, you
really have not. You are using Free Will to explore and choose and if
you affect someone in a bad way, you can make mends so you don't
cripple their path. **You want to express your understanding how it
affected them but that is all you need to do.** I'm not saying you cannot
feel remorse, but what I'm saying is to truly feel and then express it
and then leave it. **I am trying to get you to keep from emotionally
attaching and dragging yourself down further. It must be a true
effort of unconditional love that can free you from the tie.** Just saying
something isn't going to heal you but when you say it with a pure heart,
you will heal. Again, What you do isn't as important as WHY you do
what you do. We are all experiencing life and your life has intersected
with OTHERS and this has the potential to help them grow along
with you. Just understand that any problem, any choice is bound to
affect you and others. My whole point in all of this is to understand
why feeling "sorry" in a situation has a place but **it's not to take you
down a long and winding road that destroys your ability to grow.
Jesus said many times and many different ways to understand your
brother and to lay your offering at the altar, meaning do your
part, and then leave the rest to them.** We can't change anyone but
ourselves. We need to understand this at a higher level. So when you
feel some action you have done is hindering someone's walk, and you
are responsible then this is the time to give understanding and love.

From that point forward it is something they can take and learn from for their own growth. You are responsible to be responsible for you and you alone but to always respect others. And that means you need to love yourself and your efforts to take your journey. If your journey has taken you down a path a great learning, which has caused a lot of feathers to fly, then look at it from a non-emotional standpoint and decide if it has hurt anyone. ***Make right with your brother and keep going.*** See what can be refined and made into greater fulfillment but don't beat yourself up by taking all the blame for everything. ***You are here to learn and don't apologize for the lesson.***

> ***~The lesson is to teach you and if the student goes down an emotional road, he will loose sight of what he can grow from.~***

This is not set in stone but you need to take what I'm saying and ***apply it to your situation***. Keep a heart of understanding and love for yourself and all you are intersected with. Have empathy ***but don't be so fast to take away the power of the lesson.*** The power of the lesson is in how you see it and what you can grow from. ***Your perception will go off track and take you away from the power of the lesson, if it becomes emotionally trapped***. When opportunities in your journey arise and others need to hear you feel for them and understand them, then your words can help them heal. So if you need to say you're sorry, it may heal them, but just don't let it take on an emotional attachment ***where you then get your focus off of your growth.*** Emotions are good to a small degree but usually are more crippling than anything, because they become ***all there is in a situation*** and we forget everything else. ***Humans tend to blame quickly and this takes their eyes off what the teacher is trying to teach.*** Emotions that attach to a lesson are one of the reasons we loose sight of our divine purpose.

All that I have shared is only a tip of the wealth God has waiting for you to learn. ***The greatest teachings you will learn will be like I did, on your own***. Written words, such as mine do not contain all there is.

In fact my words contain so little of the vast knowledge awaiting. Go within yourself and hear your intuition. Hear the God within you. This will help you begin a personal journey. My friend, you are a special and unique individual and ***the greatest teachings you need to learn for your particular divine plan will come from the teacher within you.*** When you are ready, God will teach you what He knows you can understand and this process will continue for infinity. ***There is no final word on the vast understandings of everything.*** When you open a new door, the previous understanding you once had will be evident to you as a foundation to MORE. When you are ready MORE will be given.

THE KEEPERS OF
THE ETERNAL FLAME

I left this chapter to the end because I want you to know you are not alone. I mentioned already about the Ascended Host and how they are our teachers that guide us. We've gone thru many teachings in this book but I want you to remember that what you read here *isn't all there is to know*. There are many in this world today teaching similar and *even more comprehensive teachings far above what have shared*. Keep in mind that many spiritual beings have been sent to earth at this time in history to bring about change like never before. There also are many who have left the material realm because they are ready to help us with a higher understanding as we begin a new walk in our life and follow the inner path. I want you to know that these spiritual beings want more than ever for *you* to succeed. I wonder if you have noticed an incredible amount of very well known people who have passed in just this year. But the ones that are not famous and do not attract the attention of the world are greater in number. The reason for this is *because the foundation for a great awakening is set in motion.* I believe that there will be an awakening on this planet unlike anything that has ever occurred and this awakening is a spiritual manifestation of The Christ Consciousness.

What is the Second Coming of Christ? The second coming of Christ is when the people on earth have the Christ Consciousness and bring God's light to earth. The reason I bring this up is because I want you to know that the Ascended have the ability to help us attain a higher level of consciousness. It is up to us *to ask for their help* and thru their help the earth can become all we have the potential to be and even beyond our wildest imaginations.

The Ascended Host are the keepers of the Eternal Flame of God's pure Being. They are here for us. When you ascend to the spiritual realm, you overcome all carnal, ego-centered, and human motivation. The Ascended Host of Beings are here for one reason and that is that they love God and the unascended brothers and sisters, namely us. They also have a great love for planet Earth. Their unconditional love for every human being and their greatest hope that we commit to the spiritual growth of our souls is what *they long for.* It is based on the unconditional love they have for all of us. They work as a group but are individuals also. They long for us to manifest the Kingdom of God on earth. I want you to know something very important about the Ascended Host. *They are very committed but they cannot help us unless we call upon them.* Each of us has one assigned to helping us as our personal teacher and guide. They long to guide us but *we must ask* with an open heart and mind. They also want us to grow higher in our spiritual awareness we have the potential to become and in doing this they know how important it is for us to have a greater intuitive knowing. By sharpening this skill, of intuition, we grow closer to their instruction and we become more aware of our divine plan. *It's one thing for a teacher to teach us something without full awareness of what the ultimate goal is in our lives but when we have the knowing or at least a progressive revelation of what our plan is, we grow quicker and the joy we share with our teacher creates a bond of love.*

The Ascended Host also are concerned for the whole of mankind and their hope is to see the formation of a body of people on this planet where *we are all connected to our Christ self and our personal teacher.* You see when this happens we will have a movement of Christed Beings where the Ascended Host can be our hands and feet on earth.

This will help in removing the darkness from this planet and bringing God's kingdom into full manifestation.

I have a belief that they have a way of helping us to purify our planet and to establish a Golden Age of freedom, peace and abundance. They can help us with removing what hinders us from becoming all we can be, if we are willing to take their hand and allow them to have full reign. They can help us establish a permanent Golden Age. But because they are no longer in embodiment and the Law of Free Will does not allow them to act on their own as the law requires you to be in embodiment, *they need us who are physically in body form to ask them to help us.* We are essentially the only ones that can make this happen and they of the Ascended Host can help guide us by giving us ideas and direction. For this to really have an impact on earth *there must be a critical mass of people who hear the call to follow the path to Christhood and establish a direct connection to the Ascended Host.*

I feel an urgency to tell you that at this time in earth's history there are millions of souls on this planet who volunteered to come into embodiment at this time. They are here because of their deep love for God, and all who inhabit or ever inhabited this planet. They also have a deep love for Earth itself. They have, like I have, an intuitive knowing of what God's kingdom is like and what it will take to bring it forth. Some are aware of who they are and some are still trapped beneath illusions and darkness in this embodiment. Before I took hold of my life I felt a powerful presence within me of God's love and of a deeper reason for why I am here. I felt an awakening happening over a period of time and thru that I had a destiny altering vision of my divine plan. *I became aware that I needed to share with others how to get out of their current limitations and become a force of God's love.* What I have come to understand and what I have shared is *something that has come thru a process of my own spiritual awakening.* I have learned that my suffering and my losses in life were only to help me find a way out of all that limits all of us. My life would teach me that it wasn't about me but about what I could do to help mankind awaken to the greater purpose for which they came. Nothing was lost and everything I learned caused me to see the kingdom in all its glory.

I have been told by the Ascended Beings that the potential for the earth at this time in history is at a peak of greatness. If the earth is to manifest a change to reflect a new age then it is absolutely critical that those who came for this purpose *be awakened to the existence of there divine plan.* There is an *inner memory they hold in their souls* and if we can at least *get them on the path of awakening then the inner memory will lead them the rest of the way.* The Ascended Host of Beings are not just quietly sitting and waiting for some miracle *but they are working with those who are aware and helping them to bring the message to others.* When a few learn how to transform their own lives they can help others do the same. The Ascended Beings are totally committed to helping bring a progressive revelation in which we are always growing, learning and becoming more. The age we are in is the Age of Pisces but the next age is *the Age of Aquarius and during this age there will be such an incredible release of spiritual light from above and this light will help our spiritual growth and our ability to raise our level of consciousness very quickly.* To me the greatest beauty is the ability for the Ascended Host to be able to release new spiritual teachings that will help us even more but the only way we can be ready to receive a higher understanding is that we raise our own level of consciousness first. When we do this we also raise our ability to receive a higher level of God's light. *Giving and receiving is the balance of life.* This is why we must first take hold of our own lives and pull the beam from our eyes and become a change for ourselves.

The keepers of the Eternal Flame *ARE the most wonderful beings in all of creation, because they are aware of what we are going thru, and what we can become. They have walked the same path we are walking and they have Ascended as we want to one day do the same. They are the most wonderful because their love reaches into our world and lifts us up to stand on mountains and to feel the face of God.* They love us more than we can possibly love ourselves *given our current understanding.* They have AMAZING GRACE and they send everything to us to help us attain the same level they stand with today. They give with the purest unconditional love we could ever receive. They have the wisdom and the great love of the Father to help us in ways we never imagined. They long for us to invite them into our presence, they long for us to ask them for help. They have the power and wisdom and most definitely the love to remove all the darkness from the Earth and bring in the Golden Age of Aquarius. *But what they don't have is the authority to act directly on planet Earth. This is where we need to work together* and so I would like you to understand how this can be done. People in embodiment do not have the power to remove the darkness, but *they do have the authority to act on this planet.* So the bottom line is that the Ascended Host cannot bring the Golden Age on their own and we who are unascended cannot do it either. *The only way is when we come together in a true oneness between Heaven and Earth so that God's kingdom can be manifest the same below as it is above.*

How can you help? By taking hold of your life and begin walking the spiritual path so that you can re-connect to your divine plan. Work on your intuitive skills so that you can establish a relationship with the Ascended Beings and your spiritual teacher. *As you grow from doing these things you will begin to receive inner guidance from the Ascended Beings and this will help you get your own directions and your own instructions from within.* As you internalize this you will become stronger and more able to become the change on planet earth. The important part of what I am telling you is this is the path I took. We must become the change before our world can be changed. Focus on healing and understanding your own life and the purpose, your divine plan. Establish your connection to your spiritual teacher by becoming one with the Ascended Host. Pray to them, become a link to their realm and know that they are with you always. This is *not about you becoming a great power unto yourself. This is about you becoming one with God and all who love Him and serve Him.* As you commit to your own ability to raise your awareness keep your heart full of unconditional love and remember that we are on a quest of walking on a Universal Path to Oneness. Be willing to allow God's light to stream through you so that the world can see that it is God's light that will transform everything and replace the darkness. It is your privilege to be awakened to your divine purpose and it is your privilege to **BE THE CHANGE**.

Manufactured By: RR Donnelley
                      Momence, IL USA
                      April, 2010